NIKOLA TESLA

AFTERLIFE COMMENTS
ON
PARAPHYSICAL CONCEPTS

VOLUME THREE

MULTI-DIMENSIONAL
FIELD EFFECTS
AND
HUMAN EXPERIENCE

Channeled through

Francesca Thoman

Library of Congress Cataloguing-in-Publication data
Thoman, Francesca

Nikola Tesla: Afterlife Comments on Para-Physical Concepts,
Volume Three: Multi-dimensional Field Effects and Human Experience

ISBN: 978-1-5136-2080-0 (Paperback)
ISBN: 978-1-5136-2081-7 (eBook)

1. Channeling and Mediumship 2. Afterlife and Reincarnation
3. New Thought

Empowered Whole Being Press
www.EmpoweredWholeBeingPress.com

Illusion

The universe is an illusion, but it is not a lie.
The fundamental deceptions of lights, sounds and vibrations
Are not malicious:
Our bodies are enfolded in our souls like hand puppets,
But the story they tell is true.

Francesca Thoman

Introduction:

Working with the spirit of Nikola Tesla is an honor and as the work has evolved in the years of our collaboration I have learned a tremendous amount from him. In these channeled volumes he has trained me to comprehend what he is presenting from the Core of the Divine Mind, crafting this exceptional opportunity to view physics and reality from his afterlife perspective.

As we describe in *Appendix Two: Questions about the Afterlife*, you can meet with anyone there that has a vibration similar to yours. Nikola Tesla has been able to speak with, learn from and share knowledge with many types of people and has been quite impressed by these other souls.

Therefore, in this and future volumes, he will be presenting, second hand, some of the new things he has learned from others, such as in the articles *Living Within and Creating the Natural Self* and *Training Children the Lemurian Way,* where he shares wisdom from the spirit of Carl Jung. In another volume he might offer something that he has learned from Issac Newton, Niels Bohr or some other person, well-recognized or not, as they request.

TABLE OF CONTENTS

PART ONE:

Multi-dimensional Field Effects

Quantum Entangled Inductive Resonance

Key Points: As your own body relies on proprioception and proprioceptive sensory input to locate itself in space even without light or any other cues, the Divine Intelligence understands and communications its own inter-relationships within all aspects of reality though Quantum Entangled Inductive Resonance. This Resonance may not only be invoked, it can also respond intelligently by evoking a resonance field through your aura. Para-sound, part of psychic communication, works with other Torsion Fields to manifest specificity within 4-D reality. Quantum Entangled Inductive Resonance also helps create the specificity of the Divine Being within its own unity. The best social unity is non-uniform: a wall of uniform bricks is only as strong as its mortar and so it is with human societies. You can open your own filaments of communication with the Divine Being in the meditation that uses your Core Tone's Para-sound resonances.

Subheadings:

- Quantum Entangled Inductive Resonance Defined
- Para-sound, Torsion Fields and Divine Perception
- The Inductive Resonance of Specificity
- The Inductive Resonance of Unity
- Meditation: Invoking the Inductive Resonance

Quantum Entangled Inductive Resonance Defined:

Each part of this phrase is already known: quantum is the sub-atomic, deeply essential "points" or energy-particles of the divine consciousness's manifestation from the enfolded into the expressed, unfolded, dimensions. Entanglement is correlation of aspects of particles such as polarization, momentum, spin and position that create superposed states: two particles, once joined, remain joined, apparently each informing the other of its own state by communicating with each other far faster than light. Induction is creating a field or force from another disparate force or field, such as magnetism creating an electric current and a moving electrical current

2

creating a magnetic field. Resonance means that an existing vibration is augmented though additive vibrations of similar frequency; creating harmonics where certain tones are emphasized; similarly, certain vibrations are augmented in some materials, as when high-pitched sounds may break glass.

Quantum Entanglement embodies the original unity of the Whole: this is the divine proprioceptive sense of the manifested expression of its own nature. *Inductive Resonance* is how the Divine Being works within the incredible specificity of relativity through the "echo" of resonance. In order to operate as an intelligent unity that re-creates itself in more than one dimension, the Divine Intelligence uses the dimension of Identity and the Torsion Fields of Para-sound, Formation, Translation, Numeration and the Etheric Fields. *Quantum Entangled Inductive Resonance* is how the Divine Mind actually functions within the multiverse, sourced in its enfolded multi-dimensional core and manifested even into the lowest-energy formations. Thus, all physical realities are formed by the resonant induction of an incredible array of fields, forces, vibrations and particles created through the dimension of Identity by the Intelligence within the Zero dimension. The Divine Mind is therefore within all manifestation quite directly, continually and with awareness. It may ease some to know that the God that can sometimes seem so very remote, experiences all of your own discoveries, traumas and joys quite intimately.

Para-sound, Torsion Fields and Divine Perception:

As I have stated in Volume Two, Para-sound is a deeper dimension of sound, another "direction" of the energy-information that manifests itself in 4-D as sound waves through air or other substances. Although Para-sound is a Torsion Field with several direct effects in 4-D reality, it is also an enfolded field that manifests with a similar multi-dimensional "slant" as does Gravity and Magnetism. In this way, the inaudible Para-sound communicates information through the psychic/etheric medium, leading to hunches or prophecies, harmonious and disharmonious connections between people and the very voice of human intuition.

Thus your psychic senses perceive Para-sound overlays, whether they are in the DNA or in the historic atmosphere of a specific place. You are aware of Para-sound quite directly when you "hear" your soul's Core Tone. Using the "slope" of the Translation Field with your

3

psychic awareness, you gain enough leverage to help to shift the energy differential between 4-D and M-D reality. In other words, through using the Zero dimension, you are able to energize the "colder" energy of present-day reality up to a higher level of energy through Para-sound. In this you are emulating the Divine Being's action of impressing Its Identity into the matrix of Reality, re-infusing Its Self by means of pulses and vibration as well as by means of resonant fields, all through Para-sound.

Several Torsion Fields are needed in order to keep Para-sound enfolded and unfolded simultaneously so that it acts as a bridge, which is one of Para-sound's functions *as* a Torsion Field. By focusing the divine Intention, Para-sound structures the very processes of the Torsion Field of Formation through the Torsion Field of Numeration: in this way, vibrations of all kinds remain discrete. When you shine a blue light and a red light into the same space, their photons might or might not strike each other as they intermingle, yes. But the vibrations of each color do not alter or entrain one another unless photons actually strike one another. The blue and red remain numerically discrete: this is the combined function of the Torsion Fields of Numeration and of Formation. The "glue" that holds all these processes together is the Etheric Field: this field is the matrix through which the information in the other Torsion Fields is communicated, so that for instance the Translation field can encode the simultaneously enfolded and unfolded structures of Para-sound through the field of Numeration in order to express the Divine Intention through Formation.

All of these structures, processes and layered inter-dimensional arrangements are necessary for the infinite, multi-directional Core of "solid" Para-light, the divine Peace from which everything is expressed, to not only manifest but to manifest intelligently, instead of blindly. As it can be said, "the unexamined life is not worth living," the Reality that is unable to reflect its Self upon itself is also not worth having. This may be considered the "reason" for all these psychic layers within the Ether and the quite complex layering of several Torsion Fields. They allow the divine, enfolded realities to express themselves within manifestation and to receive information back, giving the whole its proprioception so that it always retains a sense of itself however it is manifested. These Torsion Fields are also necessary for the induction created by the two aspects of Specificity and Unity.

4

The Inductive Resonance of Specificity:

As we have pointed out earlier, the dimension of Identity limits the expression of the other dimensions quite directly, particularly through the Torsion Fields of Formation, Proportion, Numeration and Translation, though also in electro-magnetic fields and the Para-sound fields themselves. The dimension of Identity, allowing the Zero dimension that is beyond all form or physicality to become form, uses Inductive Resonance to create specificity in such a fashion that the limited interrelations of relativity are simultaneously created and overcome. The meeting of far-flung minds and psychic communication is accomplished through this resonance. If properly done, this resonant communication overleaps Timespace in much the same fashion as quantum entanglement does, though without engaging any physical particles other than, perhaps, the brains engaged in the communication, unless one of the communicators is not physically manifested.

In this way, the divine Infinite Being is able to become wholly specific and finite, containing itself within that finitude through reality's hologram. This also adds to the effects of Quantum Entanglement through the very intention of specificity by creating *relationships*. One note sung alone is unable to harmonize: a true monad cannot relate. Relationship demands both specificity and superposition. If the specificity became unlinked from the whole, as though the monad cloned itself, nothing would be accomplished but the profound separation of such discrete entities: the Whole could never know or understand its fragmented, dual Self. Quantum Entanglement is necessary for that understanding. Resonance is the result of harmony between specificities and the Divine Comprehension is created by Induction.

This comprehension must happen primarily at the quantum level because only the quantum "particles" of the Units of Consciousness are free enough to bridge the enfolded and unfolded dimensions with very little change in state. This of course also suggests that these dimensions can be bridged intentionally. That is what your human psychic and spiritual senses are for, after all: they and the very human fact that your souls are not only simultaneously enfolded and unfolded, they also retain particularly strong connections to the Zero dimension through the dimension of Identity.

This leads to the delightful paradox that, the more you are able to perceive, understand and manifest your own pure identity, the more you engage the Divine Identity into 4-D reality. The great teachers of humanity, the leaders, the visionaries and the openers of the Divine Wisdom did not ever begin by letting other people define them. Instead, they often not only came into manifestation with a clear idea of who they were already, they refined that understanding through self-reflection, yielding to the greater depths of their own Mystery. Through this, they developed their sense of self to the point that they no longer wholly identified with any aspect of their 4-D identity. When that occurred, they became actions of God. Through their action, the Divine Being comprehends its own nature at last.

The Inductive Resonance of Unity:

Unity's relationship aspect is another paradox: a cluster of identities that unify themselves to become an identity with its own purpose. The very best unity is not comprised of sameness at all! Your human self can be whittled away and your identity subsumed into a *unit,* as so often happens for war and this represents a high cost for any change which this uniform unity may create. But when disparate personalities work together towards a common objective, the results can be tremendously more effective, as they are more in alignment with the Divine Intention of specificity of experience. A wall made of identical bricks is only as strong as its mortar: if what is holding this wall together loses integrity for whatever reason, the wall is very easy to push over. The same is true with human endeavors accomplishing a specific purpose or action. But a well-built wall of disparate stones locked together by their very shapes may have very little mortar or even none. However, it can last at least as long if not longer than the uniform brick wall. This non-uniform unity of stones can withstand more shocks *because* of the specificity of the way the stones relate to one another. When this odd bit here matches with that odd bit there, when this prominence matches that cavity or when the particular size of one stone provides an anchor for those smaller stones, the wall becomes a synthesized, dynamic balance.

Many totalitarian regimes and totalitarian leaders know this and set about removing individuation as soon as possible when they come to power. Indeed, you can recognize a totalitarian mindset by that very demand for uniform unity. Yes, building a wall with differently shaped stones frequently requires far more intelligence, understanding and perhaps sheer artistry than a simple brick wall.

After all, this is why most governments don't bother promoting individuality: they are generally quite busy enough with their own affairs to worry about the individuation of the governed. Numerous governments are too often comprised of selfish individuals, rather than humble ones. The humble ones realize there is more within themselves and their own nature than they could ever know, much less the self and nature of the Whole. However, these humble ones also realize that their unity with that deeper part does not remove their identity, but rather enhances it. When you are genuinely humble in this way, you lose nothing and gain much from your "sacrifice" of not having outer power. When you are selfish in the sense of living through fear-based greed, then filling yourself with more things, power or control eventually diminishes your identity in ways you are utterly unable to calculate.

Unities naturally resonate within themselves and with each other and often enhance each other by their very specificity through psychic and Etheric Induction: whole beings, groups or unities working together can directly create symbiosis through that Inductance. This symbiosis is where both benefit from who or what they are: it rests on the fact that these interacting groups, systems or, yes, fields are each specific, whole and discrete. However, much as off-key notes cannot create a solid or harmonious chord unless by chance or very careful design, even unities cannot create resonance when imperfectly arranged and expressed. Inductive Resonance requires dynamic unity: wholeness relating to wholeness when that specificity is graced by its own internal unity. When you look for it, you can see this oxymoron everywhere: a whole unity created by specificity, or a specific unity that depends upon the integrity of each of its disparate parts to be unified. This multi-dimensional process of the edgeless infinite becoming infinitely discrete entities, forms and functions, is a hall of mirrors. However, that was the only way for the Whole Unity to discern itself into being through *becoming*.

Meditation: Invoking the Inductive Resonance:

In this meditation first become aware of your aura. If it seems depleted and rests too closely in to your body, you can "fluff it up" or expand it in any way that you wish, until it extends away from your body about 14 inches or so. Then imagine that you have an extra coating of blue-white, golden or green light upon your aura, resting like a thin film on your aura's very personal shape. Imagine that this thin coating is very alive: it is actually packed with nerve-like or root-

7

like filaments of light. These filaments respond to both your psychic and etheric field, as well as to the intelligent field of the Zero dimension.

Feel these tiny filaments respond to the Divine Mind within the Zero dimension. They begin to quiver, undulating a little like seaweed moved by gentle waves, reaching up and outward from the thin film of light. They are short and tiny: they will not reach very far. They might look rather like golden, green, or blue-white fur made from light. However, as any one of the filaments will be aware of what any other filaments are doing in less than an instant, they move in a quantum fashion to align into a beautiful pattern. Still feeling this thin, living and active film of light encasing your aura, center in your heart and feel what you want to know, learn or receive from the Core Source of the Divine Being. Or you can think of something that you want to tell or share with that Being: both things can be done through these living filaments of intentional light.

Mentally state your desire: "Give me some more love," or, "Give me courage," or, "Give me assurances about my future," or something similar; you can also say, "I am happy for my creativity, friends, success and my peace," and your gratitude will communicate itself instantly to the divine Being. Because these tiny filaments are quantum-based, it will not seem as though you are receiving or offering much energy. But when you center in your heart and focus on your soul's Core Tone [see Appendix One], you will feel a little "click" or a tiny release of energy that confirms you have used Quantum Entangled Inductive Resonance to receive and communicate information to and from the Zero dimension: the intelligence of God.

Because holding these filaments open for too long might exhaust you and give you more information than you know how to deal with, when you are done, imagine smoothing the fur-like filaments back into place, letting the thin film of light that has helped your communication become part of your general aura again.

Para-sound Encoding in DNA

Key Points: Your DNA is encoded with fields of Para-sound information, past-life memories and experiences. Because of the epigenome, DNA carries your ancestral experiences as well. The combined "sounds" of each life's symphony can be harmonious or dissonant: this is partly what causes the influx of wisdom from the Para-light core of the Zero dimension to become dissipated, waning after the original waxing. In the very process of creating Timespace, Reality has created a "chaff" of not-quite enfolded and not quite unfolded fragments of Reality that also impede, degenerate and sometimes eclipse that same Para-light's renewed pulses. This "chaff" has been created in part because in order to become Time and Space, the timeless and space-less Source needed to perceive itself within illusion.

Subheadings:

- Changing DNA through the Dimension of Identity
- Re-Inventing DNA's Identity and Your Own Identity
- Para-sound Encodings and Genetic Lineages
- The Persistence of Dissonance in Para-sound Fields
- The Waxing and Waning of Source-energy
- Infusing Source-Light into Human Affairs
- Meditation #1: Clearing Your DNA's Para-sound Fields
- Refreshing the Divine Wisdom through the "Chaff"
- The Divine Deception
- Meditation #2: Cohering the Sonic Scatter in the Para-sound Encodings
- Clearing Family Patterns
- Meditation #3: The Old Tree, the Sword of Light and the White Fire

Changing DNA through the Dimension of Identity:

DNA is particularly responsive to Para-sound in the same way it is responsive to psychic and mental fields and patterns. However, in most cases the mental fields that connect with DNA through Para-sound are sourced in the unconscious, subconscious, and only rarely in the conscious mind. The phrase from Matthew, "Which of you by taking thought can add a cubit unto his stature?" illuminates this quite clearly: it was likely a reminder of the limits of the conscious mind or at least of the ego's will. This is because the DNA reflects the higher-order, enfolded patterns in the dimension of Identity: the very personal interplay of enfolded, higher-order fields and patterns that is your human soul. People *have* changed things in their body by taking conscious thought: some have changed their eye color while others have mitigated congenital and/or chronic diseases and the like. But this is generally done by linking to the higher-order enfolded dimensions through prayer, spiritual practice or by Grace. Oddly enough, that is why re-sequencing the genome directly by adding other DNA works: the re-sequenced codes are still engaged with the higher-order dimensions through that same dimension of Identity. However, dissonance can develop between the disparate geometries, evidenced in the immune system's reactions to foreign tissue and DNA.

Nevertheless, you can help to engage and encourage the DNA pattern-change by working within your own dimension of Identity, in part by shifting your own sense of identity with any of several methods already available elsewhere. When you intentionally re-invent yourself, you literally alter the way your life might turn out. You can also shift DNA's own sense of identity by clearing ancestral patterns and energetic structures from it. This is done mainly through prayer, sometimes by work within your Akashic Record and often simply just by forgiving the patterns from the past that have formed the limitation. You can change the Identity-driven structures of your DNA by exploring, reestablishing and shifting your identity as regards to your own angelic self, your Higher Self or even a past-life self or two. This past life may be one that brings you benefit or one that seems to be the source of the miss-pattered DNA; both will respond to your shift through the dimension of Identity. You can also change your DNA by encountering the identity of the Divine Source, whether directly as in revelation, indirectly as in an NDE experience or intentionally, as when you search the divine in a mystical path.

Re-Inventing DNA's Identity and Your Own Identity:

Especially in this time of global media, many people can and have re-invented their appearances or mannerisms and thus their impact on others. Yet if you want to work with your DNA effectively, you need to work at greater depth. If you already know your own identity's Core Tone it makes any meditations regarding your DNA more effective. For your Core Tone is the very point of your human self's engagement with the dimension of Identity. But there are numerous other ways of accessing and engaging with your deeper self, through your own soul-pattern connections even without your Core Tone. The main intention here is to step beyond your current sense of yourself into the possible and the impossible.

This is actually done all the time when you choose to learn something new because your intuition has guided you to it, when you do something differently because you see that the present methods do not work well or when you move somewhere to start a new life. You are not just learning or changing your outer circumstances: you are changing your own relationship to the higher-order aspects of your own manifesting structures within the dimension of Identity. These inner structures, based in the Zero dimension's lovely and paradoxical Timelessness, forever exist and forever change. Yet you re-aspect yourself constantly since you and your life *are* their expressions. Even those whose lives appear dreadfully stagnant and deadly dull, change continually. Like a bird that can keep its head perfectly still no matter how wildly the branch it sits on is moving, the invariable sameness of such a life actually takes a tremendous amount of energy to maintain. Knowing this might actually help you to realize that the energy you need is already there: it's just that it is in static rather than dynamic form. I realize I may have simply found a fancy way of saying, "You're just stuck!" However, knowing that the higher-order energies exist is like knowing that you have a huge tank of clear spring water behind your house: it is not the water tank's fault that your taps only let drops and dribbles through. Your ideas about your identity can be considered the water taps; how tightly you turn the valves depends on your beliefs about your own nature and value.

There are many, many lessons to be learned from doing without or doing with less than you need and dealing with circumstances that are less than ideal. To mention only a few, when you are forced to choose one thing among many, you can learn lessons in

11

concentration, valuation, forbearance, tolerance and courage. But when you have come to the point of change, it is good to know that, like the water in the water-tank, a tremendously powerful energetic support is available through the higher-order dimension of Identity. Furthermore, this energy is crafted within the Divine Source of your personal identity: your point of divine origin.

On the other hand, some of the difficulty is that the gateways to that energy, or the valves that would fully open the tank, are in your unconscious. Thus they are difficult to engage, as though the gates and valves were under the sub-flooring. There are elegant methods for reaching into those deeper layers of yourself without demanding that you crawl under your whole psychological edifice; some might be considered similar to hatches, pass-ways and trapdoors: many of them have been discovered spontaneously and used quite effectively. You can take advantage of art therapy, where you can literally draw out the new possibilities. In dream analysis, you can learn to trust your subconscious or at the least learn something of what is inside it. Professional hypnosis with a skilled and ethical provider may also be of great value, for genuinely changing your identity is not to be taken lightly. Even role-playing can lead to positive change, especially if you can try on the new self ahead of time in a supportive environment with incremental, deliberate, well-considered choices. The point of all these dramatics is: like the goddess that was pulled out of her cave by people doing silly skits at the cave's mouth, your unconscious actually likes to be enchanted, the subconscious even more so. When you can offer allure, they will wish to engage.

As in a palimpsest where you can still see the traces of the first lines written upon the page, there is a tremendous amount of the child in the subconscious and unconscious. Yet this is not just because your childhood memories are laid down first: it is because these deeper, higher-order aspects of the mind also hold Magic, wonder, mystery, and the Unknown within them. And as I have said before, the gateway into the Zero dimension *is* the gate of Mystery. This child-like aspect of your deeper mind is not simply an atavistic part of the temporal evolution of the soul: someone that has lived numerous times may indeed be more child-like and more open to wonder than someone that is just beginning the experience of being human. Yet the point to remember is that the deeper aspects of the mind engage with, communicate through and are aware of Para-sound, the silent, enfolded sound that permeates reality.

12

The dimension of Identity and the Zero dimension use Para-sound's essential vibrations to intersect Time through timing: part of this timing is the development of the human self. Para-sound is also part of the psyche's structure and works through the subtle levels of the human mind/brain to create such things as significant dreams, visions and visitations as well as the sense of time and timing. The haloclines and "colors" of Time are sensed through your generally unconscious perception of Para-sound: the reason why meditation and stillness can open you up to those same dreams, visions and visitations, is because it helps you resonate with Para-sound, particularly the inaudible Para-sound of your soul's own Core Tone.

Para-sound Encodings and Genetic Lineages:

Para-sound structures work most obviously in the epigenome and paragenome, the over-layers of information on the "outside" of the DNA spiral that shift and alter the manner in which the DNA is expressed. Ancestral lineages are rich with these overlays, carrying such information as the personal experiences of your predecessors, both in the broad sense and the subtle. For instance, these overlays are part of how the Para-sound of a certain area can feel like home to someone *because* his ancestor lived and died there several hundred years ago, even though the descendant is unaware of his ancestor's travels.

Layers of emotions form a "lens" that colors perceptions: this is very important to consider in dealing with genetic issues of depression, optimism, rage or equanimity. A fair number of these aspects are genetically driven but this can only be understood by considering all the aspects of the genetic code, including the paragenome and epigenome. Yes, although there may always be a struggle to change the inherent propensities, nurture *can* overcome genetically determined emotional patterns of depression, rage, or anxiety and this may be true even in the case of inherited diseases. Understandably, there are several complex issues regarding this, including Karmic choice, the expectations of the family's own internal "culture," the local society's beliefs and their effects upon the person, to say nothing of the physical and mental effects of your circumstances. Nevertheless, as most members of a family look like members of the family, most lineages express themselves in their own rich and complex symphony of Para-sound "tones."

13

Some of these effects can be responsible for epithets and stereotyping, such as "dour Scots," "meticulous Germans," or what have you: as though each lineage were symphonic expressions written in a certain key, these biases and prejudices are in some ways a response to the combined Para-sound tones and Encodings of a genetic lineage's gestalt. This may be one of many reasons why sometimes physical and family lineages that are too close to one another cannot harmonize: when playing C# and D together on the piano, the notes are inevitably dissonant *because* they are too close. There are times when a third note can compensate for the dissonance. But if the two lineages are locked in constant friction, they cannot allow the renewal they need from growing and expanding into harmony, instead of insisting that the two notes become the same, or that one must override or obliterate the other. The analogy fails us because there is more than just one note being expressed in any cultural population. However, there are times when a higher-level harmony can override the original disharmony so that peace can be created, as when a great teacher forms a bridge of Para-sound that engages the dissonant notes within such a profound harmony that the dissonance drops away. However, some Para-sound structures have become so static that it is tremendously difficult to find a balancing note even by a great soul acting as a leader. Yet harmony may even be achieved by small actions of wisdom, as for instance through everyday people working together in those areas where harmony exists already, such as shared cuisine, thereafter reaching out from there to build rapport even in the areas of dissonance.

The Persistence of Dissonance in Para-sound Fields:

But too often, when the great teacher is no longer there, dissonance rises again because of the persistence of the epigenome's Para-sound structures. This is also in part why a philosophy, religion or school of thought may burst in, shining and powerful, and change things, yet many of the old ways will return within a generation or two. Indeed, driven by the old patterns, justifications for those very same old ways that contradict the new teaching will be found within the new system of thought! There have been so many religions that have said so many versions of, "Live well by loving God, yourself, and love others as they would be loved," that have devolved into not only merely dissent regarding issues of contention but also finding reasons for slaughtering all dissidents. The lowland chimp genes within our human symphony generate some of this: these more ancient genes

14

drive the instinct to rule by dominance within the troupe and to murder the stranger. Composed of ancient Para-sound Encodings, these instinctive mandates are sometimes difficult to override. In addition, there are many Para-sound Encodings that recapitulate the terror surrounding lack of resources: these drive many unconscious actions of fear and aggression, echoing the life-and-death struggles for resources that have actually outlasted their original impetus.

The fields that create Para-sound Encodings in the genome are also the substructures of the epigenome. These fields are formed by higher-order energies of the dimension of Identity. Even the lower-energy structures of ancient patterns are inextricably intertwined with the dimension of Identity, so momentum shifts the amount of divine light expressed. Although these original, sometimes lower-energy patterns can be altered, they need a great deal of work in order to change: they have tremendous effect because of the higher-order, enfolded structures of the dimension of Identity that include these original structures.

This momentum of the lower-energy Encodings' Para-sound fields is easy to track when you study history. Watch for the uses of excessive force, manipulations, coercion and other bitter human challenges that stop gentle and tender things from blooming and wisdom from surviving. Watch how the old motivations of dominance, aggression and rage break free and send the course of history awry: you will understand that old habits are hard to break. The old Encodings remain: they do not dissipate simply because overlays of higher-energy compassion, mercy, and kindness are offered. No, the only real way to change the momentum of the lower-energy Encodings is to quite deliberately change the human *identity*, one person at a time.

Alas: it is so much easier to destroy than it is to create and takes much less intelligence as well. Lower-energy interactions are of course easier too: much as sometimes the first words learned from another language are crude swear words, it is always easier to give in to your lower impulses. But the Encodings that retain the desire for domination are not the only reason why the light-sourced lessons of love, forbearance and compassion are often thwarted and the original messages in religions, philosophies and schools of thought become corrupted. One of the sources of this loss of the original guiding pattern is a kind of "sonic scattering" of the DNA's Para-sound within

4-D Reality itself, that diffuses or even disrupts the new, guiding fields.

This Para-sound scattering also leads to cumulative degenerations of several kinds in physical forms and systems of thought, resulting in the heavy cost of inbreeding: isolation and isolationism of cultures and the increasing effects of deteriorating wisdom and knowledge, from the "dumbing down" of school curriculums to the loss of diversity of languages, plants or ecosystems. Yet this scattering can be overcome in several ways: the quickest way is to allow a system to be refreshed through the Zero dimension, as are zygotes and stem cells, so that the Para-sonic fields' Encodings can be refreshed within the waxing and waning of the guiding light within the ages. The very Spirit of Guidance functions as wave-guide for the Encoded fields: it can shift things literally outside of Timespace long enough to re-write at least some of the dissonant patterns and remove the corrupted signals.

The Waxing and Waning of Source-energy:

This waxing and waning of knowledge and wisdom's light is one of the most fundamental natures of 4-D Reality, because *pulse* is actually one of the enfolded dimensions' major engagements into Time. As I have said earlier, Time's Möbius strip is partly curled away from 4-D manifestation because the true source of Time is the Timeless Zero dimension expressed through the dimension of Identity. Nevertheless, the function of pulse is what allows Spacetime to be created. In short, this was the way that the Infinite Now became past, present and future, allowing itself the infinitude of alternate realities in order to express itself as fully as possible within the limited frameworks *of* Timespace. But as Time must express its self as change, it must pull away from 4-D expression in order to re-intersect with the divine, Timeless Core so that it might re-create itself again in Timespace. If the Möbius strip of Time did not shift its 4-D area and level of expression, it would simply remain part of its original Timeless source. In short, pulses are the only way to create Time in the first place. Certainly, Time is needed for progression, sequence, information and the essential act of the Divine Being becoming form. In a very real sense, of course, the Source never wanes, but its 4-D manifestation does constantly.

Each breath you take in refreshes the blood in the lungs and the heart so it can flow throughout the body and return; in a well-

16

balanced system, this flow is continuous and exquisitely dynamic. But as there are times when clots, narrowing arteries or congested veins impede or stop the flow, so it is with history and human experience on a personal level. From Caligula to Stalin, there have been certain individuals that have impeded, stopped or even reversed history's well-balanced, dynamic flow of higher-energy information and refreshing pulses of love that infuse human affairs. At the same time, there have been countless others, most entirely unrecognized by History, that have acted as the capillaries to allow flow: the kind ones, the diligent ones, the honest and the principled. They have been mothers, fathers, brothers, sisters and families that believe the best way to be human is leaving the world in a better state than it was when they were born. These people have the courage and strength they need partly because of how they are raised, though surely they also rely upon their genetic heritage and their past-life heritage that are part of their DNA's Para-sound Encodings.

Infusing Source-Light into Human Affairs:

In medicine, it often takes medication to dismantle blood clots and arteriosclerosis' fatty deposits. In human experience, the medicines are courage, wisdom, integrity and honesty. It takes tremendous bravery to stand and speak up, especially when your unconscious past-life memories tell you that you kept on getting slaughtered for trying. Yet, the infusing light of the Divine Intelligence and compassion may create crafty wisdom over time: the Light can learn how to use tiny moments of leverage to thwart or at least change the course of political, spiritual or psychic juggernauts. Small moments of change are like altering the PH in a Petri dish rather than trying to kill each of the unwanted bacteria one by one. Or perhaps taking the extra time to listen to a child, whose rage and core of fear might have driven him to acts of violence if he were to be neglected one more time, can change a potential future quite powerfully.

It is impossible to prove a negative: there is no way I can prove how many such negative or dangerous potentials have been shifted in the past. But I offer the notion that when discernment, perception, courage and intelligence are partnered with intuition, compassion, wisdom and higher-level guidance, they change what might have been into what can become. Abuse, terrorism and tyranny have their own momentum. However, like a boulder sliding down a hill, even such momentum can be diverted, slowed, or even stopped if the ground beneath the boulder changes enough. And sometimes all it takes to stop the avalanche is one stone anchored to bedrock that will not budge.

This analogy also works for changing the lower-level Para-sound Encodings' momentum within your DNA and epigenome: you can clear your own Encodings quite directly, opening the channels to higher-level light from Source by keeping the flow of light clear. And as in the circulatory system's analogy, the more you open the channels in your DNA's and epigenome's Para-sound Encodings, allowing in more light to refresh and re-calibrate your own psychic patterns, the more smoothly everything else flows. As when an injury or area of systemic inflammation benefits from increased blood flow, so also ancient patterns of abuse, harm or even old hatreds and blood feuds can be eased and healed with this influx of light-patterns into the Para-sound Encodings. In short, clearing your own Encodings benefits everyone and everything else as well as you.

Meditation #1: Clearing Your DNA's Para-sound Fields:

Imagine you are on a little spacecraft high above the planet. However, instead of seeing mountain chains, islands, continents and seas, you are looking at shapes of Time: the very flows of history moving like a great, dark sea over the face of the planet. As you watch, you are drawn to certain areas that have shining golden and silver threads running through the moving sea that illuminate the dark, shifting shapes of Time. The silver threads start in one place and reach out, branching, re-branching and then folding back down into one thread. These threads are your own genetic lineage: your DNA, the epigenome and paragenome: the Para-sound Encodings that represent the countless voices of your ancestors, rich with their experiences and perceptions of reality.

The golden threads are far more variable: sometimes they shine out, thick and strong; at other times they are thin and tiny, or sometimes seem to snap and fall away. These are the threads of your past lives: your soul's lineage. There are times when the two types of thread intertwine and times when they seem completely separate. Yet even though separated by the waves and flows of Time and history, these golden and silver lines remain in relationship to one another. Watch them as the planet turns slowly beneath you, realizing that these patterns have created the person you are now and sometimes foretell the person you are going to be.

Find yourself moving closer to the roiling, shifting sea to study the thin threads, the ones that look fragile and limited. As you come closer, feeling your little spacecraft buffeted in Time's turbulent atmosphere, you perceive that some of these golden or silver threads are stained or darkened, though many of these thinner threads of gold or silver are also intertwined with other threads of several colors. Some of these colors are pleasing and some are very ugly or disturbing. Indeed, some of these ugly, disturbing colors have wrapped themselves around your silver and golden ones and that is why they look so thin: they are being strangled! Formed of fear, hatred, rage, jealousy, bitterness and revenge, the dark and ugly colors sap the life from your silver DNA and golden past-life threads like parasites. The stains on your threads are arrogance, domination, disdain, disrespect, disregard, condescension, and rejection. You have put some of these stains on your own threads. But much of the discoloration is from others and from Time itself, because lower-energy fields persist if they are not changed.

Suddenly you realize you can reach down and touch your golden or silver threads and even grab them, as though they were wire cables. Choose one thin, strangled line, either gold or silver that you are drawn to: seize it firmly with both hands, holding it still even in the shifting waves of the Time-sea. When you have a firm grip on it, say in your mind, "There! This is mine and I can clear it now: *Now!*" As you shout the word clearly in your mind, pull your gold or silver line towards you and embrace it, tugging and yanking the lines of the other colors away from it, saying, "Only my good line now, only mine: this line is only what is best in me." Feel the line respond to you, relaxing in your hold, as though it knew it were safe. See your golden or silver thread shine in your hands, becoming thicker and suppler. You feel its pleasure at being freed; it might even wrap itself gently around your hands in gratitude.

When you have cleared away all the other colors, choose some colors you like best: clear blue like the sky instead of gray-blue like a miserably cloudy day, or the lovely orange of a sunset rather than burnt orange of dry, poisoned earth. Wrap those brighter colors around your newly shining golden or silver cables as though with soft blankets, saying, "This blue is for excellence; this green is for healing; this orange is for new vitality, this white is for wisdom and this red is for compassion," or whatever meanings you prefer.

With this you have not only cleared the lower-energy Para-sound fields, you have also added new energies and fields to both your genetic and soul histories. Breathe in deeply once and as you exhale let yourself pull gently away from the sea of Time, knowing you have made a difference in your own lineages. You may not feel any difference immediately, though you could suddenly experience move vivid dreams, more moments of thoughtful quiet, better meditations and feeling more optimism. It may be that, six months later, you will finally understand why someone in your family did or did not do something. In the increased, gentle light of the refreshed Para-sound, you will feel more compassion for others and yourself.

Refreshing the Divine Wisdom through the "Chaff":

As the omnipresent Divine Mind is the Consciousness at the core of everything, so also are its wisdom, guidance and continual creativity. Manifesting as hunches and intuition that lead to miraculous escapes from danger or foolishness, as well as divination, inspiration, invention and prophecy, this responsive Consciousness delights in increasing flow, allowing beauty and nurturing love. However, as the solid core of Para-light was shattered into manifestation to create the 4-D structures of reality, it was simultaneously restrained and limited by those structures.

In this process there was necessarily some chaff, some empty husks or shattered lines of force and structure left behind. Neither quite unfolded into 4-D reality or remaining enfolded in the higher-level M-D realities, the chaff remains like fragments of straw floating in the air, constantly shifting in and out of 4-D reality's unfolded state and the enfolded Core. Each one of these tiny fragments carries little impact, yet like superfine dust, they do change the quality of the light in all of the realities and levels they are found. And, like dust, these left-behind, fragmented bits of structures are fine enough to get into everything, flickering and out of both forms and fields, occasionally creating infinitesimal structures on existing lines of force, much as dust covers cobwebs.

Needless to say, this dust changes the Para-sound "valences" that convey the essential intentions of the dimension of Identity. Much as dust would grime a lens or create excess heat, humidity and potentially static electricity in electronics, the leftover, unassigned chaff brought into being by the very process of shifting the enfolded M-D realities into 4-D expression, creates certain limits on how that reality is expressed and what parts of reality can connect well with each other. Thus, many deep-level patterns of consciousness' structural parameters of the Para-sound and Para-light Encodings were not able to manifest quite as fully as originally intended.

However, if the chaff were not there to provide scattering and insulation in many Para-sound Encodings in the DNA and the epigenome, then many aspects of the psyche itself, as well as certain aspects of entropy, could not actually have manifested without upsetting the delicate, dynamic balance they were meant to help create. The leftover, dusty chaff of the very process of Reality becoming itself has not been cleared away because, however much a nuisance it might seem, it actually softens the edges of countless interacting fields, creating very valuable semi-conductive states.

Like nebula, these encoding fragments both obscure and illuminate those realities with which they are still in Quantum-entangled Resonance. At the very least these leftover fragments are the enfolded realities of the human psyche and are often agents of inexplicable events as well. Some of the energy-structures still contained in this "chaff" create apports, mixed haloclines of Time that create "time ghosts," shape-changing and teleportation. All of these "off-side," incomplete manifestations use the remaining fragments of the original Divine Decision to manifest, the same Decision that is being made and remade in every instant in order to keep Reality from stopping its flux and congealing into the totally rigid, hyper-solid structure of its original Para-light Core.

Make no mistake: as any other kind of fragment would retain its original identity and its substance, these deeply invisible, unfolded/enfolded fragments of the original Conscious Intention *are still conscious* and therefore still parts of the Divine Intention that operates with that same Quantum Entangled Resonance Induction we mentioned in our previous article. Reacting responsively to particular quantum structures of vibrational Encodings, these fragments also shift Para-sound and psychic fields within 4-D structures. And as does Magic these fragments also create slopes within the enfolded geometries that can guide energy-flow in order to pull in energy, intelligence and love into the unfolded ones from the more enfolded, higher dimensions. In addition, these fragments create the scattering that leads to dispersion, dissolution and entropy. In a very real way, the Infinite Mind foxed itself: it has used its own conscious intentions to deceive itself into manifestation! The Infinite

21

Mind's Consciousness Fragments, the "chaff," are part of what keep the illusion of reality flexible, mobile, changeable and dynamically complete.

The Divine Deception:

On the surface, this seems absurd. Why should the bright Core of the Whole Reality deceive itself about itself? Whatever would be the purpose of it? The answer is simple, and even has been described within human myth: the Divine Mind created deception in order to leave Heaven because that allows the Whole to manifest the countless, unexpected potentials of the Zero dimension through the dimension of Identity, in such a fashion that the Zero dimension retains its nature *as* an unbroken whole even when fragmented. In addition, this shattered Whole must re-create its self continuously and simultaneously. And it does so by creatively expressing motion, change and new patterns constantly. In this way, the Divine needed to forget its true nature in order to discover it!

This may seem appalling to some. Surely, isn't the Core of the Universe, the very Self of the Divine, all good? Surely it is still the source of all that is Heaven? Of course it is. But as we discussed earlier about illusions and the hologram of reality: the source of the reflection is real, the process is real, yet the end result is both real and unreal. And the Zero dimension that is the placeless Place that is in all places, the infinitesimal point of consciousness that encompasses all the infinities of universes, remains the paradox it has always been. So in addition to the Door of Oxymoron we mentioned earlier, we now have the Door of Duplicity: the challenge that at the very least God is two things at once. And it needs the "chaff," those parts of the One Whole Being that are neither the Core, nor the specificity of full manifestation, for the scattering that keeps reality in the semi-conducting state that is necessary for completion. But in truth, the manifestation of the Divine Core creates multitudes of realities. Even though these multitudes relate to each other in an incomplete fashion because of the "chaff," this chaff allows a semi-conducting reality, a reality of layered margins, that permits far more creativity in it than would a clean, straight "Aha!" of light manifesting directly into form.

We have mentioned before that consciousness is semi-conducting: in physics, semi-conduction is only possible when a pure substance has been either doped with another pure substance (as in silicon-gallium-arsenide computer chips), or by an impurity that scatters the electron flow, however slightly. In Reality these impurities, the fragmented husks of the manifestation process, are often the means and methods *of* Reality's manifestation, though they are not Reality itself. Even some parts of the "Junk" DNA actually contain some miniscule pieces of the chaff, those fragments of manifestation processes, much as everything everywhere else does also. These bits of chaff are needed because, more than most engines of reality-creation, DNA needs the semi-conduction created by these simultaneously enfolded and unfolded aspects of manifestation, in order to shift through potential realities every time it gets recombined and refreshed. And the chaff also acts as insulation to specifically allow just enough of the Divine Creativity's "heat" to sprout the seeds of reality, but not enough to overcome them with the unthinkably huge power of the Center Core of Para-light.

However, similar to a smoggy sky, there are times when the scattering becomes too great: the delicately balanced amount of light from the Core cannot get through. And as we described earlier, when the light of wisdom and the intelligence of reality's Core is impeded, spiritual, psychic, mental and emotional processes increase their entropy and parts of physical reality lose coherence because too much of the original signal is diverted. Although 4-D reality is so deeply embedded in the structures of the dimension of Identity that things rarely exhibit *increased* entropy, such as for instance tables suddenly becoming porous and crumbling all at once, disorder in the higher levels does have physical manifestation, most usually in living systems that depend so heavily on the dimension of Identity to manifest.

It is then that the Divine Wisdom must be re-stated, the Divine love experienced again and the internal Intention of the dimension of Identity expressed anew. But as a seed can sprout in the leaf litter of the forest floor, hiding in the loess and duff of the living trees' own life-process, 4-D reality can only be re-expressed into new forms *because* the chaff gives the new forms a substrate. Though, as a seed dies if buried too deeply, it is useful and beneficial to clear Para-sound's scattering within the DNA Encodings now and then, as you can do with this following meditation.

Meditation #2: Cohering the Sonic Scatter in the Para-sound Encodings:

Though it takes a little preparation, the sonic scatter in the genome's Para-sound Encodings can be cleared very simply and with a short meditation. First, find your Core Tone, as we describe in the Appendix below. Second, center that Core Tone simultaneously in your heart, your pineal gland and the notch at the back of the skull where the head and neck meet, so that you have engaged three points. Notice: these points are not joined by lines, but allow the Core Tone to be in three places at the same time: as the Core Tone is sourced in the higher-level Zero dimension, this is quite possible. In addition, this simultaneity creates the door into the Zero dimension that you need. You will know that you have the three points joined properly when you feel your Core Tone shift to become a lens made of light that is huge and tiny at the same time.

When you feel that shift, imagine a beautiful light-tone shining through the lens. Watch that light-sound shine out like a spotlight into the roiling mists of time. Everywhere this light touches it entrains whatever Para-light it finds that has been too scattered by the chaff of reality. As the light reaches out, you can hear the original, lovely tone of the dimension of Identity. These notes, high and low, add to the very Divine Intention, creating new harmonies over broader and broader areas. Keep working and watching until you see the dark clouds shine with light of superlative brilliance and the Tones resound and mingle like the notes of full-throated organ pipes. You have now become a lens for the light of the Zero dimension and can help clear the excess scatter of the excess enfolded/unfolded chaff.

Clearing Family Patterns:

There has already been much work done in scientific, spiritual and New Age arenas about repairing the damage of a guilt- or shame-based, abusive, compulsive or otherwise traumatizing upbringings and I would not presume to add to that body of work to any great depth: the subject is too vast, individual and fraught with jeopardy if handled carelessly or improperly. However, I would like to leave you with a final meditation for healing some of the wounds that you, your parents or your siblings may have received directly from your own family over multiple succeeding generations or simply from the natural confluence of shifting temporal mores. Many things that used to be considered normal for families seem injurious now: de-facto slavery of both male and female children, prostitution of female children for the sake of hospitality, battery and domination of any other member by the father as well as abandonment and betrayal. As history is rife with these, then surely your genome and epigenome are both burdened with the frozen time created by these shocks and the grief of darkening love and light. This meditation is not intended to change the past directly, though it can: it is intended to give those silent, suffering ones a chance to speak and also change the tone of the Para-sound symphony within your own genetic Encodings.

Meditation #3: The Old Tree, the Sword of Light and the White Fire:

In your meditation, imagine you are walking in an ancient forest. The trees can be wherever tree grows in tall clusters, with the roots of one supporting the others. The path you are traveling on is easy. Even though it is getting late in the day, it is bright, with white spring clouds glimpsed through the leaves and branches. As you walk the wide, clear path, you know you need to find the Tree that is the Heart of the Wood. The path is soft underfoot because of all the centuries of leaves on the ground: it turns gently, changing direction suddenly at times, becoming narrower and rocky and then leveling out again. As you walk, you notice that the trees around you are getting older: some have broken branches, but most of them spread out as wide as they can: even though full of extra wind-blown leaves and twigs, their branches are still strong.

All at once, you come to the One Great Tree. It is not the tallest but it is certainly the oldest: its roots are very deep. As the light begins to fade, you come up beside it and spend a moment or two simply admiring it. How many centuries of rain, snow and shining summer heat has it felt? How many animals have taken shelter in it and how many times has the wind sung through its branches and leaves? You step back a bit to see it better. Notice it has several branches that are broken and still clinging to the tree, some dying or dead. Some of the branches are caught on the lower ones and some are sagging against the trunk. The light around you begins to dim, though you feel a breeze come up, moving the branches above you. It coaxes a song from the tree: a symphony of passion, wonder, courage and triumph, yet also of loss and grief, betrayal and pain.

Now you realize you have a sword of light by your side: it can cut through anything that you wish to cut. As the light around you becomes full twilight, sword in hand, you start climbing the tree as easily as going up stairs. You feel that the tree needs you to use your magic sword to cut down the dead and broken branches. You scurry around all the parts of the tree as nimbly as a squirrel, cutting and pulling the branches down no matter how large or small they are. You shove the other, leafy branches away in order to reach the branches you need to cut. One touch of the shining blade of your sword of light is enough: the branches fall away, down to the ground.

When you climb down, you see all the branches scattered around the Great Tree's trunk. Without stopping to think you use the sword again, quickly touching each branch on the ground one by one, until you have touched them all. Instead of cutting, the magic sword of light sets each branch on fire. However, it is a white fire like moonlight: the smoke shines with a myriad of colors, like ocean spray lit by sunlight into rainbows. And now you hear the voices that were trapped in these branches: the desperate cries of the lost ones or the grieving moans of the bereft. You may hear the outraged cries of the falsely blamed or the helpless rage of the abused; you may feel their horror or shock or simply sense them and know that all these broken voices are rising within the white, glittering smoke. But it is not all grief. You can hear the tree's symphony: a lovely, rich, complex sound that is full of strong beauty and splendid power.

The smoke rises and envelops the tree. Watch the tree absorb all the smoke until it is pulled into the branches. Wherever the shining smoke touches, the leaves, bark and branches of the Great Tree brighten so that the tree shines as though freshly washed by the rain. The symphony of the voices of the memories quiets itself slowly. Now the voices sound like birds calling back and forth until they become silent, one by one. Hearing the last notes, you close your eyes and sigh, falling out of the meditation gently, remembering the joy of those that were heard.

The Dimension of Identity and DNA

Key Points: DNA, like human consciousness, is simultaneously enfolded and unfolded, relating to the Zero dimension, the dimensions of Identity and Primordial Chaos in highly interactive ways. In human beings, there are more and deeper layers of the dimension of Identity: through the Torsion Fields of Formation, Translation, Para-gravity, Para-light and Para-sound, human DNA has many more points of contact with the Zero Dimension than the DNA of many other species. The dimension of Identity uses both the temporal and non-temporal aspects of DNA to create living things, engineering changes of form as in evolution, as well as creating consistency in a species' core expression. Since DNA's internal "clock" relates directly to the dimension of Identity, it can hold the "frozen" Time resulting from shock and make a species become too rigid to receive the refreshed information from the Zero dimension. Extraterrestrials use "haloclines" of physicality to manifest and your DNA determines how much of those degrees of manifestation you are able to perceive. Some of the species on Earth were actually introduced from other planets. You can become aware of your lives in alternate realities using meditation within your DNA.

Subheadings:

- Your DNA's Relationships to the Higher Dimensions
- Your DNA's Temporal Aspects
- DNA and the Involution of New Species
- DNA, Evolution and Involution
- Para-Sound. Extra-terrestrials and Introduced Species
- "Frozen" Time and Inter-layered Time
- Alternate Realities and DNA
- Meditation: Opening Your DNA's Deeper Identity

Your DNA's Relationships to the Higher Dimensions:

You can engage your DNA through the dimension of Identity and be able to discover, unlock or change specific aspects of your genetic

27

heritage. However, as the physical genetic heritage is so enwrapped with the patterns of Time and has Time's nearly infinite momentum, such changes are often beyond most meditative methods and at present still need physical intervention. Nevertheless, meditation can reveal a great deal about your genetic heritage and your own past-life heritage, since your DNA is also the place where the Akashic Records link with physical reality. You can change your past in terms of your memories and your relationship to them, in terms of the past lives that overlay this one; in this process of discovery you may actually change a tremendous number of your ancestors' experiences and physical memories for them as well. By engaging alternate realities where the genetic coding can be quite differently arranged, you can pull both past-life and genetic lineages from more beneficent expressions within those alternate realities into your present DNA 's finer structures in the dimension of Identity.

DNA's changes concerning alternate realities can happen spontaneously, as when a daughter of a lineage where all the women had breast cancer avoids it, or when a man born into a lineage of brutes and desperados breaks the mold by becoming an erudite, intellectual scholar or a bicycle repairman instead. Part of this shift is engineered through the epigenome, allowing certain genes to be expressed and others to be shut off. However, the main impulse of change is actually sourced in the dimension of Identity's own M-D geometrical patterns. Generally, these patterns keep genetic changes from becoming too facile, too liable and subject to too many higher-energy influences, particularly Para-sound effects, where resonances and counter-resonances can create ungoverned chaos. Because radiation's random emissions link the dimension of Identity more closely with the dimension of Primordial Chaos, it can create more unbalance than is best for the M-D to 4-D geometric structures within the DNA that engages both enfolded and unfolded patterns.

Although the subject of cancer, one of radiation's results, is beyond the scope of this article, I can say in short that all cancers ultimately derive from discordant, mismatched, or overwhelmed DNA patterns within the dimension of Identity itself. This is why working on your identity has both positive and negative effects with cancer, even in 4-D and why meditations to focus on being cancer-free can help, if only to a degree. Yet without more input of some kind of new energy, too often there is insufficient torque or leverage *within* 4-D reality to affect the higher-order energies and patterns. As it is, in order to keep the proper structural arrangements between the three core dimensions: Identity, Primordial Chaos and the Zero dimension, the effects of Chaos must be pulled outside of 4-D reality so much that in a very real sense that dimension is even less engaged with 4-D reality than gravity: through the Divine Being's own sense of its self, the dimension of Identity is the major factor that ensures this separation.

However, by reaching into the deeper templates of the Zero dimension, changes can and do occur in accord with both Divine and human will, particularly as with miracles, where higher-order patterns and energies are called upon. And, because DNA, like consciousness itself, retains essential connections to the three deeper dimensions simultaneously within any 4-D expression of form, DNA is often the fulcrum for this change. Working though the Zero dimension, the dimension of Primordial Chaos and then through the dimension of Identity, or from Primordial Chaos through the Zero dimension into the dimension of Identity, you can create change in the M-D geometries directly. Much as the dimension of Identity necessarily affects and alters the Zero dimension and the Divine Nature within the Zero dimension, changing your identity through Primordial Chaos, particularly in cases of higher consciousness, quite frequently literally changes the Divine Nature as you change yourself. Thus these dimensions are highly interactive, both affecting and being affected by your human consciousness.

Your DNA's Temporal Aspects:

Held in place primarily with the Torsion Fields of Formation, Proportion, Translation, and Para-sound, your DNA's "clock" relates to Time through the dimension of Identity as well, especially in the Para-sound Encodings. DNA's clock not only helps an organism relate to its environment in specific ways, creating aspects such as seasonal and diurnal responses, as well as each organism having a specific lifespan: because the dimension of Identity relates so directly to Time, DNA's clock also gives the organism its fine sense of location within Timespace by providing a steady "temporal reference tone" within the dimension of Identity. This relates directly to your soul's Core Tone, although they are not quite the same: DNA's clock mainly regulates the body's expression in 4-D, whereas the Core Tone is the point where your personal Zero-dimensional aspects focus into manifestation.

29

This internal sense of Time in DNA works with the Torsion Field of Formation to follow the proper sequences of growth and maturation, to create repair, allow the organism to receive love to its benefit or the lack of love to its detriment. These Torsion Fields also help create the wonderful coincidences and synchronicities necessary for anything from a living thing finding food or water when needed, to a shelter dog or cat finding its permanent home, to even someone getting on the "wrong" bus to meet the person he will marry. With the enfolded Torsion Fields functioning as the engines of coincidence and synchronicity, DNA thus works with the internal temporal structures of multi-dimensional geometries to align an incredible number of factors.

DNA also links with the field of Formation and the dimension of Identity in a close, nearly enfolded geometry that aligns atoms, molecules, chemicals and substances in accordance with the higher-order information, so that all living forms are deeply and continually related to the Zero dimension and its intentions. DNA not only allows the hologram of reality to be created by the substances, energies, fields and processes of 4-D physicality, DNA remains so deeply connected with the Zero dimension that it actually provides a direct door *into* that dimension and this door can be opened through human intentions or Grace.

You can communicate with your DNA quite directly, although, as it is with Magic and many other things, some people will have more success with this than others even though the potential is always there. Healing masters, masters of meditation or of visualization may find this work relatively easy, but anyone can work to shift his or her relationship to DNA and its relationship to him or her. This type of DNA work does indeed have its own identity and its own momentum to consider, however, thus we will have a meditation for uncovering and, perhaps, opening DNA's identity at the end of this article.

DNA and the Involution of New Species:

DNA engages with the Torsion Fields of Proportion and Translation to create, maintain and evolve new species. Proportion helps new forms to evolve from existing forms with a combination of sufficient speed and caution: on the one hand, the new species fills its niche as soon as it is available; on the other hand, the change is never so fast that the strange new offspring is totally rejected by the mother, herd or flock. Nor will this new animal be immediately targeted by predators, as happens with animals that look or act differently. In this sense, DNA's relationship to time includes *timing*, demonstrating an exquisite awareness of propitious conditions for both the individual and its collective. Of late, this timing has also encompassed human intervention, as with the California Condors, several species of whales, lions, tigers and the like. The whole issue of extinction is a little beyond this article, but the sense regarding timing within the species' DNA is part of extinction as well. This timing also relies upon the Translation Fields to get the information necessary for involution, by which living things respond to new, unique and higher-order patterns from the dimensions of Identity and Primordial Chaos in order to respond more ably to changing conditions.

Involution is not only expressed through creating new species: it also expresses itself within beauty. Prey animals need not be beautiful, much less predators, but frequently they are. Beauty and the concept of beauty is always a higher-order pattern, despite any number of arguments that you find beauty in what is around you simply because you are used to it and look for it or because you equate health with beauty and genetic integrity as much as any other animal. Obviously creativity itself is also a higher-order pattern; we have talked of animal creativity in Volume One, such as the patterns in a turtle's shell that compress time.

All patterns such as beauty, creativity and love; spirituality; altruism and friendship, especially between disparate species; and intuition depend upon the field of Translation to manifest. It seems odd to speak of animals having spirituality, but you may refer to stories of cats that sit with their meditating owners, or dogs that fast every Thursday. Altruism, arguably a spiritual impulse, is very clear in service animals of numerous species, even when some of these animals are not affected or trained by human beings at all. Altruism has been evident in herd behavior from the time of the dinosaurs, when a herd obviously sheltered or at least tolerated an injured individual. None of this would be possible without DNA being able to translate the higher-order patterns that continually refresh life's expressions of itself.

Because they are so important, we have particularly focused upon the Para-sound Encodings in DNA in the article above. But it is worthwhile to remember that Para-sound works directly with psychic and Etheric fields as well, which adds to an organism's responsiveness to its whole ecology and its specific relationships with its own and other species. "When you heal yourself, you heal the world," is possible because of the Para-sound links between living beings. Para-sound is also responsible for those measurable effects in times of global emotional impact, such as the death of Princess Diana, the destruction of the Columbia shuttle or the release of the 33 miners in Peru. As we alluded to in Volume One, these Para-sound linkages also allow temporal inter-communications of many sorts through the temporal haloclines; they certainly can allow communication between your past or other-life personalities with your current self.

DNA, Evolution and Involution:

As DNA is also aware of the patterns and sequences of the eons and ages of astrological time, there are times when DNA is more responsive to the changes inherent in the shifts between the Ages. In such times the DNA is more likely to clear itself of unwanted patterns that are too chaotic or that have become less and less viable in the surrounding temporal "color" of time. A new species with its particular physical form, methods of expression and niche is very much a new idea of God: DNA works with those Divine intentions through the Para-sound Encodings and its own temporal sense to determine when to create or even sometimes re-create a particular form.

This may seem a convoluted way of describing life's response to changing conditions, but what I want to emphasize here is DNA's interactions with the enfolded dimensions. Para-sound helps an organism relate to its time and place and its own identity within that place and time, as when for instance the two types of California jays, the deep-forest stellar and lowland scrub jays, will immediately leave the area they are not suited for, or when sea turtles find the same beach every year to lay their eggs.

Paradoxically, Para-sound also allows species to invade other areas where they are not original by providing resonance for them to orient upon. Species that have been mistakenly or willfully introduced by man are a slightly different issue, but animals can search for niches with as much drama as any lost tribe looking for a homeland. The DNA of invasive species not only finds the resonance of habitats similar to its needs, it can also instruct other species to allow it to fit into that new home. Para-sound working with DNA allows a moth's ear mites to inhabit only one ear, so the moth does not become deaf and thus someone's food along with the mites. Para-sound also works in the parasitic symbiosis of some beneficial worms, bacteria, or microbes that live with or inside other animals: they do not only rely on chemical messages to know that their host is healthy and make corrections when necessary as they can, they also discern this through the Para-sound Resonance in their own DNA as it relates to the DNA in the host.

And again perhaps too obviously, the Para-sound Resonances and Encodings help ecosystems to evolve, change, adapt and even repair themselves. Particularly in a limited ecosystem where there are perhaps 5 to 7 main species that depend upon one or two key species to exist, Para-sound becomes a symphony: the higher energy of Para-sound works to keep that symphony harmonious in response to the Divine Intention through the timing and temporal "colors" of any given age. This is actually one of the reasons why ancient DNA is unlikely to become viable: as a child that is born to quarrelling parents is not likely to thrive, an organism that is forced into a temporal structure that is too disparate from its own DNA symphony will not prosper. The subtle structures of the Encodings, timing, involution and each organism's sense of "place," drive it to prefer those factors and arrangements that truly support it with as much fervor as the two California jays refuse to be happy in each other's habitats.

Para-Sound, Extra-terrestrials and Introduced Species:

Although I digress to mention this, these Para-sound structures are why most extra-terrestrials and "extra-dimensionals," those that are from another halocline or Timespace, tend to either manifest on the planet only to a certain degree or often have deleterious effects on human beings. However, alas, human beings' effects upon those extraterrestrials which are able to become more physical have generally been *fatal* for the extra-terrestrials. In order to treat with most otherworldly beings, you need to encounter them within a neutral space that acts like a bridge: this would be a place where you are supported and engaged with the energies of your own higher-order geometries as well as the higher-order energies of their geometries. This inner structure of the higher-order energies is how several people might have the same encounter and yet have very different memories of the experience. As some animals hear a higher pitch than you do, some of you can perceive more higher-order, higher-level information within the experience than others.

There were more visitations from other worlds of all kinds when the ambient energies were higher on Earth; some of you may even remember those times. However, I will tell you that, although these levels of the past were kept harmonious and effective by groups of adepts, the energies of those times were not as great as the energies that you have in your world today. The reason it does not seem that way is because so much of that energy is partly masked and clouded by technology and majorly by the sheer number of chaotic minds on the planet. The resonances of the Kali Yuga that have been so slow to fade also cloud the ambient energy and limit its scope. But, as some people may see ghosts, auras, elves and other sprits, so also they can see ET's with their finer perceptions: this is because a great many ET's physically manifest to the same degree as ghosts. In this way they can be shape-changers or become conflated with other psychic impressions and inputs. For, as there are haloclines of Time, there are also haloclines of physical expression.

Indeed, back to evolution: a fair number of plants and animals originated on other planets, such as the cycads; the precursors of the raptor and hadrosaurid dinosaurs; horseshoe crabs; ants; several micro-organisms including zooplankton and several other animals and plants as well. These were introduced deliberately in most cases, with the specific Para-sound symphonies within their ecosystems clearly in mind. But in some ways, even though human beings mainly evolved on this planet, mankind has had the most impact in Earth's ecosystem symphony *because* of the small and significant genetic changes implemented by extra-terrestrials that have added another set of "instruments" to the Earth's symphony.

You are not entirely about the destruction of other living things! Instead, you are teaching animals a different level of compassion and love, one that enhances and enlarges the potentials of care and empathy that animals have already long possessed. As some natural scientists have discovered, you learn far less about the animals you study if you consider them to be without emotional or physical feeling. And surely you learn more about your own selves if you watch for the way human beings and animals resonate with each other. There is a subtle difference that exists between human beings and animals that will likely remain, however. The multi-dimensional connections to the Zero dimension that allow a specific structure of higher-order geometries that are unique to you and several other races in the galaxy, were deliberately emplaced in your DNA by races that possessed and understood those very geometries. Poetically put, you have been touched by the angels so that you could find your way back to the Zero dimension's inner Identity.

"Frozen" Time and Inter-layered Time:

Perhaps many already have guessed that DNA straddles 4-D Time and the Zero dimension's Timelessness. As it has been said elsewhere, DNA is actually entangled at the quantum level: when you talk to your cells, they all perceive your intention simultaneously. Thus, you engage your DNA though some of the subtler aspects of Time itself. As we have discussed before, Time works as a Möbius strip: a certain amount of it is "curled away" from 4-D reality so that it can appear to move forward in order to allow it to retain its infinite and eternal nature. DNA is also one of the significant links between your personal relationship to the dimension of Identity and your "location" in Time. This may seem obvious, because the DNA clearly has an internal "clock." But this clock does not simply count: it also interrelates to several aspects of the dimension of Identity, layer upon layer, within itself. These layers provide tremendously strong scaffolding upon which to build your human experience, primarily because they use such enfolded structures within the dimension of Identity as the structures of Intention and Expression.

When a shock or injury "freezes" Time and pulls it out of the continuous flow of Time's Möbius-strip, it creates certain sub-structures both within Time and form, and these can grow, like stalactites, change upon change and season by season, like crystals forming in a super-saturated solution. This has many political and social impacts, as we have described in Discharging Static Realities in Volume One; it also has direct effects upon the crystalline structures of DNA itself. The ages of the dinosaurs were rich, varied and long, yet their lives were brutal enough to freeze their DNA's expression into a static, stereotypic pattern that would not have broken through its own momentum if it had not been for the various meteors, super-volcanoes and other interventions that eventually conspired to end their most static manifestations.

Of course I agree that birds are the dinosaurs' direct descendants; however, they became so because their ancestors had enough sensitivity and impressionability, to say nothing of intelligence, to work within the new energies that were creating mankind's advent. But lest you pat yourselves on the back too soon and say, "Then surely we are at the limit of the Earth's craft," realize that the issue was not viability, but *sensitivity*. The dinosaurs, great mammals and others were undoubtedly quite viable: the bones in the La Brea tar pits speak eloquently of those animals' fitness to live. But their DNA eventually became too rigid, too encrusted with frozen Time, to retain the suppleness needed to continue to relate to Time's Intention in a gentle, forward motion.

And it is surely the same for human beings: the more shocks from abuse, disjunctions and separations you have within your own sense of Time's flow, the more rigid and brittle you and Humanity become. The more brittle you become the less able you are to respond to the new patterns presented through involution's impulses. When you cannot adapt to the finer and finer energies, you will be dropped out of Time's expression. This will not be because of divine judgment but because you will not be able to sustain the higher energies and they will not be able to sustain you.

Alternate Realities and DNA:

Yet as you will see in the meditation below, these finer energies are simultaneously strong and peaceful, demanding and supportive. When you craft them in resonance with your Core Tone and your DNA's own wisdom, their refined energy will be a comfort and not a trial. Your relationship to and the human experiences of your associations with others; dreams; the courage to create; even to Time itself, will shift as gradually and inexorably as the dawn. You are made of the Units of Consciousness that have aggregated in harmonic intention in order for the Divine Being to uncover its own nature, for those Units of Consciousness first aligned themselves with the counter-spiral of DNA as foreseen by the Divine. Because of this resonance and supreme refinement, DNA has not ever lost its engagement to the Divine Intention. Seeing into the deep patterns of the higher-dimensional geometries of DNA is catching a glimpse of the Divine Being.

However, in order for the Divine to experience its own Nature particularly through human beings, Time is inter-layered through DNA by other-life resonances: the symphony of your human self "plays" in a magnificent harmony in all the times of its expression, allowing all your lives to interact with each other by inter-layering their temporal expressions. This allows your lives to not only retain their sense of wholeness within your soul's identity: it is also another

36

aspect that helps you retain your exquisite specificity, because you are aware of the contrast in Time between each of your lives.

Generally, you are more aware of the "colors" of time than you might imagine: certainly now that you have movies, histories and the like, you can feel the temporal differences quite ably. The rhythms, directions and intentions of the human experience in the 1940's, was a great deal different than those of the 2010's. This can be sensed quite readily when watching an old film, if only to the degree the film seems silly, naive or even absurd. However, if you can notice this kind of difference, then you can notice the same temporal difference between the layers of your own lives. This not only helps you identify those lives that are yours but also lets you discern which lives tend to "curdle," or distort and separate, your soul's inner intentions from your personal placement in Time. These are the lives that will need healing and this healing can be created through attuned resonance with your own DNA.

This is true for alternate realities as well: as you might have perhaps ten flutes in an orchestra, or 20 violins, you will also have several lives that deal with, say, romantic love, perhaps several that deal with fighting in wars, living alone or living in a large family: each of those lives will also have expression through alternate realities' virtually infinite "second tiers." When you get a sense of this through you DNA you are less likely to feel trapped, static or unable to change in your present life.

And if you put your mind to it, you can discern when those alternate realities impinge you own, as when you have "real" dreams that do not mesh with your daily physical reality or even when you encounter more than one reality at once. This happens in cases when there are wildly different perceptions of the same reality: a parent may say, "I have never done well by my child," but the child says, "I trust and admire my parents for all they have worked to give me." In courts of law, when one person maintains that he or she was never violent, cruel or never even unkind to the plaintiff, whereas the plaintiff is clearly covered with bruises, lacerations and other damage that he could not have done by himself, you may very well be dealing with alternate realities in locked collision.

The frozen Time caused by abuse, the confusion of Time through over-layered resonances and unexamined structures of deeply hidden fear, grief or pain, can lock these collisions into place, affecting the intricate, multi-dimensional geometries. This leads to positive feedback loops like addictions and wild imbalances like insanity, with more and more of the stalactite-like structures we mentioned above. This can have tremendous implications for your human experience. This is another reason why healing yourself heals the world: when you change the subtle structures that create DNA you automatically change the lineages that follow and to some extent the lineages of the past as well. Certainly you change your relationships to any of several alternate pasts.

Meditation: Opening your DNA's Deeper Identity:

For this meditation, begin by centering in your heart and breathing slow, deep breaths. Feel the life of your body fitting itself around your breathing as though your breath and your body had become companionable friends. Feel the air you're breathing become an intimate part of you through your lungs and your heart, refreshing you with the element of oxygen and finer energies as well. Then be aware of the oxygen beginning to change your body: a gentle, loving shift.

With each breath, your body becomes more and more clear, more and more translucent to the love that is centered in your heart. If you are centered correctly, this will feel more and more exhilarating, more and more exciting, until you are astonished at how much energy you feel. So in order to take in even more energy, your breath becomes both slower and more refined. It is almost as though your breath is breathing *you*. But rather than distracting yourself with the vividness of the feelings, refine the breath more and more until you are breathing soft, deep breaths into the depths of your lungs, creating cellular light.

At this point, you will see that the light you have created is so focused, so clear and laser-like, that you see tiny glints shining like frost crystals or glints of mica in stone within each cell as they respond to your highly energized breath. These fragments of light are not the amino acids of your DNA: they are the higher-level, aura-like shells that contain the patterns of the multi-dimensional geometries you need in order to live in physical reality. You are excited to see them, though you may be a little amazed that they seem familiar, like little stories you remember hearing as a child or memories of old friends you haven't seen in years. You feel drawn to them. So, keeping your breath gentle and slow, you feel yourself reaching out to those points of light. Sense them reach out to you in response. When your thoughts and those structures of energy meet and feel like they are touching, draw in a deep breath and hold it for a long moment.

Holding your breath still, feel a strange, inexplicable sense of something collapsing as it expands outward, rushing forward as it stretches out or even of something roaring with the kind of sound that creates utter silence! When you feel any of those strange sensations, allow the sensation to turn itself "inside out:" you are engaging your own personal tesseract, the geometrically fourth-dimensional form of a cube. Allow your body to exhale slowly and softly. When you inhale again, know that your DNA is aware of your presence on the edge of the higher-level dimensions. Within this deeply malleable energy, you can instruct your DNA to change its identity through the dimensions of Identity and Primordial Chaos, asking it to shift many potential aspects of your body, mind, emotions and the burdens or graces of your past.

In the beginning, it is best to allow the DNA to do its own work: you can give it instructions, but as you will not automatically have the spiritual leverage you need, you cannot command it by yourself yet. But every time you do this meditation, you and your DNA will understand each other with more and more facility and will be more able to open the higher-order energies that you need for change. Allow yourself a long, slow exhalation to close the meditation, and feel your body surround you comfortably again.

Emotions as One of the Major Engines of Creation

Key Points: Emotions create fields that alter consciousness through the Torsion Field of Translation. Some believe there are only three essential emotions: anger, sadness and happiness; however a distinction must be made between emotions and feelings. Because emotions are sourced in the dimension of Identity, and feelings are sourced in the Zero dimension that is the Consciousness from which all of Reality is created and from which all consciousness is created, emotions are not only experienced by beings but also by fields and forces. Thus emotions have real expressions and consequences in all physicality and all aspects and forms of consciousness within all unfolded and enfolded reality. Feelings in particular are rich and nuanced not only in their experience and expression, but their meaning. The Divine Creation uses emotions and feelings to understand its own relationships to its self and balances these aspects with exquisite care, for only through emotional feelings and love can the Divine comprehend its own nature, for its true nature is essential Peace.

Subheadings:

- The Three Emotions

- Three Qualities of Being

- Meditation #1: Opening the Core Tone's Inner Light

- Love, Fear, Rage and Grief

- The Divine Mind

- The Metaphor of Water, Ice, and Steam

- Human Emotions and Feelings

- Meditation #2: Stepping Out of the Nightmare of Fear

- Peace and Emotions as Actions of Creation

The Three Emotions:

Sourced in the dimension of Identity, emotions are sustained Consciousness-altering fields that cause and are caused by specific neurological, chemical, mental and psychic effects of the Translation Torsion Field. The Torsion Field of Translation is first perceived in the unconscious, which rests at the edge of the enfolded and unfolded parts of the manifest and unmanifest human self. Through human intention, Translation Fields are used in several human endeavors: creativity; inspiration, vision and communication of all kinds, and they are expressed through the dimension of Identity as Individuation. Therefore, the real source of emotions is the enfolded dimensions interacting with manifested consciousness. Emotions are another way by which the Infinite discovers the multitudinous aspects of its own specificity that is discovered and expressed in interrelationships. Emotions' natures signify the natures of relationships between more than human beings.

There are those who say there are only three emotions: anger, sadness, or happiness. This suggests that love, fear and grief, as well as much more complex sensations such as courage, pride, jubilation; anxiety, shame and disgust; relaxation, contentment, compassion, patience and even friendliness, are actually *feelings*, which I define as complexly layered mixtures of the primary emotional states. Defining emotion as, "A sustained sensation in response to an outer incident or an inner experience that has both inner and outer effects," may be accurate enough, though it is a little dry. It is best to comprehend emotions and feelings in terms of the responsive actions of various forms of consciousness. After all, thinking about feeling is not feeling. Contemplating emotions mentally is rather like reading a musical score: it will not have the same meaning or impact as the symphony played from the written notes would. Although a musician might remember how the notes would sound, the silent notes in the mind are never the same as when the piece is played.

Looking at emotions from their mental definitions misses the experience altogether. There could certainly be as much interest or pleasure in the mental exercise of imagining the music, as might be mentally discerning which emotion someone is experiencing: the mind would perhaps feel similarly satisfied at the complexity or inventiveness of the score as with imagining the potential emotional effects. But its emotional experience, the very point of the music, would have been missed: with mental analysis alone, the very purpose, effects and therefore emotion's leverage to change circumstances and experience, is likewise missed.

41

For some, emotions are mysterious, unidentifiable things that seem to usurp clear thinking; for others they are what make life worth living. The original scientific belief that animals were unable to feel any emotions at all, much less had more complex feelings, has shifted a bit in recent decades: certainly there are at least numerous stories of animals grieving. Indeed, a dog greeting its beloved owner does seem to express pure joy; similarly, an animal that has lost its beloved companion certainly changes the way it acts. Some animals, particularly pets, seem to be quite responsive to their owner's emotions, coming up to comfort you when you are sad, tried or stressed. This is certainly a finer discernment than that of a wild animal that may simply be aware of your fear or self-confidence. Animals also seem to heal better when they know they are loved or needed. And certainly the long associations that service animals have with their persons suggests more than "operant conditioning."

However, I will not debate the issue regarding animals' emotions or feelings here: you need to have come to your own conclusions about this issue first, before I introduce such radical notions as the emotions of molecules, much less the rage of stars and the joy of planets. However, what is human within you was not created without precedent, no more than the human hand sprung into being all at once with no other creatures possessing hand-like appendages. From my present vantage point I must consider all that exists as an expression of Consciousness. At the very least I must also acknowledge that everything has seeds of emotions within it, whence come our human feelings. Again, as light, water, magnetism and even gravity can be intelligent, so they can also feel emotions in response to certain conditions, though inevitably these responses and conditions would have very little comparison to the human experience.

Three Qualities of Being:

Particularly as they are sustained sensations, the feelings of love, fear or grief certainly fit the description of emotions above; however they differ from emotions in three essential ways: First, they originate from the deeper strata of the enfolded dimensions, sourced in the Zero dimension rather than the dimension of Identity. Secondly, although they are expressed through the Torsion Field of Translation, as are emotions, these deeper states of feeling are also expressed through and are part of the Torsion Fields of Formation, particularly using the deeper levels of Para-sound structures. As Para-sound's "shapes" of grief, love, rage and fear directly affect Para-sound's other constructions, this Para-sound component should not be overlooked, as it shapes the encodings in DNA and the epigenome, the invisible and inaudible "feel" of a certain location or the actual rhythms of the pulses in the physical body.

This last may seem absurdly obvious: your breathing, heartbeat, pace of living or working decrease with grief, increase with fear and then stabilize quite directly with the feeling of love. Albeit in their own, deeply unique and individual ways, molecules, fields, atoms and other infinitesimal aspects of Consciousness's expression also are able to feel these experiences through Para-sound structures, even though this Para-sound aspect is not seen nearly as much with emotions as with the deeper experiences of feelings. As I said above, emotions, being drawn from the energy of Identity, do not engage the Formation fields.

Granted, there is some overlap: the *vesica picis* of the overlap is primarily in the way the three main emotions of anger, sadness or gladness and the more complex and varied feelings, directly affect one another. Indeed, there is also the fact that expressing fear, love or grief *through* emotions can heal the feelings of fear and grief and increase love. Grief engenders emotions and works with them to shift your deeper enfolded relationships with the conscious nature of Reality. In this way your human experience of feelings and emotions may interact to re-shape one another. However, because it is sourced in the Zero dimension, grief can be a situation of great opportunity, allowing deeper understanding of your relationship to the Whole. It may also freeze or inhibit even your personality's deepest structures within the dimension of Identity, causing all manner of literally frozen responses.

Thirdly: as states and feelings of being, love, grief and fear can retain their impetus and impacts even when other emotions are experienced. When you love someone, being angry with them or sad for them does not change the essential nature of the love, though it can be nuanced in the areas of overlap. A paranoid personality may have many emotions; however, since his feeling of fear engages both the Zero dimension and the Torsion Field of Formation, it will permanently stain all other emotions he experiences and must therefore be dealt with in a different way. This is much the same for depression, which is often created from an uneasy and costly mixture derived from varying proportions of fear, love, rage or grief. This is one of several reasons why depression is so difficult to overcome: similar to paranoia, it has not only a more global effect on your human experience and perceptions than any one emotion or quality: its origin is also in more than one enfolded field or dimension simultaneously. Emotions and feelings can often be antagonistically juxtaposed to one another as well, leading to ambivalence at best and a fractured sense of self at worst.

You may fear love because in order to receive it you must be vulnerable and thus would be no longer in control; simultaneously you are afraid of losing love because you know you cannot live without it. This is an antagonistic arrangement of fear and desire. Often, this can merely cause you to communicate love through mixed messages. But if you add grief to that, especially an old, half-examined grief that stems from an original betrayal such as being neglected, abused or even devalued as a child or an adult, this forms another layer of structure, as though a wooden form was covered in concrete. If the weight of what you have experienced because of the abuse or neglect is deep enough, then of course the grief and fear regarding love will become the major part of your identity and may even replace love itself. When love can no longer be reached through your identity, fear and grief deepen even more, until it becomes desperation and then despair and finally depression. Or your feelings about love may express themselves as rage: the helpless, thwarted anger stemming from your deep disappointment. In short because of your relationship to the Zero dimension, all of these four, very real feelings: fear, love, rage and grief, are part of the very core of the Divine within you: what they create has a greater impact on reality than any emotion.

Meditation #1: Opening the Core Tone's Inner Light:

One method of easing depression is to open your soul's own Core Tone. After you have done the meditation in Appendix One, continue to feel the Core Tone centering itself in the deepest and realest part of your heart. This is the place where you feel joy or yearning, that flash of feeling when you are struck speechless with beauty or when some great kindness or courage touches you. Do not be surprised to find that you want to shake your head and weep or that you must close your eyes and breathe through the sharpness of the feelings. The real core of your heart is the Divine Core and when you have been removed from this vital Center for too long, re-experiencing its power is almost a shock.

44

Much as though your eyes had been blind in the dark for a long while and then were suddenly confronted with light, the shock of the Divine Energy within your Core Tone can take your breath away. Nevertheless, work at continuing breathing, deep, slow breaths into your belly until the sharp feeling is gentled and the sensation of staring into a bright light is lessened. Doing this for several breaths is alone enough to interrupt depression and even open you up a bit, as though the sharp light had lanced an infected wound. You may find yourself understanding the sources of the depression more readily and have something new to understand and contemplate about your own self and your personal choices. The meditation can end here: one charged moment with your deeper Core Tone may even be enough to shift you away from depression briefly.

If you wish to go further with this deeper, more divine Tone, you may allow it to reflect itself back and forth into infinity, as you might have done with the stem cell meditation in Volume Two. In this way the light of your Core Tone reflects itself in several directions at once. As with two mirrors facing each other, these reflections of your Core Tone curve into infinity, yet it is as though there are a hundred mirrors reflecting one another. However, instead of dimming and decreasing in clarity, the reflections remain whole and clear like images of pure light and stay the same size however far away they are. As you watch, these bright points of light derived from your silent, invisible Core Tone will shift into fragments of Para-light. Gently increasing in size, intensity and finally in color, the points may look like clustered rainbows, mother-of-pearl or rain with sun shining through it. When you see this change, breathe in a final deep breath and end the meditation. If this does not remove your depression at least a little, by all means seek other, professional help, as you will likely need the leverage that another person can provide to make a lasting shift with a feeling so deeply rooted in your identity.

As an aside for this meditation: This impossible inter-reflection of your Core-Tone's Para-light is actually part of the Door of Paradox: where something can be infinitely large, infinitely distant and yet is still as clear as though it were close. Standing at this Door of Paradox, do not be surprised if you suddenly feel quite happy about your misfortune, dire circumstances, or the loss that may have caused your depression. This feeling of release is because you are both receiving the joy that your depression has kept away from you and also because you are likely seeing things from the soul's perspective which is far more capable of understanding the value of loss.

From the soul's perspective, your human loss, grief, frustrated rage or hopelessness that leads to depression is often a means of canceling Karma. This is not simply because you can comprehend your underlying fear or lack of love within your Self so that your soul feels less burdened by its own obligations to itself. You can also receive the lightness because the Divine Core Tone's reflection carries direct refreshment from the Zero dimension's Core of Love that is deeper and stronger than anything else. This Core is so deep it is even beyond Love and is very the nature of the Divine. Because this Divine Core Tone's intense and radiant energy exceeds fear, rage and grief, it can actually overwhelm the patterns that have gotten you caught into structures made too rigid by conflicting juxtapositions.

Love, Fear, Rage and Grief:

I have said above that the feelings of love, grief, rage and fear are all sourced in the Zero dimension, though I realize this offers a question: Why and how is it that this dimension, by description the very nature of the Infinite Source, the very Being of God, should have, not just love but rage, fear and grief as well? If fear is sourced in God, how can it be dealt with through the finite limits of your personal, everyday reality? And even though God's rage has been spoken of, why should rage or grief be part of this original pure Source? Surely grief is loss and separation, fear is the very antithesis of love and rage is often frustrated anger or thwarted control. Yet Unity and Love are the most essential aspects of the Divine! Has the Infinite Love of the Core Source, the Zero dimension that is everywhere and nowhere, somehow been compromised, lessened and irretrievably broken by expressing itself into reality?

No, the divine Source does not *identify* with fear or grief, frustration or fury: instead it has *created* them all in order to understand its own nature of love, using fear as Divinity's opposite, grief as the loss of Divinity and fury and rage as the distinct perception of boundaries. However, since all of these powerful feelings are sourced in the Zero dimension they are fundamentally important: they are the best way to manifest not just the mind of God in 4-D reality, but also the feelings of God. Fear reveals the nature of the one that fears as well as the nature of what is feared; from the Divine point of view this is essential information that could be discovered in no other way. Fear has been created from the Divine Being's desire to experience its Self. Grief similarly reveals the true nature of what is grieved for, who is grieving and why; grief also deepens the heart to allow more room for Love and thus the more direct Divine experience within manifestation and creation's experience of Divinity.

Rage at being thwarted and fury at disparity are the very real experience of God to one degree or another. Yet like love and grief, these emotions of anger are not sourced in the dimension of Identity either. Because rage often rejects the very circumstances that have created or caused it, rage may generate torque: the leverage needed to change what is into what should have been or what could have been. In this, it can be a highly positive force. However if the rage or fury turns upon itself or is used to harm others rather than provide impetus for change, rage becomes like a smoldering, ill-burning fire: it obscures its environment with poisonous, clouding vapors, destroys things without control and too often does more harm than good. This improperly expressed rage, whether human or planetary, stellar or molecular, becomes more of the chaff described above. Thus, whatever human beings of any world can do to clarify rage's reasons, sources and resolution helps the Divine manifest its Self more purely.

The Divine Mind:

I and others have already pointed out more than once that the elements and attributes, fields and factors that make up 4-D reality are balanced to a most exacting degree: that if just one factor were a tiny bit different, the whole structure would collapse, if indeed it could even have been manifested in the first place. This kind of precision in physical substance is also reflected in the divine Mind. Although I cannot describe them in more than a cursory way at this time, as I have been able to see that Mind in my new existence, I will indeed give many of this Mind's aspects some consideration later in this article.

My experience of that Mind is what has allowed me to present such things as Magic, and the meditations with Primordial Chaos as an enfolded dimension in Volume Two, and the essential forms, processes and the intelligent nature of light in Volume One. All of these are actions of the Divine Mind's intentions. But the point I want to make is that this Divine Mind has similarly balanced its own methods, intentions and areas of focus, harmonizing its manifested

47

will with as much attention to what creates meaning within life, as it has with the physical matter, fields, forces and structural aspects of Spacetime. As the Mind of God, the Heart of the Source, desires to have full comprehension, it has completed and re-completed its own expression an infinite number of times and will continue to do so beyond Time.

Similarly, God's emotions and qualities needed to be created in the way they have been created in order to enfold God's feeling nature and the depth and breadth of its Love within reality. Existence is incomplete without feeling! The divine and human qualities, emotions, feelings and empathy form a very deep structure within reality, fundamentally relating particles, fields and processes together so intricately that this relationship surpasses relativity, allowing physical entanglement and experiential unity. The Whole cannot long for its own nature without love, fear and grief or even rage; it cannot relate to its own meaning without joy, sadness and anger.

If you decide that doing without emotion, becoming computer-like or robot-like will make you better human beings and take that path, you will find that you divorce yourselves further and further from your own natures, while simultaneously remove hope of understanding the Divine in nearly *any* aspect. You have lived too long with a dry, emotionless science that cheerfully divorces itself from its own humanity and have frankly beggared yourselves thereby. There are times when quick, practiced action without feeling is needed, but to remain entirely without emotions or feelings is absurd.

The Metaphor of Water, Ice, and Steam:

For a quick, garden-variety metaphor: God's Love is like water, sometimes driven forward by rage; the divine Grief is like ice; the Divine Fear is like steam. The water collects things and nourishes them; it promotes growth and clears away what no longer grows; it is present everywhere and where it is not present, it remains always potential. But when the water, the love, becomes stagnant because it is trapped and held too long in one form, rage may be applied to break down limiting, outdated, or paralyzing structures. Grief, like ice, freezes time and is a shock to the system; yet it also can preserve love, as water stores ice through its crystalline structure. Like ice, grief closes things off and stops many processes. On the other hand, like ice, Divine Grief only rarely becomes so solid that life does not continue, because however solid ice is, it usually floats on the top of the precious water underneath, much like human grief or rage. There is always love beneath and within rage, grief and fear.

Divine Fear is like steam: it adds energy and causes movement even while it can challenge life or scald it. Yet like a geyser pulling up elements from the earth's core, this Fear can bring fresh understanding up from the depths of the heart and mind. Like steam, Divine Fear also expands things, for fear is very useful to life: like pain, it identifies danger, providing the impetus to escape or avoid danger, orienting and concentrating the mind wonderfully. You may fear for the ones you love, telling them to "Take care," and "be safe," and this is the fear that has love at its root.

Nevertheless, your human fear may also be manufactured as a means of controlling others or used by others to control you. It can be used as a whip and a goad; it can be used to create false limitations and real ones, weaving in and out of your many lives' tapestries. A hidden fear or dread can follow you through lifetimes before you begin to understand it. Certainly instilling fear is part of abuse; certainly fear can be manipulated until it creates or drives heinous ends. And yet through it all, the Divine Fear, Rage and Grief is born out of love: love of the Divine Being for Life, Life's love for itself and the value that loving and being loved creates.

When you are human you grieve for things, past times and people you loved, grieve for what has been or what might have been: your grief can keep these loved ones closer and keep your dreams within reach. Rage runs through human experience and so many of Humanity's actions. Yet rage differs from anger in that it is often silent and paradoxically helpless: because of the immense cultural pressures that capture you in their strictures, you may not be able to act when you are enraged. If your life is fraught with structures because you are the "wrong" sex, race, family, religion or heritage then you must face those limitations or overcome them every day of life. In this way the feelings of rage strike you deeper than even your identity. Rage cannot express itself easily: it can become blind and caustic or hidden and toxic, oozing out drops of poison that cannot differentiate between intended targets and hapless bystanders. Because it has its roots deeply within the Zero dimension, rage warps and even breaks the human self if held too long. The lists of fears and the costs of rage can seem endless! And grief erodes courage, will, hope and potential for dreams.

Human Emotions and Feelings:

Surely the human feelings of fear, grief and rage have gotten quite out of hand? You are surrounded and burdened by fears: fear of death, fear of things worse than death; fear of life because of what it will demand and fear that you will not be adequate to its challenges. You often encounter rage in your lives: the rage of the downtrodden and disenfranchised, the fury of those that have been unfairly wounded, hurt and abused. When this rage is controlled it can change nations, as in passive resistance; yet when this rage is uncontrolled then there is no predicting its results. Grief in itself, so based in love, has much potential for healing: by opening the heart and soul, it can humble even your proudest ego-arrogance so that, in your agony, you turn back to the Source of Love. But when grief is too painful and when it cannot be faced, it can morph into anxiety and brittleness of character or depression, leading to a constant state of being distracted from your immediate present.

We have pointed out before that it is often the wealthiest that are the most terrified of loss, whereas those that are centered in love can be either rich or poor and know how best to deal with both situations. The wealth is not the difficult issue: the fear surrounding it is. It used to be more universally known that the more afraid you were, the further you were from your true, divine Self and that fear made your soul's situation often more precarious. In much the same way, the darker, unconscious ferocity of rage shows how far you are from the Divine Love *within* yourself. You may have lost that Love because of your upbringing or as a result of tragedies and betrayals; you may have lost that feeling of divine support because you were asked for too great a sacrifice. Or you have refused to make any of the sacrifices that were needed because you rejected the reasons given for making them. Yet certainly, if rage casually and continually takes you over, then you know that you have become too distant from the Loving Source, forgetting that it resides within you.

It is clear that some of you have been heading the wrong direction for too long: looking for north in the south and depending on the darkest, smokiest of lanterns to light your way. After a while confusion itself became your compass: you may have become unable to conceive of any other direction than fear or any other direction than going into fury. For some, because of that fear, you need to control everything, dictating everything concerning your circumstances: your life, your family, everyone and everything else. Others may have lived so long in directionless anger that any other emotion feels false and weak, for it renders you vulnerable to fear. At this point some may go insane, as have some dictators, violent abusers and demagogues.

Some of you have traveled, lost in the dark, without light or compass for uncounted lifetimes and have felt as alone as a soul may ever feel. In this way, you have in fact learned the one lesson that the Divine Core could not have learned without you: *how it feels to be so totally apart from Love that you cannot find your way back by your own action of will.* Only human beings can be that afraid. Only human beings can create such a desert and live in it. Only a human being can live a loveless life and survive it. Only a human being can overcome fear through grief and love. So the human cost of your emotions buys precious comprehension for the Divine Being and in the end, Divine Love defrays the cost of human pain with healing.

Meditation #2: Stepping Out of the Nightmare of Fear:

After sitting and breathing quietly for a few minutes, take a moment to imagine that you are actually in a nightmare. In this dark dream, you are wearing a hood that partially obscures your vision; you are walking with your head bowed so you only see your feet. But looking around you would be of no help in any event: the air is dark and full of snow and sleet. There seems to be a great crowd of people around you, shuffling and cursing, as blind and cold and bitterly miserable as you are. Some are shouting angrily; in fact some of them seem so angry that they are nearly insane. They cry out paranoid ravings, vicious imprecations against the snow, the wind, their fellow unfortunates and the Fate that brought them into this miserable situation. The angry ones start accusing others, waving their fingers in other people's faces, insisting *they* are to blame for everyone's misery. Even in the throes of this nightmare that your meditative mind has created, you know that this is not and cannot be so. Yet you do not know how to speak up: you do not know what to say. You shuffle along, remaining silent.

However, as you keep pressing forward with the shivering, muffled, unhappy crowd, you suddenly remember that you were carrying something of great importance. You do not quite remember what it was: a letter or telegram, tucked inside your front pocket? Was it a bit of a candle stub and some matches? Or was it even a gem or jewel, a diamond of unusual size and brilliant color? You do not know

51

and want to find out, so you let yourself get pushed to the edge of the crowd. The wind cuts more keenly here, and the snow has ice in it, but you are burning to know what secret has been entrusted to you. Finally, there is a quiet moment in the snowstorm and a little clear space where you can stand in the light and see what you have. This secret you have been carrying will be different for every person and even for every meditation: what you draw out of your pocket may have been any of the things mentioned above, or it may be something quite personal to you. But whatever it is, it glows, softly. And then, where its light falls, the snow turns into warm, soft rain. Everywhere the light touches, there is rain!

Excited, you cry out, "Look! Look at the rain! See how beautiful it is!" You have to shout because you have moved away from the original, huddled crowd. It seems as though no one hears you with the wind and the snow they labor under. Yet you keep crying out, "Look at the rain, the sweet rain, so warm and soft!" Soon, you will see others turning to stare; you may even see others start to move away from the crowd. And wherever the rain touches the ground, the ice and snow disappear, so that green grass and flowers grow there instead of the snow.

No more churned, frozen mud; no more staggered footprints: instead, there are sweet-smelling blossoms everywhere. As you hold your shining object, feeling its warmth, you bring it close to your heart and its warmth heals and eases you. The crowd's cries of anger or fear, the sounds of frustration or self-pity, loss or grief die away and become distant. You cannot hear them in the soft patter of rain; you cannot feel them in the soft, loving comfort of the rain's sweet sound. When you hear nothing but the gentle patter of warm water, or perhaps some gentle voices near you, then close your meditative eyes and breathe the light in deeply, so that you can gently slip away from the nightmare altogether, knowing that you have found the healing power of Love.

Peace and Emotions as Actions of Creation:

Needless to say, even though they might be distilled or reduced into the three basic feelings of anger, sadness or happiness, because of feelings, the human experience of emotions can be richly nuanced, fascinatingly complex, enigmatic and frustratingly inexplicable at the same time. They are part of your identity's present sense of itself at the same time they are your self's own history. Yet they can also take you quite by surprise and overwhelm you as though they were outer forces that had nothing to do with you. Changeable, unpredictable, sometimes costly and always affecting things, emotions and feelings seem such an uncertain ground to build a universe upon! There are so many times when emotions and feelings get in your way and complicate things unnecessarily. Whatever can be the use of them if they are so disruptive?

Much as it is with God, the Core Source, your own emotions are used in order to illuminate desire, intention, relationships and a deeper and more complete knowledge of yourself. In order to create Reality at all, the Source needed its three emotions and all of its feelings, because only yearning and passion, desire and delight could create the physical and temporal structures that allowed that Divine Infinity, which is without beginning or end to manifest into form. In short, the un-created Being that has created everything, could only have created its Self without irreconcilable paradox *through* the deep meanings of feelings and essential qualities of emotions. I cannot emphasize this enough: in all their permutations love, grief and fear and all the forms of anger, sadness and happiness, are essential for Reality's existence.

Thus, even false fear, the terror or dread manipulated into being by those who wish control you and all the circumstances around themselves, is accepted into your human experience. As human beings can create, express and discern this fear's dissonant nature, this kind of fear has its own profound purpose within the structures and aspects of the 4-D manifestation of the Divine Mind and Divine Being. Although, this does not mean that this fear must be perpetuated! Indeed, you have become allergic to being manipulated by this false fear in several respects: craving it even though it does you harm. You have become too used to its agitation and have forgotten that the true core of your nature is *Peace*. However, reaching into this essential Peace again may illuminate your mind and the Divine Mind together, allowing the structures that create reality to fall back into place once again.

But Peace is not merely a lack of agitation. Like the solid, vibrationless core of Para-light or like the hidden, unmanifest energy within the enfolded dimensions and inside physical matter, Peace is the fulcrum upon which everything turns. In some ways, Peace is the truest nature of the divine Core, even more than Love, for Peace is deeper and more real than any other attribute, including the four feeling-qualities of love, grief, rage or fear. When Peace is created or discovered, Reality changes around it. When you can be in a state of true equanimity in spite of the agitations that surround you, then you can *re-create* what exists because Peace is the real engine that drives all manifestation. When you align your energy with the Peace of the Divine Core that is deeper than Love, you can literally become an action of God.

The best answer to the grief, fear or rage within a process, person, place or thing is to reach into re-manifesting the potentials within Peace. There are numerous meditations for serenity and tranquility and any of thousands of ways to evoke it. If you have a favorite method or meditation, by all means employ it at regular intervals. Or, once you are familiar with your soul's Core Tone you can center yourself in that Tone, and unfold it into the infinitely potential, solid core of Peace. This may take only a short breath or two to refresh yourself after a hard day dealing with someone else's emotional needs, expressions or occasional dramas. Understanding how emotions work within reality and yourself is a precious gift, for when you feel, and feel deeply, you become even more in alignment with the Divine Self that uses emotions and feelings to reveal the inner meanings of Its Own Manifestation to its self and its creation.

Alternate Realities: A Working Manual

Key Points: This manual is a set of mental and imaginative exercises to help you get familiar with the possibilities and experiences of alternate realities. If you can close your eyes and imagine the color of your house then you have enough imagination to do these exercises. In point of fact, you may already use creativity and imagination to gather information from alternate realities as well as from others' consciousness. When you perceive yourself as more than one type of person, your psychological stance is wider and more stable. Using meditations where you imagine aspects of your daily life differently in order to understand the difference between daydreaming and meditation, you will start noticing when alternate realities touch your own. You can even begin crafting alternate realities intentionally through conversations with your other living selves, expanding your understanding of yourself in this time and place.

Subheadings:

- Introduction
- Creativity and Imagination
- Stage One: Manifesting Play and the Play of Manifestation
- Stage Two: Dreams and Daydreams
- Stage Three: Noticing When Alternate Realities Collide
- Stage Four: Crafting Alternate Realities Intentionally
- Stage Five: Other-life Conversations
- Meditation: Shifting through an Alternate Reality Transfer

Introduction:

It may seem strange to put this workbook in the section labeled Multi-Dimensional Field Effects rather than the section for Human Experiences: surely your work with your own past, alternate and future lives is a personal experience quite separate from physics? But of course that is the whole point: human consciousness is not apart from physics: surely countless fields and forces affect you in the midst of all your endeavors. I thank Jane Roberts for bringing up the issue of the Conscious Scientist that studies the science of consciousness with his own mental, emotional, and psychic perceptions. As long as there is a gap, however small, between you and the universe, your experience will not be as complete as it might be, and thus the experience of the Divine Consciousness is similarly lessened. So we offer these meditations and exercises as springboards that you may use with your own sense of adventurous inquiry into your nature as well as the nature of the universe.

Creative and imaginative people will find these exercises easier to do. But if you believe that you couldn't even imagine yourself out of a paper bag and thus are not sure if you can do these exercises, then realize that since you have bought this book, you have at least enough imagination to speculate: that is quite sufficient. If you can close your eyes and remember the color of your house or car, your front door or your favorite pet you had years ago, then you have the image in your mind. This is the beginning of imagination: the "imagining-in" of creative thought. When you add creativity, the inward image expands its dimensions. Believe it or not, everyone is creative to at least a degree. Creativity, in essence, means to take something in one form and change it into another form that has less entropy within it. Have you ever crafted anything, whether it was your own breakfast, a house of cards or a fort made with sofa pillows in the living room when you were a child? Have you ever daydreamed and then acted on the dream? Have you ever gone on a different route to work just for the fun of it? Then, you are creative enough to do these exercises with the images in your mind.

Creativity and Imagination:

As they are energetic fields similar to mental or psychic faculties, Creativity and Imagination are based in part on the Etheric field's matrix. Creativity and Imagination frequently absorb information, images, points of view and ideas from alternate realities, allowing other realities to absorb images and ideas from your reality as well. This does not mean that there are no new ideas or that the same notions are passed around in a kind of zero sum game: Divine Creativity is infinite and therefore human Creativity could be infinite as well. But similar to the morphogenic field of the hundredth monkey phenomenon, it is easier for others to do the same new thing that others have already imagined, even though they may not be near the original working group. Because of the added resonance though the alternate realities, there is just that much more collected potential energy and just that much more multi-dimensional slope, allowing the extra momentum needed for the new idea to manifest.

This is partly why some inventions are discovered by different inventors perhaps three or four times in the same year: the collected resonance formed by the minds focusing on the same issue tends to enable the transfer through the enhanced slope in the alternate realties' geometries. In this sense, therefore, alternate realities are not separate "bubbles" of completely contained, unapproachable unity within themselves. Because of creativity and imagination's close association with Ether 's field-matrix, conscious minds that have learned a particular type of focus can discover, discern and engage these otherworld realities.

From one point of view, alternate realities are not difficult to understand. After all, when you mix eternity with infinity, what could you possibly produce? Infinite variety, experience and meaning expressed through infinitely shifting relationships forming and re-forming continually and perpetually. From this point of view, the static self-reference of the dimension of Identity seems a more astonishing creation than even the unexpectedly slow, high-density and low energy hologram called 4-D Reality: so unusual as to be highly unlikely. However, the dimension of Identity is absolutely necessary in order for the Whole to be discerned or even discernable *by* its own Self in a continually shifting cosmos that has an infinite number of relativistic expressions. Based profoundly upon the vibrationless core of Para-light that is both a Torsion Field and a state of being, the dimension of Identity allows the Divine Being to continually discover and re-discover its Self within these multiple expressions, yet rarely lose track of each specific point.

When you begin to play with the idea of alternate realities, as many already have in several creative endeavors, remember that the more possibilities you imagine, the more you can see your own identity clearly. When you see yourself as more than one or two roles or personas, you have a wider and more stable psychological stance and can actually react to shocks and strains more ably than if you have only one or two identities. If you feel that you are only a spouse, a parent or a single person, when any of these things change it is difficult to know who or what you are anymore without that one definition. However, if you are also a son, a husband, a brother, an uncle, a friend, a pianist, a volunteer at the homeless shelter, and an occasional cook, then you have not only a broader identity but also broader connections within other realities.

Using this broad stance, you can take advantage of the potential energies and slopes within those alternate realities for your own use, finding new ways of expressing yourself that help, along with loving friendship and perhaps professional care, to carry you through tragedies such as losing your spouse, child or you means of income. Or, if you are a daughter, a little sister and an aunt, a friend, a wife, a teacher, a weaver, a gardener and an occasional kazoo player as well as a parent, spouse or renter, then when any of these shift, you have some stability to work within in your sense of self. Much as geckos climb walls with the myriad tiny hairs on their feet, you can explore the myriad realities of your broader identity and find yourself able to move through changes more easily.

Stage One: Manifesting Play and the Play of Manifestation:

Think of your front door, and then imagine to yourself: "Maybe it could be purple!" Imagine the purple front door and then refine it. "Maybe it could be lavender and grape, with a big golden knob on it. Maybe it could have other patterns on it as well, such as leaves, flowers, trees, butterflies or airplanes, planets or balloons." You can have fun and be absolutely silly with this: approach it with a child-like, inventive and not at all serious attitude.

However, for this exercise take care that you do not think, "What if? What if my front door were purple or green?" Oddly enough, thinking "What if?" will tend to switch your mind out of discernment into judgment. When you start to judge your choices, you will no longer focus on the colors, shapes or potentials of that imagined door: instead you will start to think, "What if I did..." something specific. When you focus too much on judgment instead of discernment you are too likely to worry: "What would other people assume about me with such an absurd thing as a purple front door?" Or you might think, "What if I had to paint the door? I would have to wash it and sand it, put primer on it and keep people from touching it until it was dry, to say nothing of choosing the colors in the first place... "

"Maybe" is more likely to be a term that allows your subconscious and creative self to speculate freely, whereas "What if?" is usually followed by "I:" "What if I had to... wanted to... needed to..." and so on and so on. This focuses your mind too clearly in your present reality. After all, the whole point of imagining that maybe your front door might be purple is to loosen your hold on this present reality a little, so you can explore other possibilities. When you think, "Maybe the door could be round, or maybe it could be a Dutch door or maybe it could be an oval: how would it look?" In this way the subject is the *door*, and not yourself or your judgments about your own decorating skills.

Stage Two: Dreams and Daydreams:

If you never daydreamed when you were in school, then you had such wonderful teachers and so many fascinating things to learn that you were perfectly happy working in the classroom. Remember how it felt to have your mind wander off: you let your mind follow itself as it drifted away, untying it like a boat from the dock and letting the wind push it along anywhere. Of course, you were likely chastised if you were too obvious about the daydreaming, so you tended to shut down that loose, comfortable feeling in a hurry. But the ability is still there: you can still use it.

Although both states of mind use the Etheric matrix, daydreaming is more strongly based in the geometries that combine the dimension of Identity with the dimension of Primordial Chaos. You might quiet your mind by focusing your attention on your breathing or a mantra until the mind becomes still: however, daydreaming removes your mind from its original focus even more gently than meditation. In a daydream, as in a dream, you may open your mind to images, information and data that are not part of your usual physical reality. Generally there will be emotional content as well: humor, wistfulness, excitement, or even melancholy will give your daydreams impetus. Although, if you feel your emotions too keenly, it is best to just watch your thoughts' own meanders, allowing them to flow in their own way. Mental disengagement from 4-D reality through Primordial Chaos allows you to feel as though you were inside the floating "boat" of your thoughts, though you are not paddling or steering your thoughts: you are *allowing* your mind its freedom.

If you feel anxious about being taken somewhere in the drifting boat of your mind that you would not like, you may keep yourself tied to the dock of your present reality's focus by building upon something already in your immediate vicinity. Pick an object in the room where you are. If the object is something you bought, remember where and when you purchased it or perhaps when it was given to you. Work with the memory until you remember how you were

59

standing, perhaps what clothes you were wearing, whether the day was warm or cold and how many people were around you. The more real and multi-dimensional this memory is, the better.

When you feel you have the memory as clearly as you can, then breathe it into your heart and then release the image as you exhale. The mind may lose all images then; however, it will be in the state of relaxed attention that you need in order to imagine the events differently. If you were alone when you purchased the item, remember instead that your best friend or a family member came with you. If the object was a gift from a friend and the wrapping paper was yellow, remember it being blue. For now, this is all you do: make one little change to get your mind used to the relaxed attention of the daydream, and then shifting the possibilities. By doing this shift you are actually working with both the Etheric Field and tachyons: indeed, tachyons are part of *how* your consciousness encounters alternate realities. To the degree that they are "faster than time," tachyons are also "further than space," for the pan-universal matrix of Ether provides all the connections.

To work with your dreams in alternate realities, just think as you are going to sleep at night, "Tonight I will dream myself somewhere else." In the beginning, it will not matter whether or not you remember this dream: your subconscious needs time for training and your subconscious likes to do a lot of its work "in the back room," so to speak. But if you instruct yourself this way every night, gradually you will wake up feeling a little different each morning. You might have more experiences of *déjà vu*; you might have odd little moments where you forget simple things like your own address, or which way to open up a jar lid: is it to the right or the left? When these things happen to you, know you are on the right track! Your subconscious is stretching itself through infinite possibilities and getting used to swimming in different seas. Working at night is a good way to practice.

Stage Three: Noticing When Alternate Realities Collide:

Exercise One: Have you have ever described a trip that you took long ago with a friend and found that even though your friend went on the same trip there are always things each of you remembers differently? Sometimes it is simply because memory is fallible. However, there are other times when you and he actually experienced different realities. One way to check is to pick one brief, shared incident. Each of you focuses your thoughts upon it by writing it down. Describe the incident with as many details as possible and then compare notes: see how the accounts differ. Or, try to remember a book you once read or a movie you once saw and then compare your memory with the original. You may notice some astonishing differences.

Notice: the moment when your memory diverged and became different is the moment that you edged into another reality. Yes, the original book or movie or incident certainly appears to stay the same, especially if recorded in some durable medium. Yet the branching-off point is where the memory became different while still contained within the original reality. This superposition is what I call a collision of alternate realities: sometimes it creates an amalgam of realities, though sometimes the two realities mismatch, creating an "interference fit" where the two memories fight for supremacy, occasionally with disastrous results, as in cases of insanity.

Exercise Two: Another way to perceive superimposed realities is to watch one of those programs where they have a judge deciding various civil cases in real time, where people talk about how they have treated one another. Notice the difference between their accounts. You will not be seeing into another, alternate reality directly through this method; nevertheless, when two or more people see the same incident or circumstance completely differently, you will see a superposition of those realities. This exercise of watching the different stories is not meant for you to decide who is right or wrong, just to notice the incidents of superposition that result from alternate reality collisions.

Exercise Three: A third way is to discern things with different specific perspectives, as in that old novel Rashomon, where five different people have five different experiences of the same incident. If you know of an incident that involved three or four persons and you know enough of its history to understand at least a little of each person's experience, then imagine that you are each person seeing it from his point of view or her perspective. Work to see it from each viewpoint within the incident: each person's specific parallax. Next imagine the angle of the proverbial fly on the wall and finally from the point of view of the incident itself. After some practice you can even feel as though you *are* the factors in the incident being worked upon by these three or four people. If for instance you are remembering a minor road accident, imagine you could view the incident from the point of view of the cars, the road and perhaps the sun looking down.

These three exercises are not merely playing with your memory and imagination: this will make you more aware of the times when your reality brushes up against another reality or another reality brushes up against yours. You do shift realities all the time, although it is a bit as though you were on a magical subway ride: instead of stopping at a station, climbing out onto the platform, using a transfer ticket to catch a new train, it is rather as though your own seat suddenly decided to slide out from the other seats and "catch" the car to which you want to transfer. In the context of our metaphor: if you are sitting back and reading the paper or napping, you do not even notice the change. Like the eye's blind spot, your mind is used to glossing over a great many changes through alternate realities. But by starting to notice how and when things *might* change, you can learn to notice when they *do* change.

Stage Four: Crafting Alternate Realities Intentionally:

You begin this by watching incidents as they occur. Later, when you have a moment, think of how they might have turned out differently, for better or worse. If you like and would enjoy it, you can catastrophize or aggrandize each incident, so that you think of how it could have been worse, and then the worst, finally even more worse than that, feeling your mind and imagination stretch. Then think of how it could have been better and then better, until it is absolutely the best that it could have been: not only the possible best but even the impossible best. The reason for the hyperbole is that there are times when the absurd has the germ of a new idea in it and might give you a new way of seeing or dealing with something. Even though it is simply a few good ideas or just inventing things for fun, this will get your mind and subconscious working on opening the alternate perspectives and potentials.

Stage Five: Other-life Conversations:

Part One: If inexplicable things haunt you such as a fear of flying or a dread of snakes, you can put the past into the past with the help of hypnotherapy from a good past-life practitioner of some kind. Still, you do not need to get hypnotized to learn of at least some of your past/future/other-reality lives: you can simply start with what you like or dislike. This is easiest with foods. If you are happy eating rice, the chances are very high that you have lived in China, Japan,

Indonesia or India. If you are very fond of curry too, then that might narrow it down to India, but that is not a guarantee. However, if you hate rice, then that might be a clue for the same countries. The rice is not the issue: hating it or loving it is. You can follow that feeling of loving curried rice into your own memories of eating a feast of it or perhaps to a memory of having to give it up in order to feed your starving family instead of yourself.

Do not worry, you are *not* trying for total historical accuracy here: you are simply getting used to linking with a particularly clear and resonant personality, life or incident. That resonance will open the doors into alternate realities by limbering up your imagination's focus through your mind and memory. If you become nervous at the idea of "missing the mark" and getting into an alternate reality where you don't get the "real" story but get some other weird version of it instead that has nothing to do with who you are, please try to relax. You are simply trying to expand your sense of self with this exercise, not prove anything to anyone, including to yourself. As has been said elsewhere, in infinity and eternity, everything that could happen, might happen, should have happened and ought to have happened has happened somewhere and "somewhen." This is part of the deeper meaning of infinite alternate realities.

Part Two: If feelings about food don't seem to lead anywhere, start with anything that you feel strongly about: even so abstract a thing as a concept of justice or hating traitors. The point of the exercise is to experiment and discover, not to pin your experience down like a butterfly, freezing its meaning and beauty in some perfect moment of time, accurately identifying what type of thought or memory it is. Choose a method that will make this memory real to you. Then, to proceed further, imagine a particular past self that first confronted the issue is able to converse with you. Invent having a conversation with that other persona of your own self. You can even start with consequential questions: you might ask that other self, "What is most important to you?" or "What is the most important thing you have learned?" "What is the thing you like the best?" "What do you like the least?" You may get some very interesting answers!

If you cannot imagine speaking to that other-life self, allow your imagination freedom enough to write the conversation out or draw a picture of something that catches the meaning of that other self's purpose or interests in his or her life. Or you can simply feel that other person's loves or hatreds, because these feelings usually have enough signal strength to overcome the distance between your realities. If the first experiences seem vague and disconnected, again, just relax. In this kind of exercise it is perfectly appropriate to "make something up," because the purpose here is to help you encounter another part of yourself.

Meditation: Shifting through an Alternate Reality Transfer:

Part One: In this first part, sit quietly and calm your mind with gentle breathing. Imagine looking at your body from slightly above where you are sitting, though from the same original viewpoint. It will seem very much the same as when you look down at your body in the chair anyway, but you can tell you are a little higher. In addition, your point of view is just slightly off, as though it were a printed page or a picture that had lost its registration, so there is a visual "echo" of your own body, a ghostly pattern superimposed on your present body. Feel as though you were sliding over from the place of your original body-pattern, just that tiny bit, into the body-pattern that is offset by that amount.

If you do this correctly, you will feel a sudden shiver or an instant of vertigo: you have succeeded in moving a very small step into another reality. This step is so tiny that it "heals over" quickly, like the surface of a pond when you throw a tiny pebble into it. There is hardly a ripple, but you surely know you threw the stone and that it has sunk down. You may not have moved from one alternate reality to another, but you know that you have changed yourself that little bit. You don't want to change realities on impulse! But by making this little step you will be able to notice the other times that you change naturally, as according to your soul's directives.

Part Two: Now you can put everything together and really play with your own alternate realities. Invent another reality, putting in more of this, or less of that; add differences, both tiny and large. Then work on getting a sense of your expanded self by recalling or even *inventing* a past or future life. Feel the way your present reality and those other realities might collide. How would the differences really feel? Would a past-life self argue with you about the way you are living now? Would a future self look back at your present life with nostalgia, or relief to be out of it?

For the last step, wrap the new reality around yourself playfully. Don't fear forgetting anything: what you have created is your own, for if you have done it once, you can do it again. By working with these exercises, you expand your sense of your own self, become more receptive to new and uncommon ideas and begin to open lines of communication with your soul and Higher Self. The more fun you can have with these exercises, the better, because you have become part of the creative play of the living universe.

Indirectness in Living Systems: R-L Brain Aspects, RNA/DNA and the Axonal Gap

Key Points: There is a natural duality in the universe between direct, more point-focused masculine aspects and indirect, holistic feminine aspects. Two other essential aspects are handedness (right or left) and pulse: an "activity and rest." Reality might be described as an amorphous, quick-frozen non-crystalline "alloy" of energy. You can understand reality's hologram more clearly through *principles* such as balance and change, stasis and shift. The feminine aspects of manifestation allow the enfolded dimension of Primordial Chaos to express the Divine intention, refreshing reality. Healing is indirect, as are many of the body's systems and processes. The Tarot card of The Lovers shows the triangle of energy between male, female and higher-order energies. The feminine aspects are a greater part of reality than is generally supposed.

Subheadings:

- Chaotic Indirectness, Dispersion and the Creativity of Margins

- Gaps, Activation Energies and Fulcrums

- Amorphous Aspects of Reality

- Right/Left Switching and Dynamic Balances of Spacetime

- The Principles of Reality and Form

- Feminine and Masculine Energies and Wholeness

- The Feminine Connection to the Enfolded Dimensions

- The Feminine Principle in Human Interactions

- The Feminine Nature of the Universe

Chaotic Indirectness, Dispersion and the Creativity of Margins:

From the gentle fringes of the Fallopian tubes to the complex meanders of a river delta, from the essential mathematically chaotic patterns of tree branches and weather systems to the ebb and flow of seasons, wildlife populations and human fads, existence on Earth appears governed by both direct and indirect forces. These factors, masculine and feminine if you will, continually interact with sometimes stunning results, working with each other to create patterns of great beauty. Masculinity and femininity is certainly embedded in animal life and human experience. Although to speak of reality in those terms seems animistic to a degree, the straight and direct rays of the sun seems masculine to many, while the more indirect and changeable moon seems more feminine. Though, of course, those designations were not universal: in ancient Egypt, the moon was masculine and, as Sekhmet, the sun was feminine.

Nevertheless, it is elegant shorthand to think of things in this way, for this paired energy is a way of relating to the universe as a whole. Certainly sexual dimorphism is a tremendously consistent and constant factor in nearly all life. Because Duality is part of the very essence of leverage, torsion, change and the dynamic balance of forces, duality has its roots deep within the dimension of Identity. Duality is as fundamental and as necessary a principle of physical reality as Time. But as Reality's images have been created upon its chaotic interactions with the holographic fabric of 4-D expression, this creates the very feminine process and principle of mixture.

But Duality in itself would not necessarily lead to the indirectness in phenomena such as the left side of the brain controlling the right side of the body, to say nothing of the indirect and complicated enzyme-triggered transcription and template process of RNA forming proteins from DNA with M-, T-, R-RNA, and ribosomes creating amino acids and building them into proteins. Considering how each stage involves several steps and changes in a very open area of interaction, the process is amazingly exact even in the cell's inner "soup" that contains sugars and bases floating in the nucleoplasm. It is almost as though Life wished to re-create the astonishing and unlikely "first connection" of the DNA/RNA duplication every time. Certainly, the fetus does indeed seem to go through evolutionary stages in the process of its development. Yes, many cellular processes streamline over time as forms shift to become more efficient but again, the process is not at all linear: it is always subject to change, chance, shifts of fortune and again, the diffuse and indirect actions of Chaos. It is for this reason at least that I have not only described Primordial Chaos as a dimension in itself, but also aligned it with the Zero dimension and the dimension of Identity, the three elemental dimensions that allow physical reality's creation.

Another dualistic factor that I mentioned in Volume One is Dispersion: it both manifests outward from a central point, yet, by drawing information back into a point of origin, creates homogeneity through replication. Again you can perceive both the direct, masculine line of force moving outwards and the feminine, collective force of gathering, coming into center. When working together, these dualistic factors are not antagonists: they are more like the base points of a triangle that literally creates dimensions with the third point of Reality's interactive hologram.

This is one of the reasons for systems' indirectness: like the convolutions of the surface of the brain, indirectness forms margins, semi-conduction and randomness. It has been said elsewhere that if it were not for random events and the Uncertainty Principle, the physical universe would have stopped dead in its tracks hardly a millisecond after its birth! Though, as I describe in the article on The True Nature of Time below, in a universe full of beginnings and endings there never was a beginning, nor will there be an end. Created by the Chaotic Edge, margins directly promote creative responses to conditions, allowing them to change in the first place. So however time-consuming, chancy and perplexing indirectness is, it is vital to manifestation.

Gaps, Activation Energies and Fulcrums:

Axons and dendrites are not contiguous: information's electrochemical sparks necessarily have to leap the gap. This seems another way for things to be subject to misdirection, mischance and misfire and thus to be inefficient, subject to random chaos and more trouble than they are worth. Misfiring, cascades and other disruptions do occur in the brain with epilepsy, migraines and some forms of dementia, sometimes having huge human costs. Whatever could be the use of such inefficiency creating extra work every time a neuron fires or having random events break down or destroy successful systems? Clear, binary steps, straight lines and simple structures seem to make so much more sense: efficiency seems so much more valuable than inefficiency. However: the axonal gap increases the potential complexity of forms and processes and however irritating at times, complexity is essential. And especially now that many human beings are confronted with the cool, clean lines and super-fast structures of computers to the point that some wonder whether or not to do away with all the messy inefficiency of indirect processes altogether, this issue of how the feminine principles relate to the masculine is one of human concern.

This bias towards straight-line masculine efficiency has already had several effects on the way human society expresses itself, such as some museums' and libraries' desire to create an "efficient" flow of visitors by removing all the comfortable chairs and replacing them with them with uncomfortable, "chair-like" objects that make it impossible to linger. After all, lingering, taking time and being in community are not efficient! As I mention in the article about the marketplace, the very idea of computers is starting to shape human interactions: much as you have fast food, you now have a "fast-life" version of living, where complexity is constantly pared down again and again until you have mere sound-bites and idea-bites of information until comprehension and meaning suffer. Rarely is anything pondered upon under these conditions, examined at depth or given true consideration; in addition to taxing human health constantly, this is actually a shocking loss of value.

Indirectness increases the activation energy in processes, creating more able and resourceful responses to changing conditions. The universe cannot exist without change yet over-simplification *removes* change! Paradoxically, a singular focus on too much straight-line, direct efficiency leads to the worst chaos of all: the loss of purpose and meaning. Without purpose or meaning, once again the universe freezes solid, without action, because there is no impulse to respond, move forward or adapt. This was and is the essential miracle of creation: that the Core Source, the Para-light heart of the Zero Dimension, is able to engage and then transform its solid, unmoving nature into 4-D Reality through the fulcrum of the feminine aspect: indirectness enfolding the renewing impulses of Chaos, holistic unity allowing 4-D Reality its own version of kinesthesia and the elegantly amorphous and indirect focus that allows Time to become Process.

Amorphous Aspects of Reality:

Conceiving itself from the Zero Dimension within and outside of Time by using the four principles of Accretion, Dispersion, Assimilation and Dissolution through vibration [see Volume One] and through the intense local effects of several Torsion Fields, Para-light becomes vibration, motion and dynamic manifestation. By these methods Para-light and the Zero Dimension have not only created change but also *difference*. As I have said before, 4-D Reality's essential

69

construction is similar to an amorphous metal and the metaphor is exact in several senses: through deep engagement with the Torsion Fields of Numeration and Formation, Reality has been formed like a quick-frozen, non-crystalline alloy. Retaining its creativity, manifest Reality's version of electrical conductivity is Quantum Entangled Inductive Resonance. Since its first formation, 4-D Reality has been cooling and spreading out, like an alloy spun out on a disk in order to solidify it in a glass-like state; in this way physical reality remains both malleable and permeable.

The significance of this amorphous mixture cannot be over-emphasized. Where there are differences in density, content, size, rigidity, stability or malleability, there is leverage, slope, potential and kinetic energies enough to create the activation energy needed to create form and changes within form, so that change becomes a property of what is physical with more impact than with any other property or condition. It is perhaps surprising that this factor of Change is so huge, so universally constant, that although it has been remarked upon, to the best of our knowledge it has never been studied as its own subject.

However, because of this same amorphous composition, 4-D Reality is full of levers and fulcrums: enzymes providing leverage; templates and catalysts of many kinds providing fulcrums for processes such as creating DNA, cultural shifts, spiritual growth and Magic. There is also astrological energy's spiraling shifts that catapult change by means of the tiny, sequentially added differences created even within the stable referent point of the Möbius strip of Time; indeed, these differences help create the "colors" of Time. The enfolded and unfolded M-D geometries' lattice upon which Reality is placed are created through the combined leverage and templates of the three main dimensions of Identity, Zero and Primordial Chaos. In short, the amorphous nature of Reality's inner structure allows it to exist and, as we said, the amorphous is a feminine principle.

Right/Left Switching and Dynamic Balances of Spacetime:

Another duality is the difference between right and left, the two sides of symmetry. Handedness is found in nearly all species: a cat may favor its left paw for batting a toy mouse, a dog may reach out to you with its right paw first and a horse may prefer a certain lead when running straight, even incorrectly keeping to that lead when turning. This is more than just the essential duality of a cell that splits in two to grow: the dimension of Identity's very attributes of wholeness needs the duality of complimentary halves. The reason is that manifestation is actually an expression of pulse. As defined centuries ago, pulse is "an activity and then a rest." In this sense pulse reflects the feminine principle of shift and indirect action working in balance with the masculine aspects of force and inertia. When you see the manifest universe as a dynamic flutter of expression, you can begin to understand natural rhythms such as the turning of the seasons, heartbeats and waves of all kinds.

Trajectories and vectors such as light-beams or the inertial movement and directions of force, all combine disparate pulses at a very deep level, shattering the pulse's stability and thus creating the chaotic edge. One of the essential qualities of life is semi-conduction, which would not be possible without the interplay of trajectory and pulse, with lines of force mingling with the essential, particle-like Units of Consciousness within the very process of materialization. This chaotic interplay is kept in check by the very process of balance: combining right and left with a center, as it is with the brain's corpus callosum or as when walking or running, where pulse and rhythm are retained through changing sides. Whether bilateral symmetry or particle symmetry, oddly enough they retain their wholeness *because* the Chaotic Edge demands that nothing ever be exactly copied from one side to the other, at least not in living systems and generally speaking in anything manufactured as well. The essential offset, the minutely miss-matched joining of all physical things, depends on this essential factor of balance through left/right symmetry mixed with the unanticipated combinations of the three essential forms of Line, Sphere and Chaotic Edge. This offset keeps Space malleable enough to retain its connection to Time.

The Principles of Reality and Form:

To a degree, when the Divine Mind crafted the unfolded dimensions, it arranged for quite a number of automatic processes, yet since complexity itself is being continually renewed, that very same perpetual, incessant creativity is the constant and ongoing miracle. When an identity is too whole, too complete, like the noble gasses, it remains discrete but in a dangerous stasis without interaction and thus without growth. As mentioned before, the dimension of Identity limits other dimensions, particularly the manifested dimensions in 4-D. On the other hand, if it were not for uncertainty, broken symmetry and serendipity, separate identities

71

would become so robust that nothing could interact with any other thing. This shows the extreme value of the offset created by the feminine principle of Chaos.

Indirectness in many aspects aligns with the energy of Chaos, especially when higher-order energies infuse reality and the Torsion Field of Translation is engaged to manifest the indirect, unfolding energies of Chaos. Communication, creativity and healing are a few examples of this connection between the Dimension of Chaos and the unfolded dimensions that use the Translation Torsion Field in order to manifest in 4-D reality. Necessarily, all of them are indirect to one degree or another. When the body heals itself, countless factors are pulled into play. There are frequently times when a malady can become worse before it becomes better: this is certainly not a straight-light method for making things right again! Healing can be prolonged, or instantaneous; health can be stable until a sudden shock, yet sudden shocks can help the living body to bring healing forward. Moreover, in a distinctly chaotic and also indirect result, there are so many instances when a drug originally used to relieve the symptoms of one disease relieve the symptoms of another or perhaps even actually cures the other disease!

Good communication is often quite direct. But how the brain handles and interprets language is never simply direct, else why could language have so many connotations, innuendoes, puns and double meanings possible within it? Children are capable of learning any human language: they do not come with language already clear and straightforward in their minds, but must be taught and the teaching process is as indirect as it is direct: children learn from what is not said as much as from what is said, and indeed sometimes more. The human path to creative expression can be direct in terms of training. But there is always a strong element of chaos in creativity as well as unexpected, indirect means of learning and expression. In creativity, perhaps, is the best balance between the direct and indirect expression of forces, as well as the chaotic and the disciplined: ideas may come "out of the blue" but need skill to be expressed.

Feminine and Masculine Energies and Wholeness:

This is another reason why the feminine principle of indirectness is actually is given more and greater areas of expression than the masculine directness. If anything is followed to its straight-line, "logical" conclusion, it can become absurd, unworkable or

72

encapsulated in stasis. If evolution were pursued to its logical outcome, there would be only one animal left: an uber-predator that could catch, kill and eat anything and that would be that, or at best, such a straight-line evolution would create a horribly static duality of eternally continual war, uber-predator against uber-prey. Certainly that seemed to be the shape of things during the 65 million years of the dinosaurs: several chaotic shocks were needed to create change. Stasis, so plainly linked to entropy and to the masculine, one-pointed focus, does have distinct momentum. However, if it were not for the weird combination of balance and disparity that the mixture of masculine and feminine aspects create, perhaps all the planets might be like Mercury, locked in hot and frozen orbits, if indeed there were planets at all.

When you look for it, the feminine principle can be seen everywhere from planetary ellipses (instead of circles) to the very principle of semi-conduction that supports and promotes creativity so well, for indeed creativity is also a feminine attribute. The four essential processes of Accretion, Dispersion, Assimilation and Dissolution show a beautiful synergy of the masculine and feminine principles, but as all of them are patterned primarily on circular and semi-circular energies, they clearly show a bias towards the feminine energy pattern. The feminine also is triplicate: this provides torque, leverage and shift by its very nature within the function of balance. This feminine energy is inclusive, not only in the sense of gathering disparate things into groups but also the in triune concept of gestation: it is the seed, the egg and the womb's formative matrix that allows and nurtures life.

Perhaps part of the distress men have felt with feminine energy has to do with its indirectness, inclusiveness and its curved trajectories. This indirectness can seem crooked and duplicitous, false and mysterious. Yet tangents cannot become arcs unless they have change forced upon them. Indirect trajectories include the swirl and the spiral that allow the dimension of Primordial Chaos to infuse Reality with refreshed vision and inspiration from the Zero Dimension and the dimension of Identity without any direct line of force. Granted it is the same the other way: arcs must be straightened out by force, in which case they are no longer arcs. Straightening arcs engenders uneasy things from merkator projections that attempt to flatten the sphere, cloverleaf exits that confuse some people by "braiding" traffic from straight to curved travel, as well as the

73

challenges of calculating inter-planetary navigation. However, an elegant example of the two principles helping and sustaining each other is in bridge design, particularly suspension bridges and the pressure-lines of force that form weight-carrying bone.

For many centuries human bias in European and many Oriental cultures has been towards the hierarchical, straight-line, top-down ordering of peoples, resources and laws because the effects of such ordering are easier to perceive. Definitely the straight-line energy used in literally pushing someone down shows its effects immediately and dramatically, while the shifting dance of Aikido that does not use straight-line force appears too disengaged for any real effect. However, Aikido and similar arts alters the original trajectory of an attack *through* indirectness: while much subtler at times it is even more effective than confronting straight-line force with straight-line force. I grant you that for centuries, the indirect approach has been called Machiavellian and deceitful, underhanded and cunning: in short, part of the action of evil or falsehood. But the point I am making here is that while both are needed, in many ways the feminine principle allows communication with and to the enfolded dimensions much more completely than the overly straightforward methods of directed will, and thus that indirect energy should be cherished. Poetically, God and His Manifestation prefer to be coaxed.

The Feminine Connection to the Enfolded Dimensions:

For those who know the Tarot, the card of the Lovers is a shorthand image for this principle of masculine and feminine aspects connecting with the enfolded dimensions. In the card, the man and woman, as feminine and masculine aspects, stand on the same ground, i.e., they are equally important, but the woman looks into the face of the angel that represents the higher-energy enfolded dimensions from which all is manifested. This higher energy often leads to more positive human experiences: unity, cooperation and compassion. Unless forced to by culture, women generally far prefer to be inclusive and egalitarian rather than exclusive or dictatorial. Indeed, women are capable of tremendous change without despotism, tyranny or totalitarianism. By opening possibilities and perceptions through examples and stories, the tremendous powers of sympathy, empathy and wisdom, reaching out to others with understanding, women allow the energy of Primordial Chaos' dimension to enfold into reality with less damage than if that dimension's powerful and tremendously influential Chaotic energies were to emerge without buffering, thus shattering and bending straight-line order awry.

Make no mistake: the dimension of Primordial Chaos has as much effect as the dimension of Identity and the Zero dimension. Violence, upheavals, upsets and shocks result because these three dimensions are actually somewhat antagonistic to one another: the Zero dimension is total Peace; the dimension of Identity is Wholeness, and Primordial Chaos is often the very Sprit of Agitation. Yet for many women and men that are aware of their feminine aspects, violence is an act of weakness: a sign that frustration has built to a level where thoughtful solutions are impossible. The deepest strength in the feminine principle is balance: not simply a series of negotiations, but a deeper understanding of each factor's purpose, intentions and desires and how to maintain dynamic equilibrium within unity.

However, male hierarchy dominance has led to many discomforts such as having women in the military where straight-line hierarchies are imposed, often, alas, to the woman's heavy cost. Because of the disquiet too many men still feel with the indirect, "subversive" energies of feminine principles, women are too often given an insurmountable burden: to be what is needed at any cost to her, to take the full load of men's unwanted attributes and to hide away what men do not or will not comprehend in themselves. This lack of masculine comprehension shows itself in many ways, from some health insurance's long persistence of considering pregnancy as a disease, as well as laws based on far too limited perceptions of rape's shocking psychic costs. At the same time, men also have a heavy burden: to be what is needed at any cost, to take the full load of the upper hierarchy's unwanted attributes and to hide those parts of their selves that do not fit into that hierarchy's present ideas of itself. Clearly, it is the dominance hierarchy that is at fault here, neither men nor women.

The Feminine Principle in Human Interactions:

As pointed out elsewhere, human lives have been particularly short and difficult of late, partly to accelerate the pace of human learning through Karma and partly to arrive in the right place at the right time with the right people ready to open to Galactic consciousness on Earth. Oddly enough, this has meant that the feminine energies have had to be dampened and nearly stripped of impact: you have had to learn through frustration and pain and you have had to learn through dominance and greed.

Moreover, you could not have learned what you needed to know if things were too gentle, too compassionate. If you help a chick out of its egg because you hate to see it suffer and struggle, you actually weaken it enough to kill it! And if you put a desert plant in a clement, nurturing environment with plenty of water and moderate temperatures, the desert plant will sicken and die. This says nothing against the clement circumstances of the more temperate region, nor does it say anything about the unsuitability of the desert plant: it just shows that, if you want the chemicals and compounds that are only found in desert plants to use in order to create a new medication, you need deserts. Even though they may create a bitter desert psychologically and socially, there are times when even the negative masculine energies are needed.

Certainly, in times of crisis when brute strength, command and protection are needed immediately, there is no time for friendly circles contemplating the mysterious nature of the inner dimensions. You have known the social balance of feminine and masculine principles before. Wisdom was the order of the day in Lemuria: wisdom, forbearance and self-mastery. Many of you do remember the gentle, nurturing ways of Lemurian sisterhoods and brotherhoods, the kind and loving families that treasured each member. Yet particularly now because the feminine energy has been so suppressed, because the masculine energies have more control of the world than they understand what to do with, a young man's impatient impulses must struggle to perceive the value of holding back, to consider the impact of his actions and how to work within the whole. Not "*for* the whole," because that again involves top-down, or at least peer-pressure ordering. Working *with* the whole respects the contribution of each one, as each one is able to contribute. Granted, this is distinctly Socialist: "From each according to his ability, to each according to his need," so I must tread carefully here, but I will make the bald statement that feminine unity is not the "unity" of the barracks where any person is reduced to a unit of skill that must serve the whole under specific and rigid commands. The difference is necessarily in the feminine empathy and understanding.

Women do not often fight to attack: they fight to defend. As in the Second World War, many women did not see the enemy at their gates but rather a scared young boy that had been put into danger because of confused ideals: he was someone to help, not to fight and the women would rather have comforted him than shot him. Yet on the other hand, many women have showed extreme courage, facing down soldiers when unarmed so they might protect their husbands or children. This changeability is based on situational ethics: it is response to true need. Women generally understand that different situations and people have different needs at different times and that true and considered fairness must take that into account. A starving person needs different food than a healthy one, a little child needs more care than an older one and it is fair to treat each differently.

However, the masculine tendency to usurp resources for the ones higher in the hierarchy that are "more deserving" simply *because* they are higher in the hierarchy can become quite unfair. Logic can always drive any premise to absurd lengths and too often the emotional justification to legitimatize the abuses that result from misapplied logic is put in afterwards. And illogic, as many men have complained, is women's method: connecting things that should not be connected, because that thing over there has nothing to do with this thing over here, much less with the third, fourth, or fifth things, which are all just extraneous noise interfering with the straight-line action: all the extra feelings, emotions and sentimentality are just a waste of time! What after all is the use of emotion, empathy or sympathy when those feelings stop you from overtaking someone and dominating him, which surely you must do to avoid his domination of you and yours? What could possibly be difficult about that? But so many women persist in being quirky, unexpected, compassionate and absurd, insisting that everything matters to Love, insisting that there are realms beyond duality, efficiency and focused accomplishment that have nothing to do with any of those attributes: the Love that they feel but cannot define.

The Feminine Nature of the Universe:

Whether in men or women, the feminine principle's perception frequently reaches outside of logic because that perception is sourced in the dimension of Primordial Chaos, expressed through Mystery and the Zero dimension that directly embodies and manifests Love the universe. The Core Source of the Zero Dimension is not at all logical and not at all reasonable: if it were, then reality would not exist at all and any argument of the efficacy of focused thinking would become entirely moot. True, many do find comfort in saying, "There must be a reason why this happened:" the mind can find reasons all the time. However, reason limits Reality's expression far too much.

Things may indeed have causes behind them, from the prevailing energy of an Astrological Age to some person's irritation at having a bad lunch that leads to inattentive driving and then an accident. However, though Reality certainly seems to operate on direct cause-and-effect principles while manifested in the four dimensions, Reality's manifestation is without reason. As we hope to explore in the article below on the True Nature of Time, the universe is essentially Timeless in nature and thus is not subject to cause and effect, as it was never caused, as cause demands separation, process and change. However, the universe is a fundamental unity and it remains this unity because cause and effect is only an illusion. To say, "Things come to the place where they can become," is closer, reflecting the feminine, indirect, shifting nature of Reality.

In a way hard to describe, indirectness reflects that unity with far more accuracy than directness: directness actually warps the fabric of reality into cause and effect through Time and creates illusion by diverting, decreasing and attenuating the Source Core of the Zero and other enfolded dimensions into temporal form and specific structures of Time. This Mystery can be discovered, uncovered and recovered because Infinity does not forget its Self. However, Mystery can only speak its own tongue best when it is as close as possible to two things at once, communicating its nature with an indirect, paradoxical and inexplicable language of impossible juxtapositions. The feminine principle reflects these attributes quite profoundly: again this is how and why Reality is actually more feminine than masculine. This feminine principle has left its mark in countless ways, and it is a humorous paradox indeed: the very linear, forward-driving force of the scientific method has been uncovering the indirect, feminine principle for centuries now and although it has not yet comprehended it, it soon will.

The True Nature of Time

Key Points: Time has no beginning or end, yet its very nature and process connects the unfolded dimensions that manifest process and change with the enfolded, higher dimensions that include Timelessness. Semi-conducting Time is created by the ways Consciousness reacts to and within Time, most particularly in sleep and meditation. Consciousness experiences Time because the Torsion Field of Translation fragments the dimension of Identity like a prism, allowing Consciousness to create experiences through associative alignments. Using the plasma-like matrix of Ether, you can receive "non-temporal" information psychically, though sometimes the Etheric adhesions formed cause confusion in what is perceived. The Units of Consciousness' tetrahedrons create the relativistic structures that allow quantum and temporal mechanics. Gravity is to Time as electrons are to photons: Gravity cannot exist without Time or, to a great degree, Time without Gravity. Higher-order beings and energies use vibrationless Para-light as their fulcrum for change.

Subheadings:

- Semi-conducting Versions of Time

- Timeless Meditation

- Time, Para-light and Timelessness

- Time and Ether

- Time's Dual Dimensionality

- How Gravity Relates to Time

- Going "Outside of" Time

Semi-conducting Versions of Time:

Time has no beginning and no end, but it dictates beginnings and endings by its very nature and process. Time is an aspect of the dimension of Identity, chosen by Consciousness as a means of experiencing 4-D reality. Semi-conducting Time is similar to the waver of reality in Schrödinger's thought-experiment with the cat: linked to alternate realities, the potential Time in possible events regarding the cat's fate quivers on the edge of manifestation in all cases. In that quivering state, Time can be influenced by enfolded, higher-order energies, such as love or prayer that might allow the cat to live more often than not. Semi-conducting Time is also evident in the way the mind loses track of itself as it is heading towards sleep: Time can lose its grip on you and you upon it, so that what seems a moment can be nearly an hour and what seemed to be an hour can be only a few moments.

Although it may be infinitely arguable that in these cases you are merely dealing with the mind/brain's own confusion, there is a real, though alas as yet immeasurable, flutter in reality similar to the quantum mechanics that describe reversals with cause-and-effect sequences. In these twilight states of consciousness, Time actually is flowing in both directions at once and is allied with neither direction, becoming dynamically suspended between the two. Because Time is essentially an expression of the dimension of Identity, this semi-conducting state provides and unusual amount of leverage for the soul as regards both 4-D reality and the soul's relationships its own identity. People frequently die in their sleep because they can make the best and most accurate assessment of their accomplishments regarding their soul's intentions in the semi-conducting dream states. This temporally multi-directional flutter is the means by which sleep can refresh your mind and body or by which you may choose to pull up your subconscious anxieties into your conscious attention to resolve them.

I have pointed out earlier that much of Time is enfolded so that its one continuous Möbius-strip manifestation in 4-D reality is the only "side" we see. But it should be obvious that higher-order energies might be engaged to change several different aspects of Time's 4-D effect. When your sleep is too much disturbed, especially with harmful intentions as in torture, you lose your internal grip on those enfolded energies and thus on your own identity. If you have had practice with meditation or other states of awareness, the damage of sleep disturbance or even torture may be lessened. Indeed, if the mind/brain learns its way within the deep state of meditation well enough, it can stay partly engaged with those enfolded energies all the time.

This can be shown with those that are able to remain conscious and deal with physical reality successfully even in Theta or Delta brain-wave rhythms and represents yet another version of semi-conducting

Time. You have mastered the art of temporal "flutter" when you are able to access semi-conducting states of Time within the 4-D and higher dimensional levels simultaneously. States of deep creativity or "flow" may have equally positive and occasionally paradoxical effects, even opening Timeless aspects into Time/Space with little disruption, despite the huge energy differential between enfolded and unfolded reality states. The manifested form of a play, painting, business plan or the hand-built house you wish to construct may be grasped, whole and complete, in an instant, with the image's clear, vibrant image guiding the creative process both within and outside of Time.

Timeless Meditation:

Meditation and dreams represent states of temporal semi-conduction and reveals consciousness's points of origin in both the enfolded an unfolded dimensions. Consciousness is able to overleap Time in several ways, through near-death experiences, imagination, reveries and meditations as well as states of hypnosis that include past-life recall or even perceiving future-life potentials. Presently, your conscious limits regarding Time's enfolded aspects are in part because most of you have not been trained since an early age in either meditation or out-of-Time recall. As a result your perceptual bias demands temporal ordering for comprehension and rejects "off-side" or semi-conducting version of your temporal experiences.

Much as someone that has not been taught a particular language when young enough will not be able to speak it properly later, your brain has lost the fine translation structures necessary to perceive many of Time's subtler aspects. However, much as nearly all children raised with a language manage its shibboleths that become difficult or impossible for others to learn, nearly all children have the potential to work within this kind of temporal fluidity. The Navajo language, with its flexible temporal structure, is an example of both: a difficult language to learn, it arranges Time, physical reality, and personal identities in a very different way than nearly all others. The language of semi-conducting Time is similarly difficult to learn, in part because it demands that you discern your particular and specific engagement with the Torsion Field of Translation, which is another state of awareness that must be taught early.

Yes, physical Time does progress at a fixed rate. Nevertheless, by dancing through those semi-conducting temporal shifts, your consciousness can weave and interweave through personal time and Time's universal structure, approaching the hidden geometries within the dimension of Identity's temporal expressions through your own specific connection to Time. You can even pull out added energy from the areas of semi-conductive contact between Time and your consciousness in limited amounts: this happens most frequently in revelations. At least you certainly may learn how to balance your conscious energy with temporal energies so that you can actually re-pattern your physical relationship to Time. That this occurs in meditation, channeling, creative inspiration and dreaming should be no surprise. For instance, an elegant method for "slowing" down Time is paradoxically by becoming more aware of space: when you become more aware of the space you are working in or traveling though, the moments within that space seem long and deep, as they did when you were a child. However as I discuss below, reaching into the very structure of Time can be done in meditation.

Time, Para-light and Timelessness:

Another name for that the Torsion Field of Translation is Intuition: the deep, ongoing connection with the Zero dimension, the Source within all. To shape 4-D reality into its present form, the Zero dimension works through the dimension of Identity and uses the Torsion Fields of Proportion, Numeration, Translation, Para-light and Para-sound. As it is light without vibration, Para-light is Timeless and as said before is frequently the light seen in near-death experiences, especially those with "instantaneous" life reviews. Vivid and whole, without vibration or amplitude, it is light's core and 4-D light is its refection. Similarly Time is a reflection of the original state of Timelessness: Time unfolds Timelessness by selecting resonances of association. Time acts as a prism for Timelessness: shattering the solid core into rainbows of experience, it selects and re-selects specific patterns.

Reaching within Time's structure is accomplished through the psychic faculty that engages the Ether: this allows premonition, re-view of past experiences or the notifications of present but distant events. Because of the nature of Ether as a matrix, when the psychically sensitive mind is quiet enough, parts of the mind slide free of Time and the desired "unofficial" information can be perceived. Time's semi-conductive nature, hovering in between the unfolded and enfolded states, bridges the two types of information, conveying them either simultaneously or with a conscious change of focus. This change of focus is similar to when you tip a car's rear-view mirror order to change the angle of the reflected surface from direct to indirect so that the cars' headlights following you do not blind you. With the mirror re-positioned, though of course the angle allows you to see the headlights clearly and without glare, you can also see other reflections from inside the car as well, especially if the interior light is on. Meditation helps you become aware of and used to this doubled reflection, though it takes practice to discern which reflection is which.

Granted, this example is only meant as metaphor: diverting your attention from the other cars around you to watch your own face in the mirror while driving is foolish at least and fatal at worst. Yet the mirror has both surfaces coexisting in it and although it generally takes a shift of attention to see the indirect reflection that is always there, sometimes that secondary reflection intrudes. Thus it is with Time's semi-conducting aspects, particularly as regards psychic perceptions. In the dynamic, changeable human psyche, unofficial information such as traumatic past-life memories can intrude, and perhaps overwhelm, the present in much the same way. This also suggests more aspects of Ether and Time's relationship to each other.

Time and Ether:

Ether, the essential temporal/spatial matrix, allows Time to interact with space, matter, fields and forces. Though it is an aspect of the dimension of Identity, Time is not a property of matter. This is an essential point to remember: the divine Identity discovers, expresses and realizes its Self through Time and therefore uses the Torsion Field of Translation in order to express that Self through the ordered sequences of development and manifestation within Time. Ether uses the Translation Field as much as the Translation Field uses Ether. This again leads to a form of semi-conduction: Ether's changeable, "plasma-like" state interacts with the Field of Translation in much the same way as the pineal gland's simultaneously enfolded and unfolded state decodes the higher-level, multi-dimensional information in the "Junk" DNA. Without the semi-conducting nature of Ether, the Timeless, "steady-state" nature of the Divine Identity would have no recourse: it would remain frozen in its Self and would never be able to discern its own nature. Infinity needs the finite in order to be understood and Ether provides the matrix bridge.

This is also reflected in the non-temporal aspects of the psychic faculty, of course: as has been noted elsewhere, your psychic perceptions are governed by personal association and your relationship to other people that you may perceive psychically is of course an aspect of the relationships between identities. There are also minute Etheric "adhesions," channels of association that form over time and thus within Time, rather like cobwebs collecting dust. This is one of several factors that lead to the psychic momentum governing the "colors" of time and the common psychic impressions and imagery within several visions or inventions. There are times when several psychics will perceive the same future and times when more than one inventor will receive the same solution to a particular problem. Ether allows these associations to occur by enabling the semi-conducting nature of Time to interface with 4-D Reality. This tendency of conflation between psychic minds may be offset when you are practiced in perceiving the Etheric component within Reality by becoming aware of your Etheric body: this strengthens your psychic identity and makes common confusions easier to discern.

Time's Dual Dimensionality:

Time may be considered a simultaneously enfolded and unfolded dimension much like the dimension of Identity: both have inertia in 4-D and their sources in the Zero dimension that includes all others. The dimension of Identity's enfolded dimensional inertia is why it is so hard to change your own identity, tackle and finish projects put off for too long a time or remove accretions of material that have accumulated over weeks, months, or eons. However, both temporal and identity inertia benefits many processes, from sailing to the stars with an ion drive or building up a desired habit until it becomes automatic. The combined influence of the enfolded dimensions of Identity and Time may be seen in the processes of personal change, because although identity itself changes instantaneously, to engage the change with 4-D reality, Time's Möbius slope must be used.

Time is a latticework upon which all energies; processes; particles; waves and especially the Units of Consciousness and dimensional arrays are placed. The Units of Consciousness and the quasi-physical energies like the psychic function enabled through Para-sound and Ether acting as a Torsion Field, may be imagined as the unsupported parts of a gauzy curtain hung on Time's lattice. They relate directly to Time in that they are part of the hologram of Reality's expression, yet the steadily shifting shapes of the Units of Consciousness are actually

84

what retain Time's unfolded structures. In short, Consciousness creates and orders Time. Timelessness and temporal reality, two opposing states of energy, are unfolded into 4-D physical reality through the enfolded dimensions' geometric relationships within the Torsion Field of Translation.

The Torsion Field of Translation controls the flicker between enfolded and unfolded dimensions, particle and wave, being and becoming, thus providing angles of relationship through a kind of "polarization." So in a very real sense Time may be considered a series of interactions between the enfolded and unfolded dimensions that retain an overall forward direction because of the way the Units of Consciousness' tetrahedrons combine with one another. Their internal geometries create the sine waves that electrons traverse when they "go" between dimensions in quantum mechanics. Because of the unfolded relativistic interrelation that these tetrahedrons create, timing is generated automatically by Spacetime because of orders of significance within the dimension of Identity through the Etheric resonance of association.

The way Reality interacts with the haloclines of Time, Etheric fields and particularly the fields of Formation and Translation, allows contiguous movement within the strobe-light illusion of Reality without Zeno's paradox, which states that movement is impossible because before you can get to the end, you must get to the half-way point, and the half-way point before that, and so on, such that you can never accomplish a whole movement because there is always a movement before. This paradox is of course based on the illusion that the aspect of Time that you see in your reality is its true nature: something that orders and is ordered by continuous generative and degenerative processes. However, the shifts from one place to another, one processed result or another is accomplished in the enfolded dimension of Identity and not in physical Reality at all.

How Gravity Relates to Time:

As a film will have separate images that are strung together into a connective series and each image is entirely discrete, so also Time uses the medium of Ether to re-position itself into reality in a constant, steady state rather like the "solid" state of Para-light. It is only by this means that the Eternal may experience itself as temporal: by perceiving its own facets through changing its focus of attention. The fulcrum for this change of focus is Gravity. Gravity and Time work

85

together by relating to each other's semi-manifested aspects. It is this close association that appears to make time and Gravity both "properties of matter:" both of these aspects affect matter universally and both are only partially manifested within 4-D reality.

It might be tempting to leap to a conclusion that Gravity and Time are therefore dual aspects of one essential force much as Electricity and Magnetism are the same force arranged at right angles to its self. This is true in the sense that the one essential Source for both Time and Gravity is the Zero dimension. A way to imagine their relationship is to say that Gravity is to Time as electrons are to photons: Gravity manifests through mass, as does the electron; yet electrons release photons when changing state. Gravity thus contains and to some degree creates Time and yet Gravity could not exist without Time much as electrons cannot exist without photons. As photons are mass-less waves of energy, Time provides energetic fluctuations in the sense of process and yet cannot be grasped within matter.

As I have said elsewhere, Gravity is part of what engages Time with physical reality. Gravity, like Magic, is a multi-dimensional "slope," though Magic relates to physical reality more as a field in the sense that it is the area in which shift occurs, whereas Gravity is more a force, often related to the dimension of Identity. Gravity imposes action upon structure directly, whereas Magic helps focus Consciousness within structure. The difference has to do with the nature of the Units of Consciousness, as first described by Jane Robert's channeled entity Seth. "Smaller" than quarks, the Units of Consciousness are points of Divine focus that allow the translation of the Divine Intention from the Timeless, non-physical realms into Time and Physicality.

The Units of Consciousness' relationship to one another creates Space and Relativity simultaneously. You might also consider them as catalytic "switches:" rather as a blood cell will capture oxygen and then release it, the Units of Consciousness "capture" the Divine Intention and then release it into form by relating to each other, particularly with the structures of tetrahedrons. Because tetrahedrons are able to combine in a great many ways, their shapes are the precursors of all forms. They form "strings" of intentional energy that are able to fold one in upon another, coiling, wrapping, extending and weaving through one another in infinite varieties of combinations of three, six, nine and twelve. They also allow the twelve dimensions that we have described as the most mathematically factor-able dimensions in a universe with infinite dimensions. They are at once a "substance" even more refined than Ether and are essential for creating form.

Going "Outside of" Time:

Timeless "time" may be grasped in human experience in many ways and most of you following a spiritual path are already familiar with them. In a very real way, the more mobile parts of your consciousness slip outside of time when you sleep: indeed, some of the common weirdness of dreams is because you are enfolding yourself into Time's 4-D structure again after having slipped in and out of Ether's Timeless, plasma-like lattices. These same lattices are part of the reason why premonitions may occur in dreams or in the moment of waking: being pulled temporarily free of Time's relentlessly captivating focal point of Now also gives the human self genuine relief from the burden that Time represents. A lot of healing occurs in sleep partly because your human personality is not so tightly bound with your cells: the cells can re-work their own subtle Para-sound symphonies in a different way than when your consciousness overshadows them.

It is already known that you can both limit and enhance your healing by your thoughts and attitude when you are conscious; there are Timeless, unconscious factors as well, related to how your soul's energy impresses itself on your cells. But when you slip away at night, your body's identity can re-arrange itself by using different aspects of Time than those of which you are generally aware. In short, there are times that if you allow your body to find its own way without interference, it will heal faster. A thing to keep in mind is that love is not interference, nor is prayer, for both enhance the Timeless connections in everything.

Truly stepping out of time when in 4-D Reality is possible but it is often a matter of proper separation. As mentioned before, mediums, channels, healers, inspired artists and many spiritual teachers step outside of Time if only by losing their essential focus within it. Meditation also changes your relationship to Time: in some respects a good ten minute meditation may help the body as much as four hours of sleep. Miracles of many kinds involve disengaging from Time, whether it is healing or "impossible" rescues: when someone walks away from an accident that should have killed him, very likely non-temporal action is engineered by beings quite outside of Time. Such beings use Para-light as a fulcrum to shift or even sometimes spread open the temporal lattices within Timespace, in order to buffer the person in danger from injury with "temporal space:" a few instants outside of Time that parallel the incident itself so elegantly that alternate realities do not mingle.

This kind of science (or legerdemain!) by these higher-order entities or intelligences is rare, though it happens more often than is supposed. There are clearly times enough when such miraculous things do not occur and the person in question is killed, trapped or hurt. However, keeping the possibility open in your own mind and your own sense of Time helps you to notice when things change because of a "parallel side-step:" a moment of distraction leading to an unexpected decision, a situation developing in an unexpected way that seems to make sense after all or perhaps a clear sense of warning.

Granted, much of this is arranged with and through your human Intuition, but to a degree I rest my case: your Intuition is, after all, part of your non-temporal identity. Make no mistake: your power of choice as a human being remains paramount, yet the point is that the change from one path to another is often crafted outside of Time altogether. You may have chosen a path where you are provided with several opportunities to choose or you may even chosen a path where you arrange to have no choice. But often how you can change your possibilities depends upon how deeply you can become aware of who you are outside of Time.

How the Dimension of Identity Creates Stars

Key Points: Using nearly all the Torsion Fields, the dimension of Identity keeps Reality from either being solid energy, solid matter or solid light. The Torsion Fields allow the divine Mind to create Reality with intentional precision. Because many of these Torsion Fields are both enfolded and unfolded, as is human consciousness, you may be able to perceive several of them consciously. The Torsion Field of Proportion creates 4-D equilibrium; often expressed by numerology, the Field of Numeration shifts the meaning of numbers from the divine Intention into Reality, while Para-gravity fields allow the inner structures of M-D geometry to be expressed through gravity. Magnetic Torsion Fields are the fulcrum upon which stars and galaxies manifest. The field of Formation focuses the Divine Infinity into stellar and planetary specificity and uniqueness. The Translation Fields provide the calibration needed for degrees of manifestation, while Ether, especially when acting as a Torsion field, is the matrix within which 4-D reality manifests. The Torsion fields directly affect the Units of Consciousness, the tiniest points of existence.

Subheadings:

- Structures of Reality Created by Torsion Fields
- Consciousness, the Dimension of Identity and Torsion Fields
- Proportion
- Numeration
- Para-gravity
- Magnetism
- Formation
- Translation
- Ether
- How Units of Consciousness Affect the Torsion Fields

Structures of Reality Created by Torsion Fields:

To shape 4-D reality into its present form, the Zero dimension works through the dimension of Identity using the Torsion Fields of Proportion, Numeration, Para-gravity; the Magnetic and to a lesser degree the Electric Fields; the Fields of Formation; Translation and the transitional energy form of Ether. Para-sound and Para-light fields are used to create communicable information within and between the enfolded and unfolded dimensions through the Torsion Field of Translation, particularly the Zero dimension and the dimension of Primordial Chaos This allows them to link with Reality directly through the dimension of Identity. You might call the dimension of Identity the Will of God: as said before, by creating and retaining Divine Integrity, this dimension limits all other dimensions' expression and the integrity of all forms, systems, structures and processes within them.

This level of integrity is necessary and yet so obvious as to hardly deserve mention: the three dimensions of form are static, retaining their parameters even when interacting with one another, so that even in situations of potential and kinetic energy, there is rarely a tremendous preponderance of any energy, form, or field. The obvious exception is a black hole, where there is a preponderance of gravitational effects, but even black holes are balanced through Para-gravity structures, some of which are the "chaff" of reality-structuring mentioned above in Para-sound Encoding in DNA. Like the Translation Fields, these Para-gravity structures that balance black holes are both enfolded and unfolded simultaneously, creating joined areas of overlap between alternate realities.

Consciousness, the Dimension of Identity and Torsion Fields:

As we mention in Volume Two, the Torsion Fields are generally enfolded and tightly "curled" so that their local effects are generally much stronger than the unfolded 4-D fields that surround them, though the areas of effect are quite limited, even minute. This localized torque allows the divine Mind and Intention to intersect reality with great accuracy, interleaving fields, forces, matter, energy and dimensional geometries with beautifully complex and layered effects. Some of these effects are unrecognized; some are dismissed because they seem to be erroneous data. Yet discovering these dimensional effects of the Torsion Fields could change your orientation to physics as your human mind became more and more able to reach deep into itself and connect with the enfolded dimensions' points of contact. Perhaps the laws and theorems regarding physical matter will not change, but your attitude towards them would, as well as your sense of interacting with the universe more directly.

When you believed physics demanded a predestined, clockwork universe, this had certain definite effects within human culture; similarly, when you saw evolution as the exaltation of the brute and nature as the slave of man, you created a sterile emotional climate. Now that physics demands more of its scientists' minds, asking you to see well beyond the obvious, this will allow you to touch and be touched by the Intentional Divine Consciousness that uses the enfolded dimensions and Torsion Fields to express Its Self into becoming. When you are aware of that same Divine Intelligence within yourself, you will finally have the opportunity of co-creating with, becoming constantly aware of and interacting within, the living Whole Being until you are able to reflect the divine Identity itself. When your awareness expands, the Zero dimension will no longer need to work automatically: it will use all the inner dimensions and Torsion Fields as tools to unfold itself quite directly into matter through focused Consciousness so that the points of congruence between Humanity and the divine Self are increased. This will automatically create swifter manifestations from your words and thoughts.

Proportion:

The Torsion Fields of Proportion create the equilibrium needed to manifest the dimension of Identity's aspects of its Self: these fields are the main fulcrums for the arrangement of matter in the greater multiverse. You usually simply accept that planets differ in the numbers and kinds of elements that form them, as well as in their size, internal structure and their ability to sustain life; you tend to assume random chance is the operative force behind this. Granted, the dimension of Primordial Chaos is a significant factor in these arrangements, as it is in the structures underlying chance. But the dimension of Primordial Chaos remains deeply linked to the dimension of Identity: influenced quite directly by the Proportion Fields it creates individuation and coherent patterns within the randomizing structures of Chance. With the dimension of Proportion assisted by higher-energy influences from the Zero dimension, unanticipated outcomes can occur, such as Magic, Grace and random statistics, as well as ordered crystals and amorphous materials.

In fact, the dimension of Primordial Chaos aligns itself with the dimension of Identity and the Zero dimension so profoundly that the Torsion Field of Proportion must constantly regulate Chaos's expression in 4-D reality. In a very real sense, Primordial Chaos and the Zero dimension are both identities in themselves: in order for finite reality to exist, these identities necessarily need their impact curtailed within the finite structures of 4-D reality. It is not simply that if you want water from the ocean you need a bucket: you need a bucket with a handle on it. So in a very real sense, the dimension of Identity, the Will of God that shapes all things, must limit its own Self through its own will. This Divine Will is expressed through the Field of Proportion and creates a specific internal structure of intersections with Time and Time-space: a crystal lattice, if you wish.

As said before, specificity has infinity within it. By working through the Proportion Fields, the dimension of Identity allows each part of the whole to retain that specificity in spite of the higher-dimensional forces within the Zero dimension that create a state of infinite unity. By working through this Torsion Field of Proportion, the dimension of Identity not only keeps things discrete in terms of form, effect, action and placement within relativity, it allows every single thing to retain its connection to infinity and thus become a direct expression of that infinity without Infinity overwhelming Specificity. This is the first clue as to how stars are formed: as structured through the Torsion Field of Proportion, the intimate, dynamic exchange between the Zero dimension and the dimension of Identity is able to allow Space and Time to have specific areas of discrete expression.

Numeration:

The Torsion Field of *Numeration's* influence on Identity's structures is essential and profound. While this should be obvious, there are particular issues regarding the way the Zero dimension works within Numeration to create the very multi-dimensional geometries upon which reality transfers physical forces from the enfolded dimensions to the unfolded ones. As with a triangle creating leverage, the Torsion Field of Numeration is also the means by which the higher-level energies structure and communicate the *meaning* of those geometries and numbers into reality through physical form and conscious experience. I use this term meaning specifically: not only does the Field of Numeration determine how geometries interact in 4-D in ways both obvious and subtle, it also elucidates the patterns within the Divine Mind and communicates that Mind's intention in an elegant language of effect through form.

This is reflected in many things, from the differences we have already mentioned between ¾ and 4/4 rhythms, to the subtler meanings of cards in the Tarot, numerology, astrology to a great degree and even the double-slit experiment that shows light to function as a particle and a wave, depending on the observer. Plants of all kinds start growing as one shoot, becoming two (the part aboveground and the part below), and then either retain their duality, as in grasses, reeds and some trees, or diverge again into pairs of leaves on the original stem, becoming three. Light in a very real sense follows this pattern when shifting itself from particle to wave, or more correctly, demonstrating its enfolded and unfolded duality as a particle and its triune nature as a wave.

Duality can mean either continual stasis or continual agitation, but the triune expression of the Divine Mind always leads to creative change. Similarly, four creates stability and stasis, and five shifts realty into still deeper change at a more complex and subtle level than with the triune energy. Six is sacred energy, working as a function of number/meaning that allows fission in cells and realities, creating the new from the old. Seven is the Divine; 8: Abundance and Responsibility; nine carries the energy of Completion. The three "master Numbers" in numerology are: 11, meaning Illumination; 22 the Master Builder, with 33 as the Master Number of Cosmic Law: Christ Compassion. This issue is too deep to elucidate completely here, though I will say that the order within numbers is not blind and automatic, but rather allows the Divine Mind to express itself cogently to a degree that few have perceived. But some of these subtle intentions within numbers create stars, star systems' geometric periodicity and of course their complex geometries within their galaxies.

Para-gravity:

As we have mentioned in Volume Two, *Para-gravity* as a Torsion field is not strictly gravity at all but rather the structure that shifts many of gravity's own effects outside of 4-D, while at the same time having profound effects of its own. We have already mentioned that

Para-gravity regulates the way galaxies are shaped by working with the magnetic fields. Para-gravity also works within the dimension of Identity to create the uniform motion of those stars, literally by structuring the galaxies along the dimension of Identity's enfolded structures through Para-gravity's localized, focused torque. The dimension of Identity needs the Para-gravity geometries to use as templates, much as the fields of Numeration work with Primordial Chaos to form branches and branching effects with their specific patterns and limits. In this way, the higher-order geometries of Para-gravity shape how matter and gravity interact.

If 4-D reality may be perceived as the froth on the surface of an ocean's wave, then Para-gravity is the driving and shaping force of the wave itself: it forms the "surface" upon which the hologram of 4-D reality rests. Its own deep currents also structure the amount and placement of matter itself, which gives another clue as to how stars are formed and arranged while remaining discrete. Of course as I have said elsewhere, the enfolded shape of a star within the dimension of Identity is more like a sphere than any other 4-D shape: this hidden, internal shape is why they remain spheres until their own internal energies cause them to either collapse or explode.

Magnetism:

As some have already discovered, *Magnetism*, especially as a Torsion Field, has a great deal to do with the formation of galaxies and in addition to gravity and Para-gravity is yet another way by which galaxies retain their coherence. When the dimension of Identity utilizes the Torsion Field of Magnetism, it uses the magnetic, electric and electro-magnetic fields of specific manifestation to embody the dimension of Identity's intentions. Magnetism particularly creates continual communication between the infinite Zero dimension and its multitudinous, finite singularities through allowing the Zero dimension to pattern electromagnetism itself. In short, from a multi-dimensional point of view the pulse, shift and semi-conducting nature of electro-magnetism all receive the dimension of Identity's vibrational patterns, allowing Identity to create flow, rhythm and specific methods of change, thus allowing the dynamic symphony of 4-D reality to enfold Infinity within it.

Electromagnetism is also a superlative carrier of the Zero dimension's divine Thought, Intention, Will and Creativity. The 90° angle between magnetism and electricity, the point of switching, is

94

actually one of the fulcrums that the dimension of Identity uses to focus and manifest the patterns impressed through it from the Zero dimension. As shifting magnetic fields in computer chips' domains change the information in the chips, the more subtle switch from magnetism to electricity follows the same function: the dimension of Identity patterns Reality's "domains" through switching and re-arranging the tetrahedral Units of Consciousness. However, because this particular fulcrum is based within the dimension of Identity's multi-dimensional structures, it is a layered analogue coding, rather than a simple binary; thus it carries a nearly infinite amount of information.

Formation:

Even though only a field, the Torsion Field of *Formation* is as unique as the dimension of Identity because the Zero dimension continually engages and utilizes Formation's bridging capabilities in order to create the dimension of Identity itself. As is human consciousness and the conscious field of Magic, the Formation and Translation Torsion Fields are also unfolded and enfolded simultaneously. However, the field of Formation's "direction" is mainly from the enfolded into the unfolded, from the hidden into the manifest, while the field of Translation connects both directions simultaneously. The Zero dimension uses Formation's Torsion Fields to focus itself into reality through Identity into not only specificity but utter uniqueness as well: this uniqueness is the main reason why stars are stars and not simply a wash of matter from one end of the universe to the other. I may seem to be parsing my terms too finely here, as specificity certainly connotes something unique, yet the point I am trying to make exists somewhat at the limit of language: poetically put, I am trying to describe how the One is the one is the One, and how the One is both the All and the Only and still within each one of the All.

As we have explored further in the article on the True Nature of Time, the way Reality interacts with the haloclines of Time, Etheric fields and particularly the fields of Formation and Translation, allows contiguous movement in the strobe-light illusion of reality without Zeno's paradox. In addition, Formation's Torsion Field may be said to allow a continual re-presenting manifestation of each and all forms within the instantaneous communications of entangled electrons.

Similar to the old animated films where certain static objects, such as a clock on the desk or the statue of a horse, were re-drawn frame by frame in order to give them an extra "quiver" of life and presence, so also the Torsion Field of Formation curls, uncurls and re-curls in upon itself constantly. In this way it functions much as the Möbius strip of Time: as Time always moves forward in its infinite loop, Formation is always engaged in manifestation even though, like a four-eyed fish, Formation remains engaged with both enfolded and unfolded aspects of reality simultaneously. This "quiver" of constant becoming through the unique manifestation of the Divine Intention allows objects' uniqueness to be linked deeply enough to the dimension of Identity that stars, planets and beings remain whole and complete.

Translation:

As described above, the Torsion Field of *Translation* is also continually and simultaneously engaged with the enfolded and unfolded dimensions and their geometries because these fields are the way the divine Mind communicates to, and receives information from, all the parts of itself. Translation Fields might also be considered the tightly enfolded points of contact that create axes for calibration: refreshed information from the Zero dimension. This calibration is needed because there are degrees of manifestation, from the most refined, higher-energy particles such as the Units of Consciousness that make cosmic rays seem slow, to the densest expressions of 4-D reality such as white dwarfs, neutron stars and even black holes, though black holes are balanced in other ways as well.

This difference in degree results in everything from the vibratory rate of the angelic levels of being, to the vibrational rates of people in the afterlife. The "barely physical" aspects of many extra-terrestrials or higher-energy beings that inhabit certain structures and places are examples of this capacity for partial manifestation. Moreover, these degrees of manifestation allow some highly spiritual people to be able to bi-locate or appear invisible to people of lower vibrations. The Translation Fields' naturally calibrated and re-calibrated states act as a kind of "vibrational metronome," keeping the specific "pitch" of each degree of Reality steady by its continual intercommunication. This is another reason why different colors of light can mingle without altering their vibrations.

And as we mentioned in Volume Two, your personal connection with these Translation Fields is in your unconscious mind: you engage these fields in deep sleep and states of creativity, in visions and healing or whenever you change your life at a profound level for whatever reason. The Translation Torsion Fields create an inter-dimensional lattice of potentials and manifestation, formed from the Units of Consciousness, and while these fields are the most tightly "curled," they also have the greatest impact in reality and human experience. They are also embedded within the inter-dimensional and multi-dimensional geometries I have mentioned, including the geometries that work with the conscious field of Magic. Now, though it might be tempting to believe so, Magic is not part of the way stars are formed, remain, explode or collapse: there, in particular, the main engine of Para-gravity is the means. But as these Translation Torsion Fields are so tightly curled, so tiny and yet have such impact, they actually inform the way Para-gravity works

Ether:

In its function as a Torsion Field, Ether is the divine nervous system upon which the living information is communicated through the Translation fields from the Zero Dimension. Ether as a Torsion Field has been described at length in Volume Two, where I compare Ether's energy to a transitional substance like glass; it also functions as the matrix for the interplay of the Torsion fields I mention above. Ether's transitional state is the final reason why stars retain their singular identities: the degrees of manifestation calibrated by the Translation Fields through Ether's matrix are arranged along the lines of the Divine Intention through the dimension of Identity.

Ether is a rarified substance similar to plasma that interpenetrates all matter, a step down from the infinitesimal bundles of energy that others and I have called Units of Consciousness. In addition, there are units of Mind that are, in a sense, subsets of Consciousness comprised of several aspects: Intelligence; aspects of Will and Creativity that are both sourced in the dimension of Identity; the aspect of Focus. But both Mind and Consciousness are the *manifested* aspects of the Divine Being: the Mystery of the Zero dimension's core is that it is unmanifest, infinitely refined and thus has no substance at all, whether particle, field or force. Like the solid Para-light that is light without vibration, in order to create 4-D reality the Divine Core of Reality must work through all of the most enfolded dimensions and all of the Torsion Fields. Thus, there is a continual, infinite and unending state of creativity and creation being utilized within a whole reality. As I discussed at greater length in the article concerning the True Nature of Time above, Time is similar: it has no beginning and no end, but it dictates beginnings and endings by its very nature and process.

This is in part why I consider Primordial Chaos as a dimension: it allows structure and direction to be formed from this deep ferment of constant creativity in such a fashion that the Core can manifest and yet remain fundamentally whole within its true nature. It also allows this essential, primary Core to reflect its singular nature throughout and within its manifestations, including single stars, planets, forms and beings, because the true nature of Chaos is utter paradox overlaid with impossibility within contradictions created from the infinite potential of Unknown Mystery. This is why the Translation Field, the Field of Formation, Units of Consciousness and Ether are essential: the divine Will is expressed through these calibrated information processes. Indeed, the very Thoughts of the Divine Being are created and given form through the Four Essential Processes: Accretion, Dispersion, Assimilation and Dissolution.

How Units of Consciousness Affect the Torsion Fields:

Units of Consciousness retain total fluidity in all of their manifested forms: as a dynamic "substance" of Core energy, they are able to flow and create standing waves, energetic solitons if you will, like the Cultural Solitions I mentioned in Volume One. Receiving their original proto-energetic patterns within the dimension of Identity, these Units of Consciousness are actually what create particle-wave duality: their continually shifting tetrahedrons create an amorphous, transitional state that flutters between the enfolded forces and intentions of the Zero dimension and Reality's unfolded 4-D manifestation. Their amorphous, "uncommitted" state creates sine wave vibration through shifting cascade alignments: their positions realign to create the energetic lattice upon which the Torsion Field of Translation is based and this creates the fundamental "machine code" patterns of the very act of manifestation.

In addition, as the *precursors* of fields, energies and matter, the Units of Consciousness may act like all three aspects at once or in varying combinations. In this sense they are similar to Ether's plasma-like matrix state and they may provide a basis for one version of the Grand Unified Theory by providing the concept for a universal core "substance" of energetic intention. Because these Units of Consciousness remain amorphous within the enfolded and unfolded dimensions simultaneously until they form a specific entity, whether it is a wave, particle or field, they are directly responsible for quantum jumps as well as the Torsion Fields' impact upon Reality. The Units of Consciousness are a clear bridge, joining and separating degrees of physical manifestation from Para-light, to angelic, to 4-D physicality and humanity.

In short: in order to create the stars the dimension of Identity must use all of these Torsion Fields, aspects of the Zero dimension and the Divine Mind as well as Ether, because stars need to remain singular within 4-D manifestation and focus Magnetism, Gravity and Para-gravity in order to create light and molecules of life as well as viable communication from the Zero dimension.

Working with Your Core Tone and Para-sound

Key Points: This article has instructions for finding your soul's Core Tone: This Tone functions as your personal carrier wave that helps you locate yourself in Timespace. The mind's psychic wavelengths use the Etheric fields and the Core Tone expresses itself through them. At base, your Core Tone is an artifact of Para-sound. Para-sound has effects upon psychic fields and matter. Extra-terrestrials sometimes use Para-sound for the purposes of repairing infrastructures damaged by atomic explosions, frequently engaging the psychic waves and the Ether as well. You can open your Core Tone in such a way that you may glimpse the enfolded dimensions and employ Para-sound's M-D resonance to harmonize distinctly disharmonious energies and decrease Para-sound Nulls. By training yourself to be aware of how your own psychic sense functions in your brain, you can use your Core Tone energy to create change in your life.

Subheadings:

- Your Core Tone's Para-sound Characteristics

- Core Tones

- Extra-terrestrials and Etheric Fields

- Para-sound Structures and Musical Fifths

- Meditation #1: Opening Your Core Tone to the Enfolded Dimensions

- Three Methods for Working with Your Core Tone

- Meditation #2: Decreasing Para-sound Nulls

- Meditation #3: Removing Para-sound Nulls

- Meditation #4 Using Para-Sound to Withdraw Destructive Energies

- Meditation #5: Restructuring Personal Enfolded Geometries with a Psychic Fulcrum

Your Core Tone's Para-sound Characteristics:

As an appendix below, I have included the directions for finding your soul's Core Tone, the silent and unmistakably unique resonance of your whole living system: your soul, mind, emotions, memories, collective cellular resonance, DNA and personal Etheric multi-dimensional patterned geometries that allow you to engage with the enfolded and unfolded dimensions. This Tone functions as your "carrier wave:" a constant and coherent reference frequency by which you can orient yourself in relativistic Timespace. Rather than one note, it is more similar to simultaneously playing several octaves of chords and other notes on an organ: this "carrier wave" is "layered" sound and relates directly to Para-sound functioning as one of the Torsion Fields.

Consciousness uses the psychic wavelengths as the step-down transformer for Para-sound's enfolded vibrations: these psychic wavelengths are the Etheric fields. This is another reason why I consider Para-sound a Torsion Field: Para-sound focuses infinite multi-dimensionality through direct Harmonic Resonance into finite specificity while retaining all the vibrations of the whole within its multi-dimensional nature. Ether, the "plasma" that is neither particle nor field but which contains both, also works with Para-sound to retain your and the Core Tone's coherence, consistency and history through time. From one point of view, these two Torsion Fields enable the dimension of Identity to cross the bridge from the Infinite Unseen to manifested physical reality.

Now: I have spoken elsewhere about "frozen" time, where a shock can twist time into a type of super-conducting "loop" that drops out of the normal flow of Time and can even pull those energies out of your direct conscious affect. In situations of PTSD, where memories take on a "ghost-like" life of their own or when physical shocks and scars retain their form long after the cells within them could have been replaced by the body's continual recycling, this frozen time consistently alters the patterns of particles in the form of cells and neurons within space by forcing them to reiterate a specific formation: hence my image of a closed loop.

Various means of healing PTSD depend on breaking or interrupting this reiteration, whether through meditation, tapping, eye movements or other methods of changing the original rhythms of the mind. All of them work to one degree or another because they

101

engage the mind with higher orders of Para-sound and/or interrupt the momentum of already manifested Para-sound structures. Engaging your Core Tone actually works both ways as well: this Tone is multi-dimensional in nature and has sufficient signal strength to provide another referent rhythm in the psychic and mental bodies. Its higher order of Para-sound interrupts the obsessive re-iterations by providing a new point of reference upon which the mind and psyche can orient.

Granted, as one meal cannot keep you alive for weeks, a single session within your Core Tone is insufficient to alter something with years of temporal density behind it. Certainly, the essential principle of Dispersion is constantly operative and even higher-order structures of Para-sound lose focus in the unfolded dimensions eventually. However, simply focusing your conscious awareness on and within Para-sound itself automatically shifts your personal reality to a similarly higher-energy state. Indeed, when you work with your Core tone regularly, those of you that are naturally clairaudient may even find new information coming in or at least experience reduced psychic "static." Conversely, if you are so psychic that you are "on" all the time and keep hearing too much information, working with your Core Tone's higher-order energies can actually quiet things down.

Core Tones:

All physical things have Core Tones, relating directly to the dimension of Identity and the Zero dimension. This is part of what leads to a sense of the numinous: the sense of place, the sense of a living consciousness embedded in an object, whether it be a sacred thing or a child's beloved toy. The Core Tones within physical objects and substances are also what allow them to respond to love and actions of spiritual energy, creating unexpected repairs, unlikely outcomes such as the last bit of gasoline being sufficient after all and other bits of Grace. When you create sound, you interrupt the standing waveform of the Para-sound of that physical thing's carrier wave.

Both the living and non-living systems of your local reality are more responsive to you than you generally give them credit for. If you trust that animals can and want to understand you, as many pet psychics have discovered, you would be able to find out what an animal needs, wants and thinks simply by being humble enough to listen. As many indigenous tribes have long ago discovered, if an animal must die to feed the tribe, there will be one that will surrender its life when asked. All life feeds on life: the plant can be as responsive as an animal, though not in the same way and not nearly as quickly. But if you so choose, you may learn to be quite gracious about the exchange of life for life in any form.

The Core Tones of all physical things, whether defined as living or non-living, can be interrupted to one degree or another by physical action, though their responses are different. Much as some substances release light when agitated, rubbed or struck yet others do not, the Core Tones manifest as sound to various degrees. Bell-tones are the Para-sound equivalent of electrons being agitated out of their original shells and giving up that energy as photons when they return. Well-cast metal such as a chime or even a metal bowl has a coherent internal structure and will respond musically because it resonates naturally with its own Core Tone and Para-sound vibrations. However, a carelessly cast bowl or bell of poor quality metal has a dull, unmusical sound because the resonances do not match or may even conflict.

Each physical object or living thing is permanently "tuned" to its own particular Para-sound's geometric structure, its own "sound array;" thus, agitations of various kinds cause the Para-sound to manifest as sound. This, for instance, is why voices are so individual and voiceprints cannot be mimicked: the sound of your voice manifests directly from your Core Tone and its identity is distinctive and singular because of that Tone's multi-dimensional, layered Para-sound structure. In this sense your Core Tone evokes your soul's inner name through all Time and within all Space.

Extra-terrestrials and Etheric Fields:

Because of their obliteration of matter through fission, atomic explosions reach far into the Torsion Fields of Etheric, Para-sound, Formation, Translation and even the field-like aspects of the Dimension of Identity, "ionizing" those fields into new and sometimes unexpected formations, causing much more damage than can presently be calculated. The "sound" generated by this kind of damage is also increased and amplified through Para-sound Resonance. Certain forms of consciousness such as various extra-terrestrials perceive that amplified Para-sound readily. I will not open the subject of extraterrestrials at this time, save to say that many

103

human/ET encounters are grounded quite solidly in the Etheric fields. And because Para-sound relates quite directly to the Etheric, a great many inexplicable effects are created by Para-sound being restructured through the Etheric by these extraterrestrials; moreover several of these effects are created or promoted by extra-terrestrials specifically. You have little Etheric science as yet, however it is good to remember that, as do many ET's, the psychic aspects of human consciousness can perceive and particularly work with the Ether intentionally.

Fraught with confusion, delusion and illusions, including in some cases outright obfuscation, the whole issue of extra-terrestrials has long frustrated many. But as well as demonstrating their control over some nuclear bases and several other things, some of these beings are engaged in repairing the Para-sound structures that infuse and surround planet Earth. Granted, extra-terrestrials are of more than one type: some have benign intentions and some do not, some work towards the direct benefit of humanity, others intend to use humanity for their own purposes. Suffice to say that someone that has had a genuine encounter with any of these etherically skilled beings is forever changed, because the change can reach into your Core Tone's essential configurations.

No matter how bizarre or enigmatic the contact experiences, people of the light draw beings of the light to them; those people who prefer the shadows draw the other shadows too. When, or if, full contact is allowed, it will change so many things in incalculable ways, from the meaning of Humanity to the way Reality is perceived. Once this change happens, those that are not at all spiritually attuned, aware or centered in love-based unity, will not be able to "un-make" the change: Peace has such a perfect and particular Etheric Resonance that it will shift Humanity's Core Tones into deeper harmony.

Para-sound Structures and Musical Fifths:

Para-sound creates pulses and gives specific significance to rhythms and timing; similarly, work with psychic fields of all kinds including Para-sound can shift everything from the rhythms of your personal life and the life of the planet, to altering the timing of events. Because of this, it is of inestimable value to work with your own Core Tone by recognizing it, deepening your familiarity with it and then expanding its points of contact with the Zero dimension and the dimension of Identity, for this will allow you to receive refreshed instructions and information directly from Para-sound's source in Para-light's vibrationless core.

Even when done unintentionally, focusing higher vibrations such as gratitude, joy, encouragement, praise, love and other gracious emotions alters the inner Para-sound geometries quite profoundly; when you use this focus intentionally with positive purpose, it creates a geometrically progressed effect. This has been understood intuitively for millennia but is now acted upon more consciously through anything from tuning water with positive vibrations in order to change its crystallized form, to using prayer to cleanse water and other substances. All of these effects are created through psychic vibrations within the Etheric medium of Reality through Para-sound. When the Core Tone of Humanity is engaged, as many of the great Masters of Love have done, this gives direct access to Grace.

As your Core Tone is at base a psychic octave of Para-sound, this is also why singing in thirds and fifths, the chords of Earth and Heaven, is so effective, impacting the Etheric fields so profoundly. Using your voice interrupts the "hum" of your Core Tone, so that the inner sound expresses the energy from your carrier wave's multi-dimensional coherence through the dimension of Identity. This interruption sparks manifestation, adding new energy into physical reality. This results in refreshed coherence within the local Etheric fields and the Para-sound structures within and around all manifested forms. An ideal or perfect F# chord is F#, A, and C#, the diminished chord is F#, A and C, and the augmented F#, A, C##; with the fifth of course being F# and C#, because the actual vibrations of those notes are in Quantum Entangled Resonance with Para-sound structures that focus the higher-energy intelligence and information from the Zero dimension into 4-D manifestation.

Indeed, it might be said that: "In the beginning was the Song," as well as the Word: the Word being the divine Intention and the Song being the Etheric and Para-sound manifestations of that Intention. Sung prayers have more effect than those spoken aloud, and this does, alas, also refer to negative "song-prayers" as well, such as hate/trash "music." However, as negative energy represents a distorted form of divine energy, despite its powerfully localized effects it is always actually the weaker force even though, as does a Torsion Field, negativity twists all neutral and many positive energies into its own shape locally, though it must pull on positive energy in order to do so. It is illusory Magic of a very high order that negativity

105

appears so powerful and so much in command on Earth. However, as we mention in the article on Para-sound Encodings above, this illusion of negativity actually represents divine creativity.

Because duality naturally searches for balance, the exchange of light and darkness, positivity and negativity or creation and destruction seem to be continually at war: times of brightness are followed by times of darkness and darkness is followed by brightness in unending tedium. However, when properly focused, the Para-sound within your Core Tone operates as though it were the third note of a chord. The two notes F# and A do not sound harmonious, but adding the C# pulls the three tones into a different unity. So it is with the Core Tone: its note is a lower octave of the divine Unity and resonates with that Unity quite directly. And it is by that octave relationship that you can open your Core Tone into and through the enfolded higher-order dimensions.

Meditation #1: Opening Your Core Tone to the Enfolded Dimensions:

Although I have put it in the Appendix, I will review the method of finding your Core Tone first:

If you are practiced in sensing the chakras' subtle energies, you may simply focus on the Heart Chakra as though searching or inquiring for a known voice in the hubbub of a crowd, simply asking yourself to "hear" the silent tone of your true inner self. Finding this Tone gives you a gentle, welcoming elation and a sense of peace. This complex Core Tone is silent and so refined a sound that the physical body cannot perceive it directly. "Hearing" this silent sound is much like feeling emotionally touched by someone's kindness, or remembering a quiet, secret joy you once had, some special news or a present from a special friend.

If you have not had much practice with subtle energies, the second method for finding your Core Tone is to sit somewhere peaceful where you can breathe quietly. Fold your hands over your heart and breathe gently for five to ten breaths. These intentional breaths are sufficient to engage the silent, super-refined Core Tone's energy. You may not feel any difference the first few times but if you persist, you will gradually have a sense of, "it's all right now, " or, "I remember more of who I am now." You will very likely feel, "Things are going right for me at last," or, "I have something within me that works."

Three Methods for Working with Your Core Tone:

When you have discovered your Core Tone in the hidden center of your heart and can refer to it again easily, the first way to work with your Core Tone is to open your perceptions of the enfolded dimensions by focusing upon your Core Tone intentionally: it will be as though it had its own intelligence and was regarding you. In the next step, you may see yourself as it sees you! This might give you a psychic vertigo: being within the Core Tone's own perception demands much of the mind and the psyche. It will be similar to looking at the infinite spiral made by a pair of mirrors reflecting each other. Indeed, you will be using psychic "muscles" that you have not used for quite some time. This may create a strange sense of vastness and unfathomable minuteness, as though you might be a galaxy contemplating itself through one of its own atoms. Hold this perception gently within your heart and within the silence of you Core Tone, though if you feel strained, let the imagery go.

If you are a musician or you know one you can work with, another method to open the multi-dimension connections within your own Core Tone is to have you or your friend play A and the C#, two of the three notes of the F# chord, while you sing the F#. The reasons for using this particular chord are many. From a multi-dimensional standpoint, in the same way as the sphere is a lowest-energy 4-D expression of a higher-energy dimensional shape, the note of F# reflects the Zero dimension's multi-dimensional nature more easily into 4-D Reality than many other notes. Your emotions may or may not be engaged within your singing, so you may not feel anything particularly special. However, your own Core Tone will start automatically sending out "filaments' of contact into the Zero dimension, so that over time you will feel a shift in your own perceptions prompted by these multi-dimensional connections.

The third way to open your Core Tone into its true multi-dimensionality is to imagine as though you were able to spin the energies of Light, Love and Joy together into a shining, mobile tapestry that could dance and play inside the "placeless place" of your inner Tone's music. Shifting and changing its shape like a fine silken cloth blown by the wind, this spun-together Light, Love and Joy will brush against points of contact to the enfolded dimensions within your Core Tone's Para-sound structures, automatically opening them. If you have done this correctly, you will feel giddy anticipation as a result of the new, responsive energy in your heart.

Although engaging the Core Tone by any of these methods every day or every other day might be a good schedule to keep, all of these three methods have momentum enough to continue engaging your Core Tone's multi-dimensional points of contact to and within the enfolded dimensions for as long as a week.

Meditation #2: Decreasing Para-sound Nulls:

As we described in Volume Two, there are Nulls in Para-sound that create psychic and physical effects: the natural chaotic formations of static turbulence, such as the Great Spot of Jupiter, or, more humanly-created Nulls created by chaotic energy-waves that cancel each other out through the sheer psychic cacophony, as in emergency rooms or prisons. The third type of Para-sound Null is created in areas with war, inflicted abuse, extreme materialism, prejudice and hatred was well as any intentional sacrilege or wanton destruction of beauty. In this last type of Null, Chaos itself has become warped through human choice: Chaos becomes an instrument of harm and is no longer an elegant way of pulling in the refreshed information found in its highly creative enfolded dimension.

Needless to say, prayers of all kinds reverse or remove Pare-sound Nulls all the time, though there are types of prayers that hamper positive effects too: you can create a "prayer" for revenge or "prayer" for success in war and both have human costs. That too is human choice: most often each situation must be dealt with individually as regards the Karma involved. However, because just being in a state of peace is a prayer in itself, there are far more opportunities to create peace than there are war, brutality or any other type of harm, particularly once you have learned how to work with your Core Tone consciously.

To decrease Para-sound Nulls, if you know of a negative situation close or far away, first find your Core Tone and then consider the situation you wish to change for the better, for surely as you will be using the divine resonance within your Core Tone, you certainly cannot change anything for the worse! The first method, Matching Resonance, is best if you have only begun to work with your Tone, as it uses Para-sound automatically.

To match its Para-sound Resonance in order to decrease a Null, allow your Core Tone to express itself as a particular note in your mind. Imagine this note mentally as loud and as clear as you can and then, if you are able, sing that note aloud. This note's augmented resonance will clear the area around you, smoothing down and aligning all the chaotic energies you can sense within you, near you and all around you. To expand the effect, allow this sphere of Para-sound Resonance with your Core Tone to expand outward, finding similar notes already being created. You may see these points of resonant harmony as flashes or areas of light. Allow yourself to simply see them, without either judgment or even discernment: you do not need to know where or with whom these points of harmonic light connect. What you are doing is gently bringing order back into negative chaos. However, as each person's Core Tone is slightly different, you will create a non-uniform unity by aligning with other Tones naturally.

Meditation #3: Removing Para-sound Nulls:

Removing Para-sound Nulls requires deeper attunement than simply your own Core Tone: ideally you need to attune to a higher-order being, whether an angel, guide, god or goddess. Because the enfolded geometries of human identity are based in the dimension of Identity, you cannot combine with another person's Core Tone energy. However, groups of human beings can indeed resonate with one another for both spiritual and non-spiritual purposes: this is accomplished in the mental, emotional and psychic layers of the self. And although either harmony or coercion may reach into the sub- and un-conscious minds, the identity from which the Core Tone derives is inviolate.

This must be so for countless reasons, including the challenge of keeping a constant sense of self within 4-D Reality's continual changes so that the Infinite Being can understand itself. But this essential inviolability is shown in the fact that there is a place within your human self to which not even God is allowed without permission. Yes, your human self may become confused and damaged, tortured into hiding or protective self-deception. You may lose your sense of yourself when faced with massive shock, trauma or change, yet your identity, through which you may be found again, always remains within your Core Tone, no matter how long you may be lost in Chaos, negativity or Para-sound Nulls.

In this meditation, you can remove Nulls in Para-sound by opening your Core Tone into its own infinity as above. Now, imagine your were folding its silent shape of soundless sound back into and upon itself. It will be rather like forging a good Samurai sword:

layering it, pounding it, layering it, infusing it with carbon and pounding it, layering it, pounding it... However, you are layering the light within your Core Tone into a *sphere* rather than into a sword-shape: sense of the "size" and "shape" of your Core Tone and fold it over itself while retaining its spherical shape. Next, much as our exercise in Volume One, you turn your Core Tone's sphere of sound "inside out" into a hyper-sphere. Now that it is in a higher dimension, imagine infusing it with the divine Sound of Sounds, the essential hum of the multiverse, feeling this newly-created sphere of mingled Para-sound and Divine Sound flare brightly in response. You can repeat this process several times until your sphere is layered quite densely and hums resonantly with the divine Sound of Sounds.

Then, focusing on the Nulls created by situations of war, trauma, abuse, desperation or fear that need refreshed Para-sound, imagine this layered sphere coming into the situation and touching the swirls of negative energies. As you are filling the Nulls with refreshed Para-sound, you may see or hear it reaching for areas of harmony within the situation. You do not need to pray for any particular outcome, because much as happens with general prayers for wellbeing, the natural harmony within the layered sphere will shift the disharmony in the area automatically. Also, because you have asked for the Sound of Sounds to craft your Core Tone's hypersphere with you, you do not need to fear that your own energy is being used for this work, nor do you need fear that you are imposing you personal will. You are simply helping to sound a truly harmonic note by which cacophony may be transformed into a chord.

Meditation #4: Using Para-Sound to Withdraw Destructive Energies:

Think of a musical note, any note you like, whether F# or middle C and then find yourself a tone generator, bell, or chime of that note. Strike the chime or bell, listening to the sound as it begins, continues and ends. Notice how silence has changed because of the sound. As I said earlier, fourth-dimensional Reality's sound is in point of fact an "interruption," a trough or spike, in the constant tone of Para-sound. If you allow your mind to concentrate into a state of expanded attention, you can hear or feel the way sound is pulled into form from the incessant Sound of Sounds, so that it manifests into brief life through the dimension of Identity and then returns to the Source.

If you are paying attention correctly, then the silence following the Tone will have a paradoxical sense of greater space, as in an infinite sphere that is an infinitely dense and large state of "non-sound" full of potential energies. When you have become well aware of this infinite state of Para-sound, play the note or ring the bell again, while retaining your sense of that infinite "sound-space." Practice this several times until you can be aware of the 4-D sound and the enfolded Para-sound simultaneously.

When you have that sensation of spacious silence solidly in your perception, then imagine, or play a recording of, some kind of deeply discordant energy: a film clip from a war documentary, a tape of a daytime show that focuses on people arguing and fighting or perhaps a news broadcast of an angry, cursing mob. As with the specific Tone you have discovered, notice how the discordant energies and sounds interrupt Para-sound's integrity: much as the pure notes of the chime, every word of anger pulls its energy from the infinite well of Para-sound. However, unlike the chime's tones, the discordant sounds do not fall back into the Para-sound: rather, they create "chaff:" the fragments of the process of manifestation. Like silt, this chaff interferes with Reality's natural fluidity.

The next step can be done in two ways. One way is to feel the infinite, spreading plane that the enfolded Para-sound within your Core Tone creates. Imagine that the discordant sounds from the Null on this plane are like little shards of glass scattering on a tabletop rolling outwards in all directions. Yet, every one of the little shards of glass will stop somewhere on the Para-sound plane; you can intentionally see them melt and then dissolve into the surface of Para-sound's infinite expanse: by doing this you have returned the discordant energy to the enfolded dimensional Para-sound Field and thus removed it from 4-D manifestation.

The second method is to use your chime. Play the discordant sounds again, pausing a moment before you strike the note or generate the tone. When you strike the note, hear that same note in the discordant sounds. It does not matter whether or not you are skilled or talented enough to actually hear the chime's note in the cacophony: you just need to allow your Core Tone to pull the discordant sounds with it when it returns to Para-sound's enfolded state. Because you have used your own human psyche, you can create an unusual kind of "sonic magnetism" to pull the resonant, unified notes away from the discordant "symphony" of rage, hatred or despair. And when that discordant symphony is lessened, it loses power, note by note.

111

Meditation #5: Restructuring Personal Enfolded Geometries with a Psychic Fulcrum:

As it would take a true Spiritual Master to change the way the enfolded dimensions interact with other human beings, this fifth Para-sound meditation is only meant to change your personal experiences with and within the enfolded dimensions. To craft a psychic fulcrum, first consider the enfolded geometries and dimensions: the dimension of Identity in its various aspects, the Torsion Fields, the Zero dimension, or the dimension of Primordial Chaos. You could also contemplate the dimension of unfolded and enfolded Time, though of course its enfolded aspects act and react quite differently than the unfolded ones.

The first and easiest psychic fulcrum is your Core Tone, but you are not limited to that. If you are naturally psychic, depending on where the psychic information seems to "come from," you may have a sense where that function resides in your brain. The psychic impressions you get of a person might be in the frontal lobe, but receiving higher information might be on the top of the skull, or the temporal lobes. Perceiving ancient information through psychometric touch might use the back of the brain or it may engage the center of your brain near the pineal. Discerning the actual place does not matter, as long as you are familiar enough with the sensation to locate it, because you will be using that area in your brain as your fulcrum.

Concentrate upon that area where you feel your psychic sense to be, isolating it from the rest of your mind and consciousness. Put more and more of your attention on that one point, making it into the fulcrum for the shift. When you have that place in your brain clearly in your mind, see a shaft of energy rising from your Heart Chakra. Release the end of that shaft from your heart and position it onto your mind/brain's fulcrum so that can swing freely. Experiment with moving the bar mentally, from almost vertical to horizontal, at one angle and then at another, pivoting the shaft on the area in your brain that holds your psychic sense. Imagine that the front end of the bar is very, very far away: so far away it seems to reach the edges of Creation itself.

Mentally state your intention to pull in energy from the enfolded dimension with Para-sound. Once you have stated the intention, feel the bar of energy start to pivot and shift you into a state much like the Core Tone's expansive area of expression. Feel your intention through the bar of energy, feel yourself held within the enfolded dimension you have chosen as the best place to seek change. Stay with this imagery for a moment, trusting that your Core Tone is using the light in your heart to literally leverage a specific change you want to create through these higher-order energies.

Be inventive! You could wish: "I want my experience of Time to slow, so that I do not feel so rushed," or, "I want my experience of Time to speed up so that I do not feel constantly frustrated anymore." You might say, "I want the dimension of Primordial Chaos to work with me, instead of randomizing my life at uncomfortable intervals," or, "I want to shift my relationship to my own identity through changing my specific connections to the enfolded dimension of Identity." You will know when your desire for this change is complete when you feel a sudden sense of peace, of, "It's all right now." Then watch in your life to see what has changed!

The Non-uniform Expression
of the Enfolded Dimensions

Key Points: The multi-dimensional geometries that form the scaffolds of reality are not uniform in shape, content, consistency, interactivity or "conductivity" to the Divine Core or to the fourth-dimensional expressions of that Core. This non-uniformity is expressed in astrology, chemistry and human experience, particularly with issues like static realities and Para-sound "Nulls." The Torsion Fields balance the energies and manifestations of the Zero dimension, the dimension of Identity and Primordial Chaos, helping to create a dynamically balanced, shifting mixture of substances in keeping with 4-D reality's semi-conducting aspects. There are degrees of manifestation in 4-D, which explain "off-side" realities such as ghosts, extra-terrestrials, and other unofficial phenomena.

Subheadings:

- The Shapes of Multi-dimensional Geometries

- Astrological Expressions of Non-uniform Energies

- Matter and Primordial Chaos' Expressions through the Torsion Fields

- Degrees of Manifestation

- Meditation: Dancing in the Realm of Primordial Chaos

The Shapes of Multi-dimensional Geometries:

There has been much painstaking, elegant and delightful cosmological work done in recent years to discern and describe the "bubbles" of matter that form super-galaxies' arrangements with each other in order to show the nature of Einstein's Spacetime. These shapes help to clarify the actions of gravity and magnetism upon matter, but from my point of view they are the physical manifestations of a much deeper inner structure that I have called the inter-dimensional or Multi-dimensional geometries. It is for the sake of describing these M-D structures, to whatever limited degree my channeler and I are able, that I have presented the outré concepts of Para-light, Para-gravity, and the dimension of Identity.

As it is with all other fields, forces and geometries, these unusual aspects of reality also vary in their consistency, impact and receptivity to the original Source Information of the Zero dimension. However, Humanity is reaching the level of development where you can alter all of those factors and thus increase the divine Zero dimension's essential presence. You have more impact than you generally suppose: indeed, you might enjoy the chance to change the consistency of 4-D Reality itself in order to increase light, Magic or Divine Resonance, thus creating a more responsive universe. In physical forms such as bone, the structure follows the lines of force created by use: in terms of connections with the enfolded dimensions, use instead follows the inner geometrical structure, hence the meditation below.

The hugely vast only rarely seems to impact your life and your life seems to impact the vast even more rarely. But through Quantum Entangled Inductive Resonance there is a deep human connection to Reality's manifestation: this congruence of the human self and the enfolded dimensions is perceptible on the human level because of the omnipresent nature of the Zero dimension. The easiest way to become aware of those enfolded human dimensions is by uncovering and working with your Core Tone. But you can also discern your distinct impacts within those enfolded dimensions by watching the patterns and circumstances of your own life. What works in your life and what does not work? What changes bring new results and what aspects of your life remain static? Can you discern the impact of your prayers, your wisdom or your calcified habits?

Each of these aspects of your life has a different density, permeability and malleability that are determined by the inner geometries of the dimension of Identity and the interlinking shapes of the enfolded and unfolded fields. In other words, Reality's non-uniform expression is deeply systemic. However, you are an essential part of that system. After all, you are quite directly part of the structure of Life. By paying attention to what happens instead of simply how you react to it, you can begin to perceive your impact upon the more responsive and intelligent forces, such as the Ether that sustains psychic and Para-sound effects and your own responsive Magic. Eventually you will be able to work with the forces and structures that are more automatically manifested, such as physical laws, though this of course will take time.

Astrological Expressions of Non-uniform Energies:

Astrology is an obvious and fascinating way by which to perceive how unfolded and enfolded dimensions work with and through you. Those that like to study astrological patterns readily understand the difference in the way the energies of life, thought and consciousness shift, allowing certain expressions to have more impact at some times than others, because of the way these shifts are layered one on top of another. Studying the natal chart, whether sidereal or tropical, demands that you understand the fluid dynamics of its patterns and structures in a very practical sense. This may help you discern how the chart relates to real-time sidereal transits, the tropical shifts of the ages and hidden aspects such as asteroids, planets that have become dwarf planets, as well as phases and eclipses of the moon.

Reacting with one another quite gracefully, the combined Torsion Fields of Magnetism, Numeration, Proportion, Translation and Identity communicate through the plasma-like, fluid Ether, transmitting the planetary effects to the human being and to the Earth. Interestingly, these fluid layers of information are part of why astrology is often complex and sometimes inaccurate: you do not have quite enough perception of the psychic and Etheric astrological dynamics at this time for complete understanding and thus cannot yet have complete accuracy.

Astrology can be perceived as a constantly shifting multi-dimensional geometry that expresses the enfolded patterns of those inter-dimensional geometries into your unfolded, personal reality. In addition there is a difference in "viscosity" of the various elements or the signs, based on whether or not the natal chart has a preponderance of one particular element or certain specific signs. I have no intention of unraveling Astrology at this time, as there are practitioners more familiar with those specific energies than I. However, I do want to point out that Astrology is a very direct and human way you can begin to understand how fields, forces and matter can interconnect with each other as determined by the enfolded multi-dimensional geometries and structures to create non-uniform patterns.

As others have said, it is you who determine your natal chart when you decide to incarnate, with its particular blessings and challenges. Thus, when you can understand the planetary and elemental aspects of the fluid interactions within your astrological chart with your own identity, you can relate to it much more intentionally. You can also begin to work with the non-uniform aspects of the different planetary and elemental energies by studying the particular effects of each one. You might imagine each planet as a whirlpool of differing intensity and direction, for instance, so that aspects such Mercury trine Uranus might be perceived more dynamically. Interrelations between each aspect of a chart could also be understood as fluids of variable viscosity layering one on the other, as though each planet's, element's and house's energy were liquid light.

Matter and Primordial Chaos' Expressions through the Torsion Fields:

Non-uniform aspects of matter are obvious: from atomic weights to molecular density, as in the patterns formed within igneous rock by the differing weights and fluidity of the minerals. Primordial Chaos expresses itself with stunning creativity. Because of Primordial Chaos, Reality is primarily made up of amalgams, composites, alloys and mixtures: pure substances are rare because of the tremendous kinetic and potential energies of these "semi-manifested," partially unfolded dimensions. As I have mentioned before, gravity is a case in point: its affect on matter is limited because of its multi-dimensional "slant" that also leads to semi-engagements and partial effects, creating an incredible diversity of non-uniformity.

The Torsion Fields of Magnetism, Numeration, Identity and particularly the fields of Proportion and Translation, help Astrology's hidden energies to engage with human experience, allowing Primordial Chaos to manifest in dynamic balance. These fields are direct expressions of the Intention of the divine Mind and are responsive to it, allowing that Mind its superlative creativity. To the degree that you are aware of and in accord with that Mind, particularly through love, you become not only agents of its creativity you are also literally able to re-create the divine Being through your human experience.

It has been pointed out elsewhere that because this universe began from a single point, expressing itself into myriad particles, forces, fields and energies, therefore all of these points remain entangled. This functional unity continues within and throughout all expressions of consciousness, providing the platform from which Infinity re-expresses itself into more infinity through the Multiverse. And there is of course also non-uniformity in the alternate universes as well. I once called this present universe a "low rent district" that emphasizes margins, semi-conducting states and thus creativity: in short, it is for this very particular level and quality of creativity that you have chosen to live in this universe. And in a very real sense, this version of the Multiverse has chosen you to be a part of it.

Degrees of Manifestation:

I have also alluded to the fact that there are "degrees" of manifestation, inclusive of, but not limited to, "off-side" manifestations such as ghosts, angels, temporal apports and the like. The afterlife itself is a case in point, to say the least, as well as the "hidden" realms of elves, shamanic spirits and UFOs. However, there are also other whole ecosystems on other planets that are similarly "out of focus." These realms and other-planet realities are quite certainly opaque to most 4-D means of study, yet they are accessible to conscious perception through the psychic aspects of Ether, Para-sound and the Torsion Field of Translation.

From my present vantage point I can easily see a shift in your present world towards a more psychic and mental kind of science, one that will receive more data from other "densities" of manifestation. I will go into this type of science at greater length in the article containing the Meditations to Open the Lemurians' Inner Senses; for now, I only encourage those of you that want to reach out into "unofficial" input from alternate realities to take courage and do so.

Your personal reality is quite properly constructed from your perceptions of it: the wider your perceptions, the wider your reality. Here again is non-uniformity in experience and creativity and conversely, the limitations of those aspects created by the lower energy in some aspects of scientific culture. In so very many human endeavors, a restricted form of expression is easier to promote, sustain, impose and hold as the preferred standard. In low-energy cultures it is too often easier to say, "No," than "Yes," and to shut down rather than open up: that is of course the human challenge.

Some people love human chaos and even thrive on it: artists, children, rebels, manipulators and some scientists, emergency room health professionals, fire, police, and rescue teams: all of these people love responding in one way or another to mystery, drama, emergency or challenge. But the Realm of Primordial Chaos has far more than drama and tension within it: Chaos is the source of Mystery, Creativity, Wonder and Inspiration, allowing everything to be

118

rearranged and refreshed, shifting the already dynamic balance of the multiple layers of Reality into new forms of divine expression. As studies of mathematical Chaos show, there is an astonishing amount of order within chaotic expression, as well as an astonishing amount of chaos needed to create order from continual motion.

Meditation: Dancing in the Realm of Primordial Chaos:

Start the meditation by choosing something you like or enjoy watching: leaves blowing in the wind, waves crashing on the shore, people playing in a park or even the way your clothes turn over one another in the glass-door dryer: it can be anything moving that you find interesting and restful at the same time. In the beginning, simply watch what you have chosen to study, with as little mental commentary as possible. You do not want to analyze this chaos: you wish to allow it to show how your perception of Time and Space creates what you are seeing.

If you are watching leaves quiver in the wind, try and feel the layers of space that surround them, and the impulses of Time that transfer the force of the wind into movement. This should be a state of gentle, focused awareness so that in a very wonderful way you are receiving the information about the leaves' movements without thinking about them, without naming them "leaves," "wind," time" or "space" or thinking, "waves," "ocean," "beach" or "watching" at all. If you are attuning yourself correctly you will feel as though you have become larger somehow, larger yet more yourself.

Now, allow the waves, leaves, flowing stream or even the people playing in the park to communicate some of the information from within them: the salt content in the water and the feel of the wave curling; the dryness of the leaves and the temperature of the wind; the sensation of moving to catch a ball and the hardness of the grassy ground in the park. Keeping your mind out of this process may be tricky, though if you have had practice with either Zen awareness or "watching with soft eyes," you will be able to spend long moments simply being aware of forms and movements.

When you have practiced this type of attention for a while, work at feeling Primordial Chaos as the matrix in which all shifts happen, that allows all change and also exalts order by infusing creativity into existing forms and energies. As large as your soft, expanded state of mind has made you, the dimension of Primordial Chaos contains you, as well as the forces and forms of what you are watching and the part of you that watches yourself, thus creating vibrant layers of awareness and attention.

Once you have felt the impulses of Primordial Chaos shift and play around you, carefully, gently join the flux and pull of Chaos itself. As though you felt yourself jumping into the waves, the stream or the wind, allow the subtle, magical touches of the Timespace shifts acquaint you with the feeling of Primordial Chaos itself: a tremendously powerful field of force that does not work against order, but continually balances it, keeping it from becoming solid and immobile, without any possibility of change.

Through forming the dimension of Primordial Chaos, the Divine Intention allowed the motionless, timeless Para-light to enter into Time and become fluid. So also, your own life may become more fluid and responsive in Time and Space when you have learned to flow with that inner, Divine Mystery that is the unexpected heart of Chaos.

Part Two:

Human Experiences

Solition to Axiom: Civility and Gratitude

Key Points: Civility and gratitude are solitions in all cultures, allowing a group of people to work harmoniously with each other and with strangers. Both of these gracious interactions require a certain degree of self-responsibility: they are interfered with by entitlement, greed and blame. In addition, gratitude has often been mishandled by turning it into an obligation or chore, while civility seems too tedious to be managed. However, if both civility and gratitude can be viewed as benefiting *you*, not just the other person, this will have a positive effect on civilization as a whole and the solitions can more easily and naturally become axioms and cultural norms. There are many deeper aspects regarding gratitude and civility: issues of the difference between guilt and responsibility, or how a sense of entitlement skews human interactions. The answer is to evolve selfish reasons for gratitude, civility, responsibility and even compassion. This can shift negative civility and living in an uncivil culture towards the positive.

Subheadings:

- Gratitude and Civility: The Arts of Dynamic Harmony
- Cultural Solitions: Consideration and Aggression
- Choice and Responsibility
- Refining Civility
- Drowning Choice with Addictions
- Addiction, Responsibility and Blame
- Self-responsibility
- Entitlement
- The Addictions of Greed
- Selfish Gratitude
- Selfish Gratitude and Selfish Civility
- Overcoming Solitions of Negative Civility
- Living in an Uncivil Culture

Gratitude and Civility: the Arts of Dynamic Harmony:

Gratitude and *Civility* have long been solitions in all the world's cultures, representing mainly methods by which each culture relates to the members within its own boundaries and necessarily to strangers in order to diffuse tension, encourage unity, harmony and agreement, deepening bonds of all kinds.

Gratitude, the quality of thankfulness and appreciation for the kindness, action or intention offered from one person or group to another, is an acknowledgement of the betterment to your own life or circumstances because of another's actions through gift, service or favor. However, gratitude seems poorly defined for many, leading to confusion and anxiety, as well as resentment, especially when gratitude is abused and has ancillary demands of future obligations freighted upon it. Ideally, gratitude acknowledges a debt and cancels it: as long as the favor, kindness or sacrifice of one for another is acknowledged, especially between friends, gratitude balances and closes the transaction of giving and receiving.

Some have misunderstood and mishandled the meaning of gratitude by demanding gratitude from others for any and every thing. However, similar to respect, gratitude must be earned and not demanded. And particularly when you were young, the reasons for gratitude might have escaped you unless you received thoughtful answers to your questions. If you got something you wanted, you were happy: shouldn't that be enough for everyone? Why go to any extra trouble to say, "Thank you"? Perhaps some of you remember being reluctantly thankful, especially when you were told repeatedly, "Tell your Uncle 'Thank you' for the nice gift he gave you," when the gift was nothing at all like what you wanted.

Gratitude is too often presented as a just another chore: something you must do because you are told, not because you want to do so because you understand it. And the sarcasm some used was even more confusing. When you were a child, you acted upon impulse with little reflection: if you had what you wanted, you simply felt the joy of possession. You could not yet empathize enough to understand the effort, care or work that was put into the gift until you had to go out and buy or make one yourself. So often you were expected to understand the nature of gratitude as an adult might have understood it, yet you were left with mystification of one kind or another: a hard base upon which to build a value for gratitude.

123

Civility, defined as courtesy, consideration, politeness and respect, demands a fair amount of self-control, kindness, attentiveness and even selflessness. It is the fine art of dynamic harmony: seeing that the needs of the many do not overwhelm the needs of the individual and that the demands of the individual do not fragment the collective. Because the nature of civility changes as each culture's evolving solitions give it a new form, specific aspects of civility have been given greater emphasis at various times. In some cultures hospitality to strangers is given a specifically high rating; patriotism and sacrifice for one's country has been emphasized in others, while respecting family unity is the gold standard of courtesy in some cultures. The most important consideration in other cultures is deference to authority, whether to a king/queen, a military regime, a cultural tradition's ideological code or a newly created social structure's expectations. Most solitions regarding civility work because the genetically inherent nature of human beings is to be social, to allow needs and desires to work within the chosen definitions of social bonds. The sense of the tribe, the loved and beloved ones, is very deep in the human psyche, as well as the sense of "not my tribe," a competitor or enemy.

Within these social bonds there are ideally aspects of even personal civility within your own character: ideals of self-improvement, self-reliance and honesty to yourselves and others. When you respect yourself, then you promote your own courage, self-trust and emotional stability. When you consider yourself and your actions important within the structure of your society, then you act with integrity, inventiveness, creativity and flexibility. Frameworks of character have given prominence to all of these aspects at one time or another, sometimes with cultural support, sometimes without it. When your culture does not support you giving courtesy to yourself, you must rely on your own past-life history, a wise and gracious teacher or teachers, or simply lessons from the school of hard knocks to achieve a personal sense of self-respect.

Cultural Solitions: Consideration and Aggression:

Consideration, an aspect of civility, needs special mention here because it has had other connotations added to it over time and so I would like to re-view the word. Consideration definitely means to consider: to take thought, to contemplate, reflect and take into account. It does require at least a little empathy: the ability to put yourself not only into the other person's shoes and feel as they might

124

feel concerning your or another's action upon them, but it also can mean valuing the other as you value yourself. The Golden Rule may be stated, "Do *not* do unto others as you would *not* want done to you," and this demands a more thoughtful empathy that simply giving to others what you would like them to give to you.

The lack of this larger empathy is part of what drives prejudice, wars, many types of abuse to children, women, cruelty to animals and inhumanity in general. Some of this harm perpetrated upon others is displaced aggression: it stems from aggression to your own self. This aggression often forms when you have been so shocked by unnecessary punishment which you were unable to resist, whether because you were too young to speak or you would not have been heard even though you could have spoken. This later, projected aggression is the protest against what is seen as unfair treatment, because the child only imperfectly understands that his needs are not after all intrinsically paramount. If this frustration can be diverted into positive action or channeled into learning, then the child and parent both benefit. Punishment, though often easier than training, is far less effective. However, unless a child's natural senses of compassion and consideration are noticed and emphasized at the time, the child himself will not likely understand and value either one. Very young children are quite capable of compassion, yet it needs to be reflected back to them diligently.

Granted, a child can be quite selfish, thoughtless, forgetful, self-centered and self-serving. This essential narcissism can be explained and perhaps forgiven by considering where the child-consciousness came from originally: Heaven itself! In Heaven, where all needs are met instantly and all preferences are fulfilled, where you are never asked to do anything you don't like or want to do. You don't even have to remember where you put your sweater: after all, Heaven is fully climate-controlled. Once the soul has recovered enough from life to receive love or has repaired itself from the shocks and challenges of that life which might have driven it into despair or disbelief, Divine Love matches the soul's every need before life and between lives with an unmistakable, unconditional caring that the soul feels constantly.

Leaving Heaven for Earth is worse than traveling to a bitter, alkaline desert and the discomfort can be felt as depression or rage, both of which can lead to aggression. On Earth aggression is common and often is an effective response to your sense of loss and despair, because if not overbalanced or unwisely applied, a directed sense of anger and frustration accomplishes things. Indeed, you are actually aggressive towards yourself in a very real sense when you correct yourself on errors, determine to change or keep yourself to a standard despite the impulse to slide into the easy, lazy, indulgent ways.

By this yardstick I was a very aggressive person! Yet as I had a clear purpose to my life and was both sure of my desires and humble toward their power and impact, the aggression had somewhere to go and a way to have its energy be used. Living in the bright shadow of this purpose, I did have tremendous self-control. Alas, it seems that in America and several other countries, self-control and self-restraint are not often taught in these times: this is a loss for all. "Freedom" does not mean becoming a brute towards others because you feel free to indulge your egocentricity through selfish, inappropriate aggression. You can even become a brute when you misdirect the positive aggression of self-control out onto others, especially when you do this in an attempt to dominate them without taking responsibility for yourself and your impact upon others.

If you do not look at your own actions with the courageous scrutiny that a sense of responsibility creates, then you are propelled by your own and others' reactive emotions and have cut yourself off from your priceless human power of free will choice. Unfortunately, free-will choice's human authority is too often surrendered to circumstances, obsessions and addictions, other people and any of various social collectives. But if our ability for free choice were one of our most precious possessions, why would we arrange things so that we could resist exercising it? Oddly enough: because of our confused understanding of responsibility.

Choice and Responsibility:

There has been an erosion of certain kinds of civility of late; this has resulted in abusive behavior in electronic social networks, deceptive, cruel and vicious manipulation of those networks, including nefarious, criminal and excessive use of leverage in some websites, politics and society at large. You do not stand on a knife's edge, where civilization is about to go under. But you do stand at a point of decision: you can allow yourselves to succumb to bad feelings, to outrageous behavior that becomes so normal that it is never questioned until you redefine humanity through deteriorating to lower and lower levels. Or, you can focus upon self-determination and harmonious self-definition, finding a new balance between the

126

needs of the collective and the needs of the person. In short, you can decide to *choose* what to feel about how you are treated and then how you react. You can learn to be kind and choose to be. Unless you are so damaged that you have become full of toxic harm, you can learn the means, methods and mores of being civil and choose to make them you own. This power of choice is always within your reach.

This is true even though you might be in a dire situation where everything is stripped from you. There may be circumstances when you are threatened, coerced, and imprisoned. I do grant you, there are times when the number and type of choices given to you are manipulated with such cruelty that there are no right answers, for all choices that might lead to any kind of freedom have been ruined and any action leads to death or worse. Especially when certain cultural structures and forces have been usurped by the insane, this cruel manipulation has been far too often the case: those with so little humanity left within them that they delight in engineering fear and pain in others in order to obliterate them, too often allow brutality and malice to triumph. Brutalities such as these have happened throughout human history, surely, but you are more aware of them now: you are able to feel the first-hand or second-hand effects of cruelty more clearly.

Refining Civility:

And as your personal sense of humanity has gained sensitivity, you are even more aware when something is not in accord with kindness, compassion, or mercy. Many times you simply long for the gentler things because Humanity's inner vision has clarified enough for you to see how else it all might be and to feel the peace that you feel when you are not being brutalized. One clue from civility itself is: do not automatically assume malice on the part of others. Be wisely aware of what might happen, of whom they might actually be if they are pretending otherwise, but hold the judgment of their character off as long as is sensible. To assume malice, to live your life in a constant state of tension between fight or flight is no way to live at all and can cost everyone dearly.

On the obverse, don't assume that silence is either compliance or acceptance. If you are comfortable with something, it never automatically follows that the other person is as comfortable with it as you are. Sometimes being mistaken this way can lead to minor gaffes, such as the person that was so happy to discover good, salty, strong Dutch licorice, and gave it happily to a friend to share... but the friend absolutely loathed licorice. Or as in the time when another person showed her friend an absolutely beautiful picture of an emerald green tree snake, having forgotten or never known that her friend was so afraid of snakes that she had nightmares for the week afterwards.

In a more serious vein, taking advantage of someone for any reason, simply because it would help you, or be easy for you or because *you* are certainly "okay with it," is quite unwise and might be worse than unkind. For instance, assuming someone would certainly babysit your children because their doing so would help you out a great deal, yet meanwhile you are conveniently forgetting that your intended sitter has a compromised immune system and the child's germs might actually kill the sitter with flu, pneumonia or the like. Or assuming that just because someone *does not object* to your proposal or to your taking him or her somewhere or setting him up to do something with you, whether it is a loud party or a museum tour, is not necessarily the same thing as the other person desiring or accepting your proposal is foolish, and under certain circumstances could be criminal.

In short, not everyone is as you are. Not everyone likes what you do because you like it. The best thing you can do for the sake of civility is to remember to ask first.

Drowning Choice with Addictions:

Yet the power of choice is so huge a thing, so full of meaning, mystery and power, that too many run away from it. You choose addictions or obsessions, hoping you are solving things by drowning your anxiety surrounding this power of choice. With obsessions and addictions, too often you believe you are freeing yourself by exercising your free will choice to attach a foreign influence to your body, mind and psyche. For some, this is truth: you have had lives as shamans: solidly grounded in your own identities you have learned to watch and regulate the effects of the semi-toxic substances upon your own minds and emotions. As some animals live with parasites of several kinds and still thrive, there are people that can to coexist with addiction's parasitical energies well enough to function. However, there are too many others for whom addiction has too many memories of escape from the hard lessons of life within it. And yes, a hard life can drive you to seek escape, to return to any type of

Heavenly bliss you can find. When you are planning your upcoming life in your comfortable place in Heaven you forget how easy it is to over-estimate your strength and abilities for handling a difficult life, so too often you plan and determine to accomplish too much, over-burdening yourself.

Too late, you find that the "friend" you have hoped for, the support, surcease and ease you have looked for in the addictive substance, is never *in* or even part of that substance or obsessive process in the first place. Instead, these things too often rip away those very fragments of your character that might have helped you find the peace and strength, determination and grace that would help you with all the troubles in your life. And only then, when those precious things have been despoiled and lost, does the substance or thing reveal its true nature: the nature of an unprincipled, vicious parasite. Like the vampire bat's saliva that numbs the skin on the bite so that the bat can lick up the blood without its victim noticing, the addictive substance or process deludes you as to its nature early on, making your feel especially good, particularly well or simply dulling the pain of your life. And its primary lure is: "This is exercising your free will the easy way: you do not have to face remorse, guilt or regret, no! If you take me into yourself, you will be able to live *without* any pain in your trammeled, frustrating and painful life, without any responsibility or accountability." Too often its deception is total: by the time you notice *it* is getting high *on you* and that *it* is getting drunk *on you*, it is frequently far too late. There are few larger lies in the multiverse.

Addiction, Responsibility and Blame:

The deep issues regarding addiction particularly are far beyond the scope of this article, but I bring them up here because I am talking of the fear of free will. Too often, with or without addictions, rather than taking up the burden of saying, "Yes, I did this evil thing to hurt this other person, acting thoughtlessly and foolishly," and facing the consequences, you find numerous ways to distract yourself from the dread of your own human choices and being held accountable for those choices. This dread is a deep human agony, but paradoxically it only becomes so deep *because it is avoided.* Consider: if you have made a mistake, done something unwise or wrong, you can do several things. You can ignore it and hope others will not notice, as when a child might think, "If I keep quiet and don't say anything maybe

129

Mommy won't find out." Although, upon reflection you will see that the major flaw is that *you will always know what you have done.*

If you cannot ignore the error you have chosen and cannot hope that others will, you might try to deflect responsibility through blame. Frankly, this happens far too often. However, making someone else more wrong by picking up on even the tiniest of misdeeds the other has done and blowing it all out of proportion to try and hide your worse misdeeds, doesn't ever make you more right. This distraction and deflection is used too often in bureaucratic and political stonewalling, prevarication in sales and run-arounds in businesses in order to give the true miscreants time to set up their scapegoats. This is as much legerdemain as the magician that says, "Look at my right hand," when he is manipulating the trick with his left: in terms of self-responsibility, this misdirection is deeply false.

Another way you can deal with the looming threat of payment or punishment for your free-will mistakes is by trolling for pity through excuses, pleas or manipulations of various kinds: lying is actually a form of this. When you lie about what you have done, it is generally because you dread the cost of honesty so much that you compromise your own sense of truth and everyone else's in order to avoid honesty's pain. For, obviously, you could of course take responsibility for something in the sense of taking the blame, facing the consequences and feeling the remorse. However, you cannot do this if your character is not strong enough in the first place.

If you are not civil with yourself, if you do not respect yourself, then you do not have the courage, resilience, self-trust or emotional stability you need in order to realize that you have even *made* a mistake, fallen into thoughtless negativity or harmed another. In this marginal, lower-energy reality within your present 4-D system where the amount of energy present has very specific limits, it is far too easy to do the feckless thing, to take the way through your difficulties that uses the least amount of energy. Much as the planet is arranged so that there are only a certain number of beautiful coastal habitats where you might build your perfect beach house, only a few mountainous places where it is safe to build and oh, by the way, there is a strictly limited amount of water generally, human character can be limited as well. Not everyone can shine with the pure energy of character, resilience, civility and honesty just by wishing for it.

However, even the limited amount of energy here will allow and support that valuable outcome if you are able to start forming your character when you are young or to reform your character later on by small increments. This is obviously another reason why training in civility and gratitude is best when started early: you have time to build up the momentum that carries the empathy in civility and the generosity in gratitude forward. Although it seems to be too often forgotten of late it is still true: if you work hard with something in the beginning rather than later, it is easier to succeed. When you create structures for civility and gratitude in yourself early on, then you gain not only momentum but also the facility of familiarity, so that civility costs you little to maintain and you reap civility's benefits thereafter.

Yet for many, the restraints of gratitude and civility seem to frustrate their sense of freedom: "If I cannot be free to say what I want when I want to, just feel what I feel so I can act on it in the moment or arrange things to my liking, what would be the point in living on Earth in the first place? If I can't have any fun, which means any actions that I can do for free just because I want to, then why should I ever bother? What's the point in leaving Heaven after all?" Thus for some their Heaven on Earth *is* to act irresponsibly! However, the paradox of self-responsibility, self-control and self-honesty still remains: by holding yourself to responsibility's inner structure and thus limiting the "freedom" of ill-considered, immature, thoughtless or manipulative actions, you actually become even *more* free. At the very least you are less likely to be put into jail, which would be most certainly a major curtailment of freedom!

When you take it easy in the beginning because it seems too troublesome or arduous to correct yourself, then, as with the parasite of addiction, you will unexpectedly find it too late to change and you finally comprehend that you can no longer realize what it means to be a responsible human being. It is so easy to *not* notice how your actions affect others, to *not* stretch your mind and heart to include empathy: in short to take the path of least resistance with your limited ego. It is certainly true that correcting small things in the beginning consistently and with forethought can be tedious. However: once your irresponsibility has been left to increase on its own through expediency, laziness or even willful resistance, correcting the small errors that created incivility in the first place increases in difficulty *geometrically*. In this sense, lack of civility is like a degenerative disease: if not caught early, it gets steadily worse until it's too late to even try to change.

Self-responsibility:

Responsibility seems a burden because it has been miss-applied in most cultures. "Responsibility" as in, "who is responsible for this?" has generally come to mean, "Who will we blame and punish for this?" There are those who define "responsibility" by breaking the word down a little, and say, "It is those that are able to respond to a situation." While that does ease the confusion a little, it is not enough. If there is only one person able to respond to a situation, such as only one parent that is able to respond to the unintentional or even intentional mayhem that her or his children may create in the family home, this is of course a burden. When there is only one parent that can manage the child's training, arranging the child's betterment by working long hours and then catching scraps of time with the child, that is a burden for parent and child both. This sours the meaning of responsibility for all concerned, especially when the over-burdened parent snaps from sheer exhaustion and acts thoughtlessly. Dreadfully, the responsibility has become a cage and all of your choices have caused you to lose your freedom. You cannot respond if you are exhausted, weary, taxed beyond limit and there is no help in sight. And in most cultures, when you cannot respond to the overwhelming demands of your life, you are blamed for that as well.

But the main misapplication of responsibility in many cultures of this time is variations on the theme: "See how you made me feel," or, "See what you made me do." More than emotional laziness, this can be a form of emotional blackmail or extortion through guilt or shame, leading irretrievably to the terrorism of punishment. Guilt and shame have powerful leverage against a child because being unloved by his caretakers is synonymous with death, if not indeed annihilation. This is not just the comprehensible death of, "If I do this, then I will die," but rather is the unclean terror of, "If my caretakers are faulty, then I must go it alone, even though I cannot remotely predict what will happen. At the same time I know I am too young and small, too weak to help myself at all."

That pain remains within your past lives as a deep, unsolvable terror that is often lodged in the unconscious. This same deep level of terror shapes those that have been abused by neglect; if further abuse is added on, there is little wonder that some crumple under it and some attempt to overcome it by pushing it back out onto others, or driving it further into their own selves through addictions. Though surely abusers sometimes expect or demand your gratitude, no one should ever have to be grateful for abuse, even though the abusers feel entitled to "respect."

Entitlement:

However, entitlement is one of the most irresponsible and artificial states of mind known. This sense of entitlement is both a sickness and an illusion. It is a sickness because it leaches your own powers and strengths from you: the power of valor and the strength of self-reliance. The attitude of entitlement is an illusion because it depends on sources of validation that are not intrinsic, that are not a true part of your whole being. Instead they are a series of manipulations leveraged through your false ideas of your identity in order to create actions and reactions within loved ones and others. More than simply a method for taking and usurping something you do not deserve, entitlement works at creating false valuation for yourself that is dependent on others' willing or unwilling participation in the charade. In short, it is without substance: it needs a tremendous amount of stolen energy to be maintained. By choosing to feel entitled, you lose your power of empathy, compassion and fellow-feeling: you then live in a world where everything and everyone is an object crafted towards your gratification, instead of a human opportunity to encounter the face of the Divine through personal engagement.

Because entitlement divorces you from any sense of your real power as a human being, this attitude of self-serving helplessness actually sucks your self-confidence dry. When you have no faith, no self-confidence, every choice becomes an anxious thing driven by weakness that you must hide through pomposity, bombast, arrogance or other forms of fear-based, inauthentic manipulation. In this way you lose your true power of choice. Demanding is not choosing: it is based on helplessness, particularly on the kind of helplessness that is willfully recursive: it re-defines itself with its own definitions. You cannot receive new input when you demand, for far too often your sense of what is right is based on blindly denying the affects of those very demands upon others.

This static state actually freezes your human experience in place. Certainly, as any parent of an entitled child can attest when they try to move their entitled offspring out of the house, the child's unyielding attitude quite solidly freezes whatever situation you are experiencing. Much as when a child feels an insoluble shock when he is punished by being told he is responsible for another's feelings, cutting yourself away from your own power by falling into entitlement's extortion cannot be solved: the real issue, that the child *has no control over your feelings in the first place,* is nothing the child can make right. Similarly, because entitlement is a desperate attempt to avoid being vulnerable, you cannot become human if you remain entitled because you cannot be vulnerable. Being truly human and humane: tender, responsive, loving, caring and as aware of others as you are aware of yourself, is only possible when you are able to be sensitive. When children have not been taught that they can withstand vulnerability, that they can overcome trials and survive, then they will have no sense of themselves, no sense of their personal power or strength, much less a sense of the nature of any real weaknesses.

When you feel entitled, you divorce yourself from others' realities and therefore your own reality. This means that you can never feel whole and complete in yourself. When you do not feel complete, you too often try to fill the empty self with the very same things that caused the original lack. Therefore entitlement becomes another obsession and the nature of all obsessions is that they distract you from the real issues. When you cannot perceive the real issue, you cannot deal with it. Thus it becomes something like a psychic tumor that steals your very life from you; furthermore, this tumor-like attitude of self can be passed on to others. The psychic entity of the obsession, addiction, craving, blind habituation or compulsion acts towards your sense of identity as a tumor does to the body: it steals away other living parts of you, perhaps a little at a time, perhaps all at once. Yet it inevitably takes up more and more space in your identity, eating up more and more substance, until the original self is starved to death. Like cancer, this attitude of entitlement can be cured, but the cure demands true effort, grace and pure healing.

The Addictions of Greed:

I have spoken earlier of the Infinite Need and Infinite Fear that some experience, and how the greed for total control of all resources is based in the fear of not having enough, of not being able to command enough. The sense of lack that drives these individuals is so implacable they are unable to ever feel whole. You all know certain

134

people that can never be satisfied no matter what you do or refrain from doing: the bullies and dictators of totalitarian regimes, whether they be the draconic leaders of a suffering country, or the hateful and exacting family member that will allow no one any peace but would rather have his hurt feelings totally rule the family.

Granted, sometimes this implacability's root is insanity and sometimes it derives from complex personality disorders of one kind or another. Such disorders can be foreseen and forestalled in time if there is the cultural will to do so: there is every chance that they will be foreseen and forestalled in the future. However, many times this slide into infinite, implacable starvation is caused by only two things: a deep lack of the self-reflection that self-civility provides, as well as disengagement from the dimension of Identity, which creates a gap between you and your experiences. This gap keeps you from perceiving anything that is not in yourself already. Since you will not respect yourself, you can respect nothing else: thus you are utterly abandoned.

Like the in-depth discussion of addiction, the issue of coercive insanity is also beyond the scope of this article. Though I will suggest that demanding entitlement starts with improper mirroring or even a lack of mirroring from others in the family: either because of poor training or because the damaged individual is unable to process empathy in the first place. Much of the mirroring that you might have missed in your early development can be reclaimed, but there are some aspects that cannot ever be recaptured, such as the blithe, unconscious grace and ease with which you could have understood another person when you were a child. If you were roughly handled by abuse, neglect, living under threat of emotional abuse or sheer incompetence, this makes everything more difficult later, if not nearly impossible.

You can only retain your grace when you have been mirrored with that same gracious and supple ease that is potential in all humanity. Generally, kind people create kind people and of course the obverse is true. Some people do choose lives of little mirroring for reasons of spiritual or personal development; there are many reasons why. However, I bring it up here because mirroring is an aspect of civility. Mirroring means that you have been granted the benefit of emotional interaction within empathy. When you are angry, others react with honesty and apprise you of your impact, showing kind understanding; when you are kind, the same occurs.

135

Yet if because of lack of mirroring, you were never shown what happiness looks like in yourself or in others, if you were never instructed about the scope of your impact, you are working in an emotional vacuum where your true feelings are never heard. Thus you are unable hear others' true feelings either. This vacuum's fundamental nature is the same unclean terror an emotionally abandoned child experiences: however much this terror must be resolved and demands to be resolved, it cannot be eased unless new ideas and new input are presented to bridge the emotional vacuum's gap. This vacuum drives entitlement: it divorces you from your human experience, driving the degenerative processes of addiction, obsession, irresponsibility and despair.

However, in the present, for yourself and your children, your friends and people you know, nurturing civility through selfish gratitude is a potential answer to the degenerative processes that results in irresponsibility and entitlement.

Selfish Gratitude:

As we described above, *Gratitude*, defined as thankfulness, gratefulness and appreciation, is actually a state of recognition: being aware that someone or something has given you energy, whether through emotional communication or in some form of action, solely or at least mainly for your benefit and betterment. Gratitude perceives that something is given to you that you lacked; it also causes you to recognize and be aware of another person or being, including the Divine Being. Thankfulness is often the first response to such kindness, while gratitude is the deeper state that follows thankfulness: a state of contemplation where you can assess what has occurred. True, you will often weigh and measure thankfulness automatically, yet certainly with contemplation you become more aware of the fact that energy has been given to you and can discern that energy's nature. Gratitude shows that you acknowledge the kindness, love, thoughtfulness and generosity that have been given to you, recognizing the full value of what has been exchanged, as well as the person, persons or beings that have given you this energy or substance.

Selfish gratitude seems an oxymoron, but it truly isn't. Even though it is generally presented that way, gratitude really isn't for the other person's benefit: it's for *yours*. If you say, "Thank you, you are so kind," to someone that has given you kindness, you are not so much stroking the other person's ego as you are telling yourself: "Today, someone has been caring and thoughtful to me. Someone went out of his way for me! Someone stepped forward on my behalf and she or he made a difference in my life that I could not have made myself. Someone else believes I am worth his trouble: therefore, I am valued. I am valued by this person: therefore it follows that I can value myself." That's it: pure selfishness!

When you value yourself, you are in far less pain than when you feel without value and empty in an emotional vacuum's void. If you feel you are worth something, you will act like it. You will be so much less likely to take the easy, negative and reactive ways that will hurt other people with your own feelings of abandonment and loss. You will even be able to refuse outright to act out because of your hurt feelings or the feelings of malice that may have developed as a result of an earlier situation where you did not have love enough inside of yourself to counteract their burden. And again, selfishly, when you make it easier for others to be kind by being grateful to them, they will find it far easier to be kind to you, again and again. Obviously, you will experience much less friction if you are gracious and kind! This is as clear a statement of physics as: if you agitate a pot full of water, then some will likely spill out; yet if you carry the water carefully, you'll keep it in the bucket.

Another way that gratitude is selfish is that, when you say, "Thank you," for a gift, compliment, or praise, then you will make it your own. The "thank you" discharges that object, gesture, or act of grace from the other person's possession, allowing it to become *your* possession. The compliment can become part of you, free and clear: now you can add it to your self-image. And even though receiving gifts, kindness or compliments from others might be hard for you this moment of gratitude allows you to *digest* the things others have given to you. But it is wise to take the time for the sake of general civility and your own civility to yourself. Many acts of civility, from bowing to curtsying to handshaking evolved or were created in order to give the participants in social interactions time to collect and center themselves. This allowed everyone to absorb the situation and act intelligently instead of reacting blindly or thoughtlessly. Bows and curtsies, handshakes and bringing a gloved hand to your lips in courtly greeting allowed you to be at your best, without reacting thoughtlessly. Again, this is purely selfish!

137

Alas, it is true that there are any countless number of things that you have been given that you have not wanted, that you never asked for or that have been frankly injurious to you. Emotional, physical, sexual and spiritual abuses might be examples of such "gifts." Too often, your had to deal with so many irresponsible demands from implacable family members, business associates or even the general public that you had to make yourself hyper-responsible for those that refused to take responsibility for their own selves: if you did not they would surely make you responsible through accusations and guilt. The deep wrong of blaming the victim, holding you responsible for someone else's bad actions costs everyone very deeply and is not easy to repair. However, I will discuss those later, as at this time I am mainly offering ways in which the civil act of gratitude benefits you.

Selfish Gratitude and Selfish Civility:

If you can discern how gratitude, kindness, consideration and ethical behavior benefit *you*, you are not only more likely to do it you will also help to change the solitions of the various culture-driven forms of civility into *axioms*. By being wisely selfish, taking in gratitude as your own and embracing civility as a way to peace, you can even help bleed off the dark energies of Infinite Need and Infinite Fear that are potential in your own self, until, perhaps, such imbalances no longer exist. By no means is gratitude or civility a panacea for insanity, trauma, tragedy or any remaining abuse or abusers: not even an axiom of self-healing civility can clear all pain or loss away.

Yet civility and gratitude can help each of you, one at a time, to alter the potential direction of cultural degeneration that hurt feelings and revenge drive forward all too easily. Similarly, the costs of thoughtless cruelty and inconsiderate behavior can be lessened or even removed, with the result that there are fewer hurt feelings in the first place and therefore less desire for revenge altogether. Selfish Gratitude can nourish your emotions and spirit in a way that nothing else can. And when you are no longer starving for a sense of self, you will no longer rob people of their rights to joy, grace and a peaceful existence: you will not need to, because when you are grateful, your soul is fed. When your soul is no longer starving, it can let its kindness shine.

Paradoxically, it is because the deterioration of the cultural *solitions* of gratitude and civility that an axiom needs to replace them. When you are civil, thoughtful, and wisely grateful all the time or when you realize that being selfishly grateful is as important as breathing, you can automatically perceive other people in relationship to that wisely selfish gratitude or civility. This becomes a superlative freedom: on the one hand, you can choose what to receive, how you receive it and how it will shape how you feel about yourself; similarly, you can choose methods of civility that nourish you and are able to find methods of civility that prevent you from offending others or yourself, thus keeping you out of danger. Indeed, when you have learned how to be selfishly kind and considerate towards yourself, you learn how to contrast that to abusive behaviors' pitfalls. When you see the difference and have strengthened yourself enough to act out of wisdom, you inevitably become so much more readily aware of how others feel, of what others need, that you know how to give to them wisely: not only for your own needs, but for theirs.

It is granted that sometimes you must bear the freighted strictures of gratitude that are culture-driven by guilt; you may be asked to withstand unbalanced, brittle civility as when a servant must always be kind, generous and patient, no matter how poorly he or she is treated. But because civility is the partner to gratitude, you can build a strong counter-agent in your own soul. In short, civility: courtesy, respect, politeness, good manners and consideration, is being dynamically and even pro-actively empathic with others and yourself. Selfish civility means to learn how to manage social situations with the kind of grace that does not take too much from you, or demand too much from another. And of course as when you are selfishly grateful so that you support and nourish yourself, you will find that thanking others and supporting others much easier.

Overcoming Solitions of Negative Civility:

You have been taught for so long that you need to be gracious by paying the cost of yourself. You have so long been told that you need to be kind to others before you are kind to yourself, that you must respect others without respecting yourself, taking the high road when others have entrenched themselves into your very soul with their own blind needs. This is Negative Civility: it takes something away from you, sometimes quite catastrophically; eventually of course it breeds bitter resentment, dismantling the whole dynamic flow of civility between people altogether. When you give yourself away and have no means of replenishing the loss, your emotions, psyche and spirit

139

begin to waste away. And as we mentioned above, this spiritual starvation is part of what drives addictions and much abuse.

As has been pointed out elsewhere, if you give everything of yourself to your family, there is only you left to take care for you, and if there's nothing left of you, then who will care? Worse, the ones that have been taught that you will always carry their burdens are unlikely to understand the nature of those burdens if they have never had to carry them. So you have no outward means to replenish your self with the very kindness, thoughtfulness, respect and grace you have given away! In your growing hunger for the very thing you are giving to others, you eventually or sooner become unkind and ungenerous because you have given all of your kindness away. You may even feel entitled out of sheer desperation.

You become thoughtless if only out of sheer exhaustion, for it is always harder to respect anyone else when you have saved no respect for yourself. Because you have allowed yourself to become hollow, you lose your sense of grace, your aplomb, and even your sense of your own purpose. That there are those who still love others freely and easily after giving everything of their selves away says much about the tremendous courage and strength in the path of a saint. But such saints are actually rare indeed. And it is a particularly vicious species of cruelty to ask someone else to be a saint for your own convenience: this is only entitlement once again.

And if you have decided to live your way through your life by taking instead of giving, asking another to necessarily be a saint is surely abuse. At the very least thoughtless and unbalanced demands for respect, consideration, attention, kindness and such are at base sheer emotional indolence on your part. When you demand that another twist himself into the shapes you need and call it "respecting me," you have surrendered your happiness, if not also your wholeness, into the hands of others. You make them liable for *your* wellbeing at *their* cost and in addition have charged them the extra tolls of guilt, shame and manipulation.

Living in an Un-civil Culture:

And far too often, the kind of gratitude imposed upon you by religion, family tradition or some other cultural leverage has a sour and bitter taste. As said above, because gratitude has been described as something you must give to another person, it leaves you hungry for recognition of your own value. With selfish gratitude, the other

140

person may or may not give kindness: because you understand the true nature of giving you will always receive what you choose, making it an exchange whose currency is under the dominion of your power of choice. With selfish civility, you can keep yourself away from compromising, tense, dangerous, or unhappy situations because you will not treat yourself shabbily, nor allow others to do so. Thus you will keep yourself clear from much hurt and injury.

Yes, it is indeed most unfortunate that in the presently unkind, thoughtless and occasionally cruel cultural landscape, you must quite deliberately recognize your own value. It is sometimes too much to ask that you have to detoxify what others give you in order to assimilate anything of value from it. However, selfish gratitude and selfish civility is metaphorically like vitamin D: you can make it yourself and you don't need much sunshine to do it. Just a few acts of kindness given to you can be enough, if you can take them in, digest them and graciously make them your own. And selfish civility is like cool water in a burning desert. It feeds a need so vital you hardly recognize it: the need for *peace*. True, your Human Self may find peace in countless places, from meditation to even tiny moments of solitude or friendship. Yet if you are civil to others wisely, you find nearly everything in your human relations working better and more peacefully.

The world is too close to itself now, the effects of unkindness too magnified by social media, the speed of travel and the tremendous number of interconnections between people, to ignore the need for a universal understanding: that selfishness becomes selflessness when it is wise. The culture-driven structures of protocol, gratitude and the cost of human interaction must be turned into the *axiom* of civility: the deep comprehension that, however different, we are human. There is too much competition for limited resources; there are too many old wounds, deep hurts and cycles of vengeance to allow you to be careless with anyone. There are too many that do not have enough and too many of the few that have too much. When you can understand gratitude and civility in a new way, in the wisely selfish way that is selfless, you can change everything and put so many demons to rest.

And it is not that hard. It has already been discovered that children are innately compassionate and altruistic. Civility is already part of the natural grace of the human being. When it is wisely handled, gratitude always adds positive energy. So many frustrating irritations, so many feelings of emptiness and the emotional vacuums of those that feel the only way to be real is to create drama, havoc or horrors, can all just fall gently away. For when your soul is fed and you feel the ease of peace, you reclaim the human joy: gracefully interacting with others and yourself in a truly human civilization.

The Hypnosis of the Marketplace and Media

Key Points: With the combinations of advertising media, recreational media and social media, your conscious minds have been steadily diverted, sidetracked, hypnotized and too often overwhelmed. This leads to not only a lack of peace and sometimes even a lack of meaning but also burdens your subconscious mind to the point that it can shut down. The human cost of trying to emulate the super-fast speed of computers through social media is driving many of you away from stability and peace and can lead to addictive behaviors and worse in a futile attempt to cope. Paradoxically, this frantic activity can also lead to profound boredom because you never perceive the whole depth of any one thing: lack of connection to what is whole can drive addition as well. To become aware of not what you do but also *why* you do it helps you navigate all the disparate, ceaseless input. By suspending your belief in this present version of reality, you can return to a more human reality, one with more and deeper meaning.

Subheadings:

- Manipulative Advertising: a Brief Review

- The Nature of Hypnosis

- The Conscious, Subconscious and Unconscious Minds and Persuasion

- The Super-Fast Challenge to the Mind/Brain

- The Addictive "Choice"

- The Loss of Meaning

- Lack of Stability in the Self

- Advertising

- "Pushing Your Hammer"

- The Cost of Time

- Belief and Suspension of Belief

Manipulative Advertising: a Brief Review:

It may seem strange that I present this issue in a book primarily on physics and metaphysics but there are several issues here that I wish to address because of the explosion of media devices that operate continually and that many of you keep close to you. In a very real way, you are diverting your conscious attention, as well as having your conscious attention diverted: this encroaches on the subconscious. Diverting attention from the conscious to the subconscious like this is a species of imposed hypnosis and does not have a simple solution. You can become so outwardly directed, so focused on what is coming into your mind and thoughts through social media, television, movies and other amusements that over time this changes your relationship with reality, sometimes to such a degree that not just personal identities shift but also Humanity's identity as well. There can be great cost in trying to absorb rapid and incessant input: the mind/brain eventually enters a dissociated state in order to deal with all the details, especially if those details are varied, continual and particularly designed to command your attention. And if your attention is commanded by something else, you are unable to command it yourself. And when you cannot command your own attention, you have lost your human core.

With the computer-driven Internet surely there is exhilaration, a sense of easily won accomplishment, of delightfully fast gratification and feedback. Yet too often it is just movement itself that gives you the satisfaction, not the human state of contemplation or understanding. To ask the human self to be in a state of perpetual arousal is not something that allows you to stop, consider, discern or even just process the barrage of ideas. This is not a human thing. You are most human when you are most in and within your Self. You need your Self in order to live and need rest in order to have a human self, instead of a self that is created by the super-fast technologies that are at the base of social media. When you are in continual motion there is no possibility of wonder: you go on to the next thing and the next and the next, without processing any of them fully.

At that speed your mind slips into a low-grade terror: it has not finished with one thing before you must deal with another. This is being harried: you can never rest. And to be human, you need to take time to understand what has happened to you. You sleep every night in order to process your day and in order to repair what you can of the shocks or challenges you have experienced within that day. But if

144

you are never, ever, ever given time to process, then you are in a continual state of "hover:" you cannot have a whole, still moment to yourself but must continually receive, react and repeat. Peace is virtually impossible in this situation: this kind of continual input leads directly to the debilitating false fear of anxiety. There are those who say they feel peace in this continual motion, however, this kind of peace is simply a shell, a covering over unhealed emotions and feelings, particularly the feeling of grief.

The Nature of Hypnosis:

Clinically, hypnosis is both a highly subjective mental state of intense focus combined with dissociation and a particularly high-level of response to suspended disbelief. It is generally an interaction between the practitioner and the recipient, though you can move your mind into a similar hypnotic dissociation by your own efforts. This change of focus is done for emotional reasons all the time. If for instance you don't want to look at the real reason why something is going poorly in your life, such as the fact that you have an entitled, negative and abrasive attitude, you can focus on the way someone has betrayed you in some little thing like being late to dinner instead. This way you can sidestep the pain of facing your own responsibility for your difficulties.

Or in a more positive way, you can focus on the good things in your life, appreciating the sunsets, rain and gentle breezes of spring, in the midst of some huge challenge to your life: a chronic illness, a recent devastating loss or even long-standing abuse. There are limits to this: not everyone has the strength or the broader sense of self that allows you to perceive your situation in two different ways at the same time. You need to realize simultaneously that yes, the challenge is real, perhaps intractable and won't be solved soon; yet you need to see that yes, it was so utterly wonderful to watch the ducks in the pond this morning, because, after all, you woke up being able to see, and you know that some people are blind.

Hypnosis speaks through the conscious to the subconscious and unconscious minds in metaphors and imagery, because these are the language of those inner minds. In a very real sense, hypnosis means entering into a state similar to dreaming, where you briefly accept outré data as normal. This strongly suggests that the hypnotic state is not extra-special: instead, it is as much a part of your minds and brains as a mathematical ability, the ability to remember several

145

recipes or to keep focusing on the road at the end of a 14-hour drive, as well as the ability to dream. In short, your minds are often stronger and have more capabilities within them than you generally suppose. Shamanism, psychic impressions and reaching into your own divine connection through intuition are actually fairly standard human abilities, as is the deeply unconscious ability to change realities, heal emotional wounds and retain your creativity despite shocks and abuse.

These deeper parts of the human mind are the ones that allow you to strike out on a new path, overcome incredible trials or uncover hidden truths in yourself and others. The subconscious can relieve pain or exacerbate it; the conscious mind can train the subconscious as well as the subconscious trains your conscious thoughts. Your subconscious can open up your perceptions or close them down, so it is a good idea to understand your subconscious as much as possible. This keeps the subconscious from being able to act blindly, as it can with negative and even Toxic Magic, which could shift your inner mind away from the deep intentions that are preserved in the unconscious, the more human root of the Self.

The Conscious, Subconscious and Unconscious Minds and Persuasion:

As it is, it has already been proven in a great many ways that your conscious mind edits out a lot of the input that your senses and brain actually receives: there's just too much data to keep track of it all consciously even in normal reality, much less the hyperkinetic barrage that computer-driven technology can produce. By actually functioning in a higher dimensional level, the subconscious can retain and process more information than the conscious mind ever could. However, although it still takes in the subtler kinds of data that your conscious mind may reject, the subconscious cannot communicate with the conscious mind directly if it does not feel they share a language. However, some know that if the two minds are kept apart because the conscious mind is too distracted to take in the subtle imagery of the subconscious, then the deeper, higher-energy levels of that subconscious can be actually manipulated, at least to a degree.

When movie and television advertising was new, there were a lot of attempts to manipulate people subliminally, such as flashing one-frame messages inside the film itself saying: "Hungry. Hungry. Hungry. Popcorn!" Even though your conscious mind would not recognize that a message was on the screen, the subconscious processors of the brain would receive the message and very likely act upon it. This particular kind of subliminal message has been part of the media in one form or another since the 40's if not earlier; there is no current legislation forbidding use of subliminal messages in any of the media: television, radio, billboards or the Internet. I do not want to create fear: like any other hypnosis, no subliminal advertising can work to make you do what you truly do not want to do. The subconscious mind is different than the conscious but it is not alien: both minds are part of your structure of identity.

Yet as any con man knows, even without being subliminal, there is a lot of room in the gray area of persuasion. If the con artist can start with something you already believe in, desire, hanker after or wish for, he can conflate the existing wish with a new one and make the new idea have the same currency as the old. If you already believe in rescuing cats or really like skiing, then a product that is presented along with images of cats or skiing seems much more palatable to you as the consumer than a product presented just in "bare bones" form, much less with something you dislike, such as changing a tire in the rain.

Too often, though, you do not realize that your sympathies are being usurped. There are surely many things that are used to distract your attention so that you can be nudged into acting from subconscious drives or even unconsciously and persuaded to do things that you do not understand why you are doing them. For instance: some time when you watch a favorite show on TV and it comes time for the station break, just close your eyes gently and let your mind drift just a little bit, while still thinking of the show you are watching. There may be times when you suddenly want to open your eyes and look at the television: it's almost as though something wakes your eyes up and you need to look. Watch: what are you looking at when your eyes open? What are you seeing? It might be totally random or it might not. If it is not, then what seems to be getting your attention, even though you don't know your attention is being caught? And does the same thing happen when you are only playing a recording of your show? If there is a difference, this might be a fascinating subject for you to pursue.

The Super-Fast Challenge to the Mind/Brain:

You can defend yourself from these persuaders by having a strong sense of identity, including a clear sense of what motivates you, what you want out of life and what things you will and will not do: in short, a good sense of ethics. But as healing, creating and learning do, discovering your own ethical system in the context of your community takes time to uncover and understand. You can never grasp the lifetime of thought that goes into a deep philosophy, spiritual wisdom, humanitarian comprehension or even a new mode of perception in the 2 seconds that a fractured attention span demands: it cannot be humanly done. If your process of contemplation, comprehension or even consideration is overwhelmed by super-fast input, by the exhilarating speed of doing this thing and then right away the next thing and then the next and the next without pause, your brain actually slips into low gear. Because it has to deal with an input speed it is not designed for, your mind must actually reduce its points of contact with Reality! So you are actually seeing less and less of more and more, until you have a potential blizzard of white noise, like the classic random static pattern.

Your mind, however, can become so used to making sense of its reality because it must that it does not realize that it has grown deeply opinionated, rigid, or even paranoid, in an attempt to classify and codify the input. And, because this input is so demanding, you are actually distracted from the process of being distracted: you don't realize that your attention has been asked to do too much. This distraction and your reaction to it also creep up on you. When you cannot think, when you cannot stop and focus, then you have to deal with less and less, both in terms of input and in terms of any other connections, including purely human ones. One rose might be the subject of an hour's contemplation. But a hundred roses all at once do not allow you to have the benefits of a hundred hours of meditation! And this lessened perception is another way in which your attention can be diverted, so that "invisible" things, that are only invisible because you are not looking at them, can be paraded past your scattered awareness. Too distracted to perceive, you may have no control of anything that may be riding on the carrier signals of the barrage, so you may even receive input you have no notion you are receiving in the first place.

The Addictive "Choice:"

In addition, this becomes a state of continual, low-level excitement, one that may only apparently be driven by your own interests and sense of your own self. Surely, and of course, it is only you who are punching the buttons, turning the dials and choosing where you are going to look next, right? But this paradox of deliberately reaching for something that can command your attention that you must yield to at the same time, is a good definition of addiction. Addictive substances "lie" to your bodies by commandeering the craving centers of the brain. Like the parasites that can drive a snail to climb up a blade of grass so it is obvious enough for a bird to find and eat it, thus spreading the parasite's eggs around in the bird's droppings, the addictive substance or thing manipulates you by lying to you. It tells you that you want it, when in fact it may want you.

Most relatively simple substances like alcohol, nicotine, heroin and cocaine actually have a far lower energy profile than a simply joyful human being. Do you get drunk on the alcohol that actually has a much lower level of energy than you do or, rather, does the alcohol truly get drunk on you because of your native multi-dimensional geometries and energy? Does it want what you are so much that it becomes addicted to you? And then, as with so many other drugs, recreational or otherwise, does the lower-energy drug or substance actually crave becoming part of your own internal, higher-energy, Para-sound structures, so that it arranges to have you drink, eat, snort, inject or absorb more of it for *its* sake, the same way the parasite arranges things with the snail?

From my perception, this is exactly what happens. Say that the alcohol or heroin "want" to get a "jazz" of energy from you: it goes about it very cunningly. Like that parasite, it tells you that it's just fine to climb that blade of grass, there's no problem at all: you feel *good* about climbing that blade of grass. Well, at least there's no problem for the parasite, because this is what it wants in order to keep living. Similarly, hyper-fast, media-driven inputs can become a kind of "mind sugar:" something sweet and fun that you have "decided" that you want, even though it has very little real mental nutrition but that nevertheless your mind can crave as much as your body might crave sugar.

Note: I do not suggest that social media itself is any kind of parasite or addictive energy. But despite the fact that the continual harassment of super-fast input makes it almost impossible to think deeply on anything, it might be frightening to contemplate: at what level of complexity could the electronic interchange of information evolve desires of its own, even ones as primitive and straightforward as a parasite's? What benefits might be derived from keeping people anxious, harassed and stupefied? For one thing, if you are in a stressful and totally demanding situation where you are anxious and you do not know what to do, wouldn't you listen to anyone or anything that says, "Look over here: I have the way out?" And if you have no time to consider things, no time to dwell on things, you might take any offer without foreseeing any consequences.

The Loss of Meaning

In this state of continual input, in addition to the possibly of addictive effects from perceiving less and less of more and more, there is also a loss of the meaning of words and of language. This meaning is lost in several ways. When in the state of torrential bombardment, you have less time to contemplate what is happening. Not being able to linger over anything, you may find that you will accept only three definitions, synonyms or antonyms for something as being sufficient, instead of twelve. Even though twelve synonyms or definitions would add depth richness and subtlety to the meaning of the word you are using, you are too rushed for more than three; frequently you use even fewer.

Yet by using these easier, faster, "more convenient" three definitions, you have suddenly become poorer in your words, without noticing. And perhaps you even feel better about it because using only three definitions is faster! Even modern Thesauruses have less diversity than ones of 50 years ago, especially those that are attached to computers: many have become too limited for precision. And if your words are imprecise, they can be misinterpreted, misused, manipulated and misconstrued. It is difficult enough dealing with homophones, words that sound the same but are spelled differently and have different meanings that voice recognition software does not comprehend. Homophones are words such as rain, rein and reign: the phrase, "free rein" originally meant to ease your hold on the horse's rein to let it choose its own path, though I will certainly allow that "free reign" makes too much sense. There have also been tremendous consequences for misinterpreting idioms, as in the phrase at the beginning of the Cold War, "We will bury you," that only meant, "We well be so successful, you will eat our dust."

The other loss of meaning that excessive input causes is when the meaning of things is manipulated by conflation and equivocation: this happens in the media all the time and it is not always something you notice. No product is sexual gratification in and of its self, social

150

success in its self, or love or any other human thing, but too many products are presented in this way. And once again, if this happens fast enough, it will be very hard for you to notice when the switch is being made. No product can be purity, but many products are presented as though they were. Some advertisements even ask you to equate their products with integrity, beauty, power, joy or love. And thus you have lost definition and meaning again! It has become manipulated through equivocation: "This product we are selling is (fill in the blank with your favorite desire)!" This product is the love you want, the happiness you want, the success or even the vindication you want, not what it truly is: something that is useful most times, needed some times, but generally quite inert otherwise.

Lack of Stability in the Self:

And in this state of confusion added to the state of harried overwhelm, how emotionally, mentally or spiritually stable do you think you can be? How deeply do you think you can perceive things; how varied or rich will your world be? There are a lot of people complaining that they are bored simply because their life does not skitter like a drop of water on a hot griddle, popping and snapping and scurrying from one side to the other at every moment. But paradoxically the boredom has more to do with never stopping, never pausing to be in a whole moment, much less being whole *in* a moment. If you were to take your bored mind and quiet it with contemplation, meditation or simply careful consideration of something, situation or person outside of your own sphere of self, your mind might have a tantrum and tell you that you can't stand being still. However, if you persist, you will reach into a different rhythm, a rhythm more closely aligned to your breath, heart, mind and soul.

Yet the boredom created by undigested inputs takes on a life of its own: like an addictive parasite, it wants you to keep feeding it at your expense. And in the most terrible paradox of all, many of you try to escape this arid ground of meaninglessness by becoming addicted to something else! Many say that they drink, do heroin, painkillers or other means of forcing attention away from their pain because life hurts too much. But from my point of view it is not always that life hurts too much, though I do understand that some things can be terribly painful. Rather, it is that being divorced and divided *from* life by the continual state of anxious distraction and the continual

151

demands on your attention, that actually make you less able to bear pain in the first place.

You cannot know who or what you are, you cannot be stable in your sense of self if you cannot be still. Many of you that have become overwhelmed by despair and are without any internal base of your human Self may commit suicide, whether suddenly or slowly, as with using drugs or letting them use you. This is not only a loss of meaning in words: it is a complete loss of your human meaning. But again, this is the tremendous difficulty: if you are continually barraged by demands, deluged with other peoples' opinions and kept on the surface of your mind because of the rapid speed of the input, you have no time for reflection into your own Self, much less into the deeper nature of that self.

Advertising:

I will not get into my irritation regarding the fact that you are actually paying for the advertising you watch: the snazzier brands often are the most expensive to buy because, in addition to using their funds to improve their product, the sellers also use your money to convince you to buy them again and again. There are many products that are genuinely useful, created thoughtfully and with your best interests in mind: thus I by no means disparage advertising itself! After all, every living thing uses advertising in various ways: the complex songs and feathers in birds, alluring scents as with flowers or mammals, to say nothing of bright colors advertising how poisonous an animal is to eat. Yet I will point out that it is wise to watch for the real meanings of words from the point of view of the sellers of products, goods and services. When something is called "convenient," you may ask, "convenient for whom?" What would be the consequences of this convenient product or service? What will it cost in terms of pollution, deforestation or use of crude oil? Is the new change in the packaging more convenient for you or for them? It is easier for them to use oil-based plastic rather than cellophane created from plant cells or do they really want to give you something that is truly easier to open?

Again, this kind of awareness does take time and this is difficult, because time is being robbed from you continually. And in the anesthesia generated from extreme stress, often you do not notice the loss, through either being numb to it or you may even feel good about it. Efficiency! Streamlining! Speed! Convenience! These are good for the industry of the Industrial Revolution and you have been taught that they are good for businesses of all kinds. And so they must be always good for people too, mustn't they?

But in the rush, where are the simple afternoons just watching clouds? Where are the calm, quiet moments when you are simply aware of breathing? I grant that to some I must seem something of a hypocrite: it was, after all, my alternating current that began all of this and I pushed myself almost beyond human limits to discover, uncover and unveil it and my other inventions. My visions sustained me, though: they were basis of my sense of myself. My desire to help the world sustained me: that was the thing that made my intensity possible.

"Pushing Your Hammer:"

There is another aspect to advertising that spills out into the common culture, related to the adage: "If all you have is a hammer, everything looks like a nail." All too frequently, someone does the equivalent of inventing a certain type of hammer, and then looks for places to use it. When insufficient numbers of people seem to want it, advertising can slip into the "pester" mode. Level one is, "Here, this is the solution to the problem you didn't even realize you had!" The second level is, "I see you are suffering for lack of the solution my product represents. Buy what I have!" The third level: "You have to buy this hammer because I have it to sell!" None of these respect the buyer's true needs.

At other times this desire to push your hammer can be related to the attitude of some engineers and tinkerers, "If I think something needs a fix, I will fix it, even though it isn't broken." A sub-genre of that attitude is, "Because I know and am familiar and comfortable with this new technological improvement, therefore everyone is. Indeed, they will love it as much as I do and really want it, too." But the end result of all of these attitudes is your attempts to overwhelm the buyer's personal assessment of what the buyer needs for the sake of selling your products. You, as an advertiser, provider or practitioner have, in short, become both unaware of and unresponsive to the buyer, and this will actually interfere with your own prosperity quite directly.

However truly excellent your solution is, if your buyer feels rather like prey, he or she will very likely run. Furthermore, it is unwise to allow advertising to replace or usurp the natural passions of life for

153

any reason. Granted, some of this is urgent attitude is based in true concern for another. However, there are times you must be aware whether or not you are more concerned for yourself and how you might look to others, than considering the real needs of the person. It can be hard to believe, and sometimes harder to remember, but there are actually times when help doesn't help.

For instance, if someone walking with a cane trips and falls, too many people descend upon the fallen all at once, grabbing arms, hands, shoulders or whatever to help the person up, without realizing that the person himself might still be in shock from the fall itself. Suddenly being mauled by strangers, however well-intentioned, is frightening! It is far, far better to ask, "Do you need assistance?" and then if the person says, "No," then for goodness' sake, please take them at their word! Even though they must work and struggle to rise, it is far more respectful to not push your help. It may be hard for you to watch, but realize that by standing back until your help is actually requested you are offering this person one of the few things he may have left: his or her dignity.

The Cost of Time:

There is a delightful story about a man showing someone from another country the new subway system in New York. He told the visitor, "If we take that subway, we will take twenty minutes off the time of our trip and so be at our destination earlier!" The visitor nodded and, very impressed, went with the man on the subway. When they arrived, the guide started dashing off to run the last few blocks to their destination, but the visitor found a bench and sat down!

When the guide saw this he asked, "Is there something wrong? Are you all right?" And the visitor replied, "Certainly: I am quite well. But now that we have the 20 extra minutes you have saved us, I thought that would be time enough for us to meditate." You can imagine the guide's consternation at not "taking advantage" of the extra time by hurrying all the more and the visitor's perplexity at not taking advantage of the time to rest. It was all the same amount of time, yet it was valued differently: one for living in agitation, the other for a moment of peace.

So the thing to watch out for is not what you are doing, but *why*: are you acting from your own inner strength and vision or are you acting from undigested inputs? Are you acting from your knowledge of yourself or the version of yourself that others want to create so that you will buy their products? Or as in social media: are you bombing others with hateful things anonymously because this is the best way you can think of to relieve your own anxiety about your own inadequacies? Or are you continually and unfailingly positive with everything you say because you are afraid of the consequences if you are accused of "passing judgment," when you are merely discerning something? It isn't only what is done: it's the why it is done. A kiss, given in love, is dear. A kiss forced on someone for your own needs is heinous.

Belief and Suspension of Belief:

And, back to hypnosis: as you can guess after reading the articles on alternate realities, both belief and the suspension of disbelief can be either tremendously useful or tremendously disruptive and may have some deep connections to creativity. There is clearly suspension of disbelief in hypnotic states, which you enter perhaps more frequently than you realize. Creativity similarly demands at least a small suspension of belief: how else might you see the stack of boards in your workshop as a couch, a door, a go-cart or a playhouse? There is a profound reason why you need this suspension of disbelief: it actually allows you to shift from Reality to Reality without feeling the jolt of the change. At the same time, it allows you to keep past, present, future and alternate other-life experiences from intruding in the present flow of your chosen route into this current life's future. Just to be human is to believe: you must believe that you are this body in this time, with these demands and concerns, instead of the shining, multi-dimensional and many-faceted part of the Divine Being that you are. For the sake of discovery, you have fooled yourself into believing the play of Reality in front of you, as has the Divine Being fooled its Self.

There are myriads of ways to reclaim that shining Self within your life, from meditations to retreats to numerous therapies. You may choose what works best, though we have included the meditation for finding your soul's Core Tone, the inaudible note of your own soul, in Appendix One. Small suggestions, such as emphasizing your exhalations to help steady you or centering in your heart, are often effective. Asking yourself, "What do I *really* want?" again and again until you know that you have found your true answer is also a good device to clear though the overload.

155

Yet the first and main thing is to ask: "Do I want to be changed by everything coming in or do I want to be a person that can choose to change?" It is easier to allow yourself to be acted upon: when you are anesthetized by distraction, you cannot be aware of the anxiety and agony of losing your Self to forces other than your free choice. Nevertheless, your deeper self will always try to grasp you attention again, even though at times it must ask for it by causing you pain. For not all pain is bad. Some pain, if discerned and healed, brings deeper freedom, not less joy.

Examining the Costs of Emotional Pain

Key Points: Trauma can cause a gap between what you feel and what you express. At times, you craft your sense of self from others' unmet needs too often and so your self-worth can be so fragile that you will shut down emotionally. Some of your own emotional liability is because the Divine Being searches to understand its Self even in pain, frustration and loss. But in the process, Self-pity is created: a Chimera-like amalgam of emotions that often masks itself by mimicking other feelings and emotional effects, from manipulation to obsessive-compulsive disorders. Older souls are most prone to Self-pity because you often have had to put off dealing with lifetimes of pain and hurt due to exigent circumstances. Self-pity acts as an emotional clumping agent to gather the dross of emotional pain so you can clear it from your soul.

Subheadings:

- Sources of Emotional Pain

- The Challenge of the Iron Age

- The Nature of the Emotional Chimera of Self-pity

- Manipulative Control

- Self-hatred

- Self-righteousness

- Stereotypical, Obsessive and Unconscious Actions

- Self-pity's Roots and Causes

- Time-scars and Soul-wounds

- Healing Self-pity

- The Reason for Self-pity: Refining the Gold

- A Note on Introversion and Extroversion

Sources of Emotional Pain:

Emotions and feelings are the expression of your whole human being, based in all of the unfolded and enfolded dimensions and

157

using all of the Torsion Fields to one degree or another. This is one of the reasons why human beings are all such rich, layered and complex beings. However, if any part of your wholeness is damaged, this creates a gap between what you feel and what you say or express. This gap can run so deep that what you say can even have no love in it at all. The widest gap between the heart and your feelings and emotions is pain: pain of loss, of betrayal, of abandonment; of being tormented, belittled or lied to; of taking on too heavy a burden of self-sacrifice or having dreams deferred as in a situation of continual frustration, denial or disenfranchisement. All of these have significant effects: all of these pains deal directly with your identity as a human being as you relate to others.

Even self-hatred, self-judgment and impatience with any aspect or part of your body or personality, are all derived from others' examples, usually resulting from their own frustrations, sense of inadequacy or thwarted dreams that they have reflected towards you and from which you have crafted your sense of self. As you are based in the Zero dimension through the dimension of Identity, you are a pure expressions of the Divine Intention: revealing the Divine Being to Its Self through your body, mind, soul, spirit emotions and feelings. Thus you retain your core value whatever the circumstances of your life or any of its blocks, challenges, miss-steps or cruelties, though at times this value is too often at the cost of strained and sometimes profoundly damaged feelings and emotions.

A tremendous number of plots, sub-plots, stories, songs and dramas are based on one essential theme: "I was badly hurt/betrayed/frustrated or grieving: this is what happened to me and this is what I did about it." This is certainly not meant to trivialize any aspect of human pain in the least: all pain is real and certainly the scars it creates can last though several incarnations, perhaps even for thousands of years. Yet as many spiritual human beings know, the core of any pain is the pain of separation from the Original Source of Love. To become human means to become alone and separate: deaf to the Eternal Song; blind to the Living Light; numb to the Presence of Love and in addition, thwarted by crippling beliefs, axioms and the expectations of those that are supposed to be close to you. When you are human you may be tormented by the fires of rage, hatred, viciousness and contempt and then flung out into the fields of error and confusion with few, if any, instructions on how to restore your own humanity.

In short, living in 4-D Reality cripples the human soul in pain of one kind or another for that lifetime at least. That you can still find Love, hear the Song, see the brilliant Eternal Light and even overcome limitations and disabilities of a particular lifetime so well that you are still able to love is extraordinary. And that some of you even ask for more burdens, in lives which you choose to be born without arms, legs, hearing or speech: that is the measure of your superlative love for the Divine Being and a measure of your courage as human souls and spirits spun from the living Core. Frankly, most angels are quite abashed by your courage, strength and perseverance: some angels feel as timid around you as you might with your most favorite movie star appearing at your door, while you stand there totally unprepared because you haven't heard the star is coming.

Even though, as the Buddha put it, "existence is suffering." always slightly out of true, un-centered and marginal, yet, as I have pointed out before, physical existence was not created to be torturous: dealing with the marginal, semi-conducting factors in Reality leads to tremendous creativity. Both fear and pain are emotional goads: emotional hormones, if you will: fear and pain insist on certain changes in your human self that might not be accomplished any other way. Some spiritual breakthroughs can only happen when the fear of treating with the Unknown is less than the pain of staying where you are. Sympathy, empathy and compassion cannot be fully understood without experiencing someone's difficulty as your own. It is wondrous indeed that you, all parts of the Living Unity of the Source, have to re-learn how to reflect others within your own experiences consciously: you must choose to be aware, to see things as others see them and to see yourself as others see you. Yet each time this happens, even though fear and pain may drive the experiences, the divine Being rediscovers and recreates Its Self with invaluable specificity. Only in this way can the One altogether be the One and still discover the One. And yet, there are high costs for this re-discovery: high emotional costs that lead to much human grief.

The Challenge of the Iron Age:

Although you might imagine that when things are going well in your life and you have enough and sometimes more than enough, you would relax and open your heart to others, instead of closing your heart and hanging on to everything as you used to when you were feeling anxious, too often neither your generosity nor your checkbook open. Why? Part of the reason is that you are dealing with

159

others' emotional damages that remain inside of you. This damage results from the very punishment, selfishness and greed with which others have unthinkingly handled you: too frequently they have dealt with you just for their own needs at the expense of yours. Blamed for things you have never done, wounded by others' frustrations, belittled by others' fear of inadequacy, you may be deeply misunderstood by someone who can only give minimal effort to looking outside of himself. This lack of spiritual energy in the current time perpetuates expedient actions for the sake of immediate results because expediency needs less forethought. Thus the generalized lack of your emotional vigor is a direct result of the damage caused by the same lack of emotional vigor and mental focus of those who associate with you: thus the lower-energy problems and solutions are perpetuated.

This is one reason why pulling in energy from the higher-order, enfolded dimensions is so important. Whether through fostering creativity, contemplation, spiritual practice or meditations on love and light, if you reach into higher levels of energy intentionally, you automatically add to the ambient supply. And every time you lie, prevaricate, use verbal, physical or emotional abuse to pull yourself or anyone else down or use denigration to distance yourself from the challenge they represent to your fragile sense of self, you not only tie up the potential spiritual energy into knots of frozen time, as happens with shocks and wounds, but you also burden the Manifested Self of the Whole in perpetual moments of pain. This may seem absurd: what, a little white lie causes the very Self of God pain? It does: every lie adds to the pain of separation.

As has been said countless times before, the Self of God is Love, Light, and Truth. And as we said in the article describing the Para-sound Encoding in DNA, in order to discover itself, this Self of God had to create an illusion strong enough to deceive itself. The perhaps unanticipated difficulty was that because this lie was sourced from the Core of Life, the deception would gather its own life-like momentum. But certainly something crafted using the substance of the Divine Being must surely and certainly at least reflect the same intense durability, creativity and sustainability of that Divine Source.

Although it is heresy for some to say that God is the author of sin and evil, from my vantage I feel that in its ache for self-discovery, the Divine Mind and Being used Its Self to create something as close to being Other Than Itself that could possibly be fashioned. So, yes, you

160

may see where I am leading: the divine Being has cast its own shadow upon itself through lies, deception, illusions, harm and evil and must perpetually live with that choice. Yet the thing to remember is that if the Light casts a shadow and while the shadow seems separate from the light, a change in the nature of the light creates a change in the shadow because they are ultimately the same substance after all. And you, as expressions of that Divine Being, have a similar truth: you are your own light and your own darkness: you can always choose between them.

The Nature of the Emotional Chimera of Self-pity:

As a psychic and emotional creation that has no real consciousness, the Chimera of Self-pity neither thinks nor has malice but it does have tremendous momentum: it is ruthless in its greed for its limited understanding of life, which is to feed, continue, and replicate. It can create and perpetuate its reasons to exist. Acting like a strange attractor in a chaotic mathematical system, it can become the seed-crystals around which your realities form so that you are continually hurt, thwarted, frustrated, betrayed, disenfranchised and disappointed. Like a recessive or even dominant gene, the attitude of self-pity can be passed down in families in both DNA and the paragenome. Moreover, because it is an artifact, a semi-living entity, this Chimera can become part of the living systems of families and the people in them long, long after the original incidents, impulses or causes for the self-pity have ceased to have any real meaning.

Self-pity is so painful that it drives many of you to seek anesthesia, whether of drugs or power or willful blindness to your own effects on other people. It also actively promotes those effects in you and others by itself. Sometimes you cannot look at the harm you have caused others because it would mean to look at the torturous agony that Self-pity constantly creates and re-creates in your life through your subconscious and unconscious selves. Self-pity's miasma leads to misery, depression, rage, helplessness and despair in all the layers of your Self. It also, paradoxically, keeps you from perceiving and learning the information within your pain. Self-pity is so self-centered that it brings your sense of who you are down into its own tight, unhappy ball of misery: it shuts you down so much that you cannot reach out for healing, especially not for the healing that demands that you face your real pain, however sharp it is, in a real way.

161

Self-pity is a form of quasi-emotion that has become complex, deceptive, self-organized and self-perpetuating enough that it acts as a polarized lens: it pre-selects and sometimes warps the reality you see to the point that it dictates what you are *able* to see. Like the thought-forms that feed on fear or the psychic parasites in addictive drugs, Self-pity also has its own shadow-consciousness. It is insidious, as well as depressive in its effect and so is one of the major roots of depression. It is also a chimera in that it has many aspects that can manifest at once that do not look at all related to their true source, which is your feeling that life is particularly unfair to you and for you. Make no mistake: Self-pity is strong enough to exacerbate your feelings of abandonment, betrayal or injustice to the point that you may feel that God has only disdain and devaluation for you and your life. Self-pity can make the worst things you fear entirely true in your human experience, because it has a tremendous amount to do with control of your reality, of others and even of the Divine Truth inside of your human self.

Manipulative Control:

One of the heads of the Chimera is the kind of weakness that commands others to do your Self pity's bidding in a very unclean way emotionally: by manipulations of whatever kinds that work to further its aims. Psychic, emotional, mental, physical and even spiritual manipulations are all the tools for Self-pity's control, at whatever cost. Another of the heads of self-pity's Chimera creates continual, unremitting, inexplicable and indefensible injustice in your life to whatever degree Self-pity deems necessary to get the energy it wants. It has both tremendous leverage and tremendous weight: it gives you an emotional load so huge that you become the camel for whom even a *feather* is too much to add to the psychic and emotional burden you are already carrying. In this way Self-pity quite thoroughly hampers your ability to be pliable, adaptable, responsive, loving or kind to yourself or others and you become impatient, controlling, hurtful and vicious instead, even to yourself.

Self-hatred:

For that is another of Self-pity's heads: self-hatred in all its forms. A little discernment and impatience towards yourself might be a goad towards improvement: if you see where you are lacking in kindness, generosity, patience or graciousness towards other people or yourself, you can use your discernment to see what needs to be changed and perhaps how to change it. And frustration with a body or mind limited by illness or disease is sometimes warranted. However, although it can break through blockages at times, frustration can become corrosive. All self-hatred is actively toxic: not only in terms of making you feel smaller, less worthy of love, less valuable and so on: it leaks out to other people constantly. When you hate yourself you do damage to yourself and this not only cripples you because of the pain that damage causes, it also makes you less responsive to others because you are hurting so much and literally don't have the energy to care.

Pain of all kinds takes tremendous energy: to feel it, to deal with it, whether actively or by avoiding it, to change it through healing or to accommodate pain's original damage. The sad fact that there are so many who cut themselves and do other violence to themselves because that pain hurts less than the pain inside, shows how dangerous Self-pity's Chimera-head of self-hatred really is. In a very real sense self-hatred is the ultimate betrayal of your Self by yourself. Furthermore, the punishment you inflict on yourself only breeds terror inside of you, the terror that freezes action and stops communication with and to your Center of Self: the divine Core. Not only does this aspect of Self-pity become toxic to love itself, Self-pity is also highly manipulative and can distort your reality around itself in sometimes truly dangerous ways. You can bring yourself down to nothing through suicide or you can project the agony outward and murder others. And at the root, it's all Self-pity.

Self-righteousness:

Another head of this Chimera is when you would "Rather be right than happy." This head eats out all joy in life until it is only a hollow shell. Creating one Pyrrhic victory after another, you win battle after battle, but lose the war and get overrun by the sadness you cannot name. The desire to be vindicated at least costs you human contact, because surely no one wants to be tested at every turn, proven wrong at every turn or faced with your implacable (literally, unable to be pleased) refusal to be happy. This utter lack of anything but unholy glee at trumping someone else's good suggestions with yet another, "Yeah, but..." beggars your spirit and starves your soul. You continually confront friends with your problems and many will help from sympathy or empathy. But in the end you will have re-created net gain zero: a lot of froth just turning around in yet another endless circle: this way you can "right" yourself into a life of appalling misery,

163

meanwhile completely no longer looking at the fact that you are the only one who can solve your own righteous Self-pity.

Your friends, counselors, teachers or spiritual advisors cannot break through your adamant rigidity, for in order to remain victorious, Self-pity refuses all solutions. At some point, not even God can solve things for you! A great archangel of mysterious majesty and power could appear in your living room and Self-pity would find something wrong with the angel, its presentation, its suggestions, its timing or even the feathers it dropped on your precious Oriental rug! There will always be something wrong, because much like "frozen" time, this righteous Self-pity is driven by fear and terror into another tight, super-conducting circle of emotional affect. It can become out of reach of anything in Time or Space and even of the enfolded dimensions, until your only solution is to radically change yourself.

Stereotypical, Obsessive and Unconscious Actions:

When your life follows the definition of insanity of doing the same thing again and again and hoping for different results, leading you to addictions of all kinds from gambling, bad love affairs, hoarding; continual, inventive and terribly effective self-sabotage such as eating, using or imbibing things you really know aren't good for you or anyone else, then you can deduce that the engine behind all of these is Self-pity. Hoarding, for instance, tries to fill a real void such as the death of loved ones or betrayal by others with momentary flashes and sparks of beauty and excitement: the next lovely collectible, another lovely plate or dress or baseball card, or Yet Another of My Favorite Things. This is because Self-pity has trapped you into a state of continual avoidance in its own super-conducting loop. You are truly in real pain, usually in a state of excruciating grief, loss, abandonment or betrayal. Yet if you have no means of dealing with this kind of pain in the moment, then you must distract or anesthetize yourself in order to cope.

Unfortunately, the distraction and anesthesia work for the moment and when that moment wanes, the original problem, the grief or betrayal that you have not been able to grieve because of the depth of its pain, still remains. Indeed it has gotten deeper because you have become even a little more separated from yourself. This deep lack of awareness within you leads to anxiety and because your instinct is to avoid pain, that drives the pointless, obsessive-repetitive

164

actions. However, when pain becomes Self-pity you cannot resolve it and it always remains with you! It can remain with you for lifetimes.

Another unfortunate thing is that this kind of repetitive anxiety/avoidance loop can create mental ruts, then emotional ones and then physical ones, altering the brain itself. When you incarnate into a body with a brain that has already been pre-programmed for obsessive-compulsive disorder, hoarding disorder or a tendency to addiction, you are likely dealing with the costs of the Chimera of Self-pity from past lifetimes quite directly. In this way, what is called Karma is actually an expression of habit: you fall into this kind of infinite, self-replicating loop in this present life because you have fallen into it before. You could not resolve it then and cannot resolve it now without a great deal of work.

Please understand: this is not punishment, not by God, not by your soul, nor by the universe: it is entrainment and the attraction of familiarity. Better the devil you know than the one you don't, particularly if the devil you don't know has a terrifying, fearful aspect that looks as though it would fundamentally challenge your sense of self and reveal all of the unmet needs and grief that have burdened you for so long. Many old souls do spend lives as hoarders or in addiction because of this: because of the demands at the time of the original grief, from dealing with war, widespread tragedy, a mission to act on someone else's behalf that costs you too dearly or something similar, you could truly not deal with your own pain at the time and had to keep it with you. Though, when you choose your lifetimes from the comfort of Heaven, it is too easy to forget how intractable and implacable Self-pity is and how very easy it is to fall into it in the first place.

Self-pity's Roots and Causes:

Most old souls are inevitably burdened with self-pity to one degree or another. And because Self-pity is a Chimera and a Chameleon, it can hide very well. Wanting to be right rather than happy, hurting yourself so you can be comforted again and again and God's Love for you be proven again and again are some of the reasons. Truly feeling better than others because you really can do things better than anyone else is a trap of arrogance and oddly enough such arrogance can turn into self-denigration. Granted, although you might hate to admit to your arrogance, because to do so would wound your pride, Self-pity's hold is a difficult one to resolve: after all, you really have been the hero and saved people, things and situations with aplomb, panache and great success. You really have been the kindest parent, uncle or aunt, child; friend, governess, teacher, leader; spiritual advisor that there has ever been and sometimes you have even solved the unsolvable. As it's said, "It's hard to be humble when you're perfect." But for some, you fear that you must always be perfect and being *only* perfect is barely good enough. You can't make any mistakes because you aren't permitted any. That leads directly into Self-pity because there is no way out.

Self-pity's various Chimera-heads can sometimes act to retard your ego's control over your life by keeping you humble, but this is a dangerous method because Self-pity more likely helps you find ways of humiliating yourself. It feeds on your arrogance with the "rather right than happy" game, the "yeah, but..." game, the "nothing ever works for *me!*" game and the final game of saying, "See? I told you: God doesn't care!" to all and sundry and even to God Himself. Often Self-pity will engineer a spiritual crisis where the only way out of your misery is to go straight to and through the gate of whatever is your greatest fear, again and again, until you realize that it is clinging to your Self-pity that is causing your agony, not God.

If you have grace in your soul, you may laugh at yourself at this point and settle back down into the business of living with the Divine Being as the friend, agent of Love, and Co-creator it is and you are. As an agent for the Light you pay attention to His, Her or Its instructions; as a friend of God you remember God constantly; as a Co-creator you learn how to listen to your intuition and act in synchronicity instead of with your own sense of timing. In Eternity everything is done now; however, being in Time requires finesse: a delicate balance of paying attention to your own intuition and simultaneously yielding to what exists in front of you. If what you need is inside of yourself and you *only* look outward to psychics, spiritual counselors, runes or Tarot or any other means of divination to give you instruction, rather than fathoming your own inner truth, then the answers can become contradictory, confusing, frustrating and seem utterly useless. This leads to disgust and disdain for these methods and the practitioners, rage at and rejection of the God that is supposedly the source of these messages and your self-pity deepens as a result of your hurt confusion.

To manage that kind of pain you can become brittle in several ways: hyper-controlling of yourself, circumstances or others in your

166

life; mentally rigid and exacting in any of several ways, from espousing an inhuman science that treats all things and people as objects, to the paradox of an ancient soul acting like a soulless brute because you have turned yourself away from the pain and hence your humanity. Though, rather than becoming crippled by your pain at the root of your self-pity, you can re-claim your own responsive tenderness and find relief in helping others. When you solve someone else's problem you can sometimes find the means to solve your own. You still may not be dealing with the original root of your self-pity directly but just working from a heart-centered place can be palliative at least and transformative at best.

Time-scars and Soul-wounds:

As we have discussed already, some of the sources of your self-pity seem obvious: tremendous loss, unhealed grief, shocking betrayal, bitter injustice, torturous punishments or spiritual violation. Your spirit can be ravaged when it has been given impossible choices as in a war: when you must decide whether to reveal the hidden secret you carry or see your wife raped to death and your children murdered in front of you. Or when you are an abused child that must run away from home in order to keep from being molested and in order to live you must end up selling yourself on the streets for strangers to molest for money. In these cases and many more like them the tender, responsive spirit inside of you is desecrated. Unsurprisingly, this kind of heinous crime leads almost inevitably to a grief so huge that it cannot be properly grieved; therefore it is not but, instead, is kept frozen within your soul's own eternity until you can discover healing.

Favoritism in families readily creates jealousy, envy and self-pity, particularly when you are in a dysfunctional family and labeled as "the perpetually poor relation," "invisible child," "the keeper of all the dirty secrets," the "designated patient/problem," or the "replacement parent/child/sibling." When your talents are denied expression or are belittled and willfully misunderstood, when you are seen as a non-person for any reason, when you are never give peace or rest, all of these things lead to self-pity. When you are held to an impossible standard and judged harshly for simple mistakes; blamed and punished for others' actions; when you have been consistently told lies and given nothing but false promises; when you have been told to do something beyond your ability and then excoriated when you fail, your spirit is crushed and the pain of it leaks into your soul.

All of these things lead to soul-wounds: the pain, self-pity, shame, worthlessness and guilt that you can carry through lifetime after lifetime until you can renew your sense of self.

Healing Self-pity:

Healing Self-pity is neither simple nor easy. Sometimes the hardest part of healing is that many can help you a great deal but there are some things that only you can do for yourself: self-forgiveness for putting yourself in danger or allowing yourself to be used. You may need to recognize the truth of the part you might have played in arranging, allowing, or even creating the harm that has been done to you or the harm that you have done to yourself. Self-harm includes addiction; refusing to accept wise advice out of willful pride; not listening to your own intuition in order to be accepted by your peers even though you may have received warning after warning, thus putting yourself into an untenable situation instead.

Reality's several cruelties are not malicious punishment, but they are necessarily as automatic as any mechanical, dynamic physics. This is partly because, instead of the One Referent Tone of Love that is the solid Para-light of the Divine Core, 4-D Reality mainly has the solid reference point of Time as its core. And Time must continue in as close to a fixed rate as possible lest space itself become compromised. The "frozen" time of shock with its minute super-conducting loops that I have mentioned elsewhere, is as close as eternity can be allowed within the 4-D, temporal macrocosm, though the eternities of pure Grace and total enlightenment are rare exceptions. The other exception is meditation and also finding your Core Tone.

So the first part of healing is forgiveness and forgiveness never means saying, "What was done to me is acceptable!" It means, "I no longer choose to be part of the drama that those people/person/situation created for me. I no longer choose to identify myself as attached to that harm, identified with it or at the mercy of it." You may comfort yourself by knowing that the person or persons that have harmed you will feel every bit of the agony they created for you in their own Life Review; you may comfort yourself when you realize that you were never meant to be perfect on the Earth Plane. Perfection already exists! You came here in order to make mistakes, to live in the margins, be foolish and occasionally stupid and often misguided: that was the stipulation regarding God's own re-discovery of the Divine Nature. Your own fascinating route from

168

wholeness to fragmentation to wholeness again can be as enchanting as the dappled dance of light on moving water and can display your artistry, your success and your elegance.

Because unrecognized Self-pity stops your dance of healing, the first thing that needs to happen is to realize that you have been feeling sorry for yourself. Because Self-pity is such a Chimera, this is an adventure of self-exploration: to discern where you are angry, frustrated, feeling hopeless or lost. You may watch how often you say things such as, "Oh, of course!" when another bad thing happens or you once again loose the job, the friend, the recognition you wanted or you even just spill the groceries. If it helps, realize that Self-pity has been getting its nourishment from all of your grief, frustration, lack, loss and immobility. This may help you to demand that Self-pity no longer be a part of you. If you can trust what you know of that higher guidance, you may ask for higher-level and higher-energy help for this removal process.

But if trust is hard to embrace, you can dig and dig away at the quasi-living construct of the Chimera itself directly. As though taking a bitter pill as medicine, you might decide that yes, indeed, you do actually create (and sometimes allow) your own reality. Yet you do not accept this with self-recrimination: instead you decide, "Well, if I made my reality and I know what's in it, even though I might not remember choosing it, I can fix it! I can find out why I might have made such a mess for myself, whether it was because of past-life Karma or, perhaps, some strange agreement I made with myself about personal best to make up for the times I let myself fail. Or it might be from some agreement I'd forgotten I'd made with my mother to never outshine her or with my father to never succeed. This way, I empower myself, take control and command; this way, I can create the joy of my own success, for and by myself."

The Reason for Self-pity: Refining the Gold:

Though too often "you create your own reality" has been a way of blaming the victim, there are times when outer circumstances demand that you yield control to someone or something as the lesser of two evils or perhaps the lesser of two insanities. As in some of the horrific examples above, there are times when you have arranged things (in your comfortable place in a Heaven without any pain) so that you are faced with a merciless situation that allows you absolutely no choice in order to refine, or prove, yourself to your Self.

169

Proving the gold of the self is as lengthy, painstaking and difficult a process as proving gold from within the earth that uses fire and then skimming off the dross when the gold has been heated to 1,000°. In your human self, you could remove impurities by pulling them away from yourself little by little; if you are impatient you might take the other approach of using the psychic or emotional equivalent of hydrochloric and nitric acid to remove the impurities as you would in earthly gold. In order to remove what is not your true self you might put yourself into implacable situations of great danger, slow, agonizing, corrosive family situations that seem to take all the heart and spirit out of you, sometimes even engineering situations of misery for yourself that seem totally unfair.

And this, oddly enough, is the "reason" why Self-pity is allowed to exist: it acts as a clumping agent, something that draws the impurities together on the liquid gold's surface so that you may skim and remove them all at once instead of atom by atom. This is another reason why old souls have to deal with self-pity so often! You have mined the gold of your selves already, moved it to where it can be extracted from the ore and processed, so now it's time to refine what you have learned, felt, experienced, created and discovered. Removing Self-pity is part of the healing process for all of the several lifetimes' worth of distress you have felt, the wrongs that have been done to you and the wounds you have received. Self-pity has been collecting them for you, especially when you have had lives that were too short, too frenetic or too complex to allow yourself time to deal with the wounds. Sometimes, however, you have to put the healing off for too long and this is why self-pity is so "sticky:" it helps the wounds in your spirit cling to each other. This is not to exacerbate your pain, but to help you clear more of your emotional wounds with the right moment of comprehension.

A Note on Introversion and Extroversion:

Refining your gold by removing the dross that Self-pity has collected demands introspection, the courage to investigate, discern and deal with subconscious and unconscious issues inside of yourself, so that you find where all the detritus has collected. But most people, even old souls, are reactive instead of reflective or introspective: most people are focused outwards instead of inwards. Some of this is the natural extroversion of the human species: only a third of human beings are natural introverts, whose brains actually take longer and use more energy to process experiences, ideas, feelings and thoughts. This extra time not only means that ideas and experiences are digested more thoroughly. It also means that the mind/brain is given time to create new connections, both likely and unlikely, between your experiences, thus allowing more foresight, wisdom, patience and alas, more anxiety, worry, impatience and obsessive self-recrimination.

Introverts may take so much time and energy to process things that sometimes spending an evening with three people is quite a full evening. Such an evening may even demand that the introvert spend several days in quiet, contemplative recovery from the influx of data extracted from fully listening to what was said. But introversion on the spiritual path is valuable indeed because it allows you to clear the emotional scars of your life's experiences to such a depth that you do not have to carry them into the next life. Many older souls are introverts and most are quite fascinated with what has been hidden from them by their own wounded souls. But this self-concern need not be self-absorption: it is again part of refining your soul's and spirit's gold.

Language, Meaning and the Divine Intention

Key Points: Language is one of the most human things about us, but too often it is treated casually and manipulated so that it becomes divorced from the heart and human feeling. From voice-recognition software that cannot recognize homophones to incomplete and sometimes incorrect training in school, the meaning of language has lost its precision. Language is driven by emotion, yet your feelings and emotions that have not been recognized put hidden pressure on your sense of self: when that self is damaged enough, this damage creates emotionally toxic disdain that is communicated through verbal slurs. But at the core of language is Divine Love, which language itself can evoke. Language is communication between people, but when there is a gap between emotions and love created by pain, language can fail its purpose.

Subheadings:

- The Human Meanings of Language
- Mistakes and Confusion in the Language of Modern Media
- The Heart of Language and the Language of the Heart
- Lies, Epithets and Calumny
- The Schism between Love and Emotions
- The Wounding of the Self and the Desire for Revenge
- Love and Other Divine Feelings
- Cultural Attitudes to Emotions and Feelings
- Emotions, the Wisdom of the Heart and the Sacred Power of Language
- The Gap between Emotions and Love

The Human Meanings of Language:

Question from Melany G: Language means so much to me and so I try to speak it fluently, though it seems that many just toss it and its emotional meaning aside. Why is that?

172

Nikola Tesla: Language has tremendous power and is surely one of the greatest human gifts, being far more than simply communication. All things, "living," "non-living," fields, forces and energies, communicate in the sense of imparting information of the state, placement and intention of that thing or being in relationship to other things and beings. All of your body's cells communicate with each other and the whole. Save for the times where there is cancer or teratomas, the cells draw their patterns directly from the dimension of Identity, remaining discrete by retaining those same patterns through Quantum Entangled Inductive Resonance with that dimension. Organs have distinct boundaries and edges: the nerve cells of the brain, spinal cord and the body are all distinct in their form and function and the three layers of the skin rarely mix. These boundaries are not simply caused by the programming data in the DNA that handles proteins: the dimensions of Identity and Primordial Chaos use the Torsion Fields of Translation and Formation within the "Junk" DNA to manifest the patterns of Divine Intention into 4-D reality and to do this requires continual communication.

It has been said elsewhere that language evolved in order to communicate with strangers. When a child grows in a family, the parents and siblings often understand it without any words at all: a look, an expression, or a simple grunt may be enough to say, "I'm tired, bored and hungry: feed me now." But a stranger will of course not know the child's cues, so the child must at least experiment with other ways of getting his message across. Herd animals generally share the same basic physical signals: the horse's flattened ears or the bull's pawing the ground is such a clear communication they are recognized from species to species. Yet depending upon which ocean they spend most time swimming in, whales and dolphins both have dialects: indeed, subspecies of birds are created partly by the evolving disparity of their songs.

In this very real sense, communication is given form in this way. The continual re-iteration of the Divine Intention's pattern through the Multi-dimensional layers within the higher-order DNA in the "Junk," creates a standing wave of meaning through communication that becomes the 4-D form. However, language is more than communication: it is highly creative and can act as a Torsion Field in itself. Both fleeting and durable in human experience, language is an amazingly potent bridge between form and the formless, as any shaman, worker of magic, one who uses prayer or spiritual teacher already knows. Language can heal and it can harm; language can build and create ruin; language can guide and can confuse. The brain itself loves language, as any parent with a babbling child can attest or anyone that has recovered from a stroke or brain injury and learns to speak again. What takes language away from you harms you more than you might realize; what impoverishes language impoverishes you.

In the body, teratomas are created when cellular communication breaks down and teeth grow inside of toes, or hair grows inside an organ. This happens because of the haploid germ cells that are not gametes (or stem cells) have migrated or spontaneously formed in unusual parts of the body, creating real but non-functional structures. It is easy to see that language, being more fluid and more volatile in its energy, can rapidly develop verbal teratomas like the body as well: these are some of the hidden manipulations that abuse language. Rather than a haploid cell, verbal teratomas are created through incomplete empathy by half-truths, misperceptions and incomplete comprehension.

Such things as implications, subtexts, innuendoes or even poorly expressed emotional freight are examples of this deep confusion in language as well. The consequences of these verbal teratomas can be quite dramatic: with an adroit abuse of meaning you can too easily be seduced into a world where you are manipulated deliberately. This has already happened with some advertising where love and need are confused with objects. I will even go so far as to say that the deliberate manipulation of meaning in order to confuse, abuse, misuse and control others are verbal cancers and can be as pernicious and deadly as physical cancer to eradicate and overcome.

Mistakes and Confusion in the Language of Modern Media:

Language is finely balanced between the fleeting, as with slang, new scientific or psychological terms and the more durable terms, phrases, idioms and such. But with the Internet and social media, the rapid shifts have increased to a tremendous degree. Unfortunately, that speed gives an overwhelming scope for repetition of errors to the point that opposites can be equivocated and equal things divorced from their original unity. I do understand your irritation with the sometimes casual and careless manner with which language is treated. However, it is nearly impossible for some to admit they misunderstand their own use of language or, worse yet, have been taught incorrectly and have been perpetuating the original errors.

This reluctance to admit you are incorrect has resulted from the equivocation of "incorrect" and "wrong:" the term "incorrect" is pure information without judgment, whereas to call something "wrong" means that there has been harm done and judgment passed. Alas, the harm being done by this confusion is that it often makes it impossible for you to admit that you are incorrect! A crime is doing wrong by deliberately harming or abusing someone or something, especially without remorse. But when you can't tell in what way you are mistaken then you cannot change.

There are several errors of punctuation, spelling and other mistakes that have haunted English for decades. For instance, not realizing that the apostrophe is truly a contraction and not a possessive element is an error, though it is not a crime. Yet when "it's" is seen as "belonging to it," instead of its real meaning, "it is" in a contracted form, leaving the pronoun "its" dangling in the winds of perplexity, that is a perpetuated error. The muddle was entered in decades ago because of some original errors in presenting the concept of the apostrophe. The so-called "possessive apostrophe" is actually a contraction that joins two words, the same way "do not" is contracted into "don't:" the "apostrophe s" is derived from the ancient English convention of saying, "You know John, his house?" or, "John, his wife?" When you say those words quickly, it becomes, "John's house" and "John's wife." It was forgetting the real origin of the contraction that led to the awkwardness that has haunted English for too long. When an apostrophe is put in odd places writing plurals, using "house's" to mean many houses, confusion is given free reins and thus reigns even when it rains.

I play with the words here because, with voice recognition software, the difficulties with homophones are increasing. Homophones, "same sounds" such as "their," "there," and "they're" all have the same sound, but very different meanings and if the meanings are lost because the software renders the sentence as, "We are going to there house," absurdity soon results. Puns are most often created from homophones after all, as well as assonances. But if someone says that sentence with the misplaced homophone in the earnest conviction he is correct, then meaning has been tarnished at least, lost at the worst. Nearly all of these mistakes are promulgated and perpetuated because of unclear training resulting from expediency, overwhelmed teachers and too many exigent dramas removing the peace of learning. I hope to address that issue in the article Training the Lemurian Child.

In the article on the Hypnosis of the Marketplace I have spoken of the poverty of social media's quick-time paring down of words and that is a force to be reckoned with: if one word must serve for too many things that word can be manipulated more easily. Consider the word "buck:" a young man; a male deer; the fighting action of a horse; to resist; a military degree ("buck private" being the lowest); a pejorative slang word for a young black man or American Indian, a dapper fellow, a herd of antelope, to gather courage, to resist an unfair situation, to struggle for something and so on. You need to depend upon context and connotation to realize which version of the word the other person is using. But if context is impoverished, as with the rapid thought-bites of social media, connotation is impossible to decipher. When there are no verbal cues there is little chance to avoid confusion. Hence of course the clumsy necessity of emojis and similar cues yet they, too, are an impoverished version of human facial expressions.

Confusion leads to anxiety: it must, because billions of years of being prey have taught you that when something doesn't make sense it is best to pay attention to it so you don't become that something's food. But when confusion is continual, pandemic, and unrelenting, in order to cope with the continual state of emergency the overtaxed mental and emotional systems fall into apathy and learned helplessness. In short, carelessness is not a small issue, not at all.

But as long as the words "wrong" and "incorrect" are used interchangeably, many will resist being simply corrected on their grammar, trying to buck off what they see as an attack on their intelligence instead of bucking up and simply saying, "Oh, I was mistaken!" Mistakes are easy enough to fix if you are not feeling damaged in your sense of self as regards your error. Accurate words clear confusion. Accurate, clear communication eases many connections and allows for the whole to recognize its own unity elegantly. There is no easy solution for this except perhaps to define "wrong" more correctly. However this re-definition will not come from adding more rules, but rather by searching into the meaning of language. This is why you already understand that the true source of language must be the heart.

The Heart of Language and the Language of the Heart:

MG: Despite the fact that the heart is where the true power of language lies, many people seem to manipulate language and the heart though labels: epithets and name-calling. What is going on with this gap between emotion and love in language?

NT: Several things create the gap between emotion and love: amongst them is the fear of emotions' power: their ability to overwhelm and direct your human actions and experiences. This fear is fueled by the fact that emotions and feelings are often out of your conscious will's control, whether because of subconscious drives or because of mental, chemical, physical or emotional patterns in the brain. Feelings and emotions that have not been acknowledged and recognized create tremendous pressure in the Self.

Strictly speaking love is not an emotion, though certainly it evokes both emotions and feelings, because love is the responsive harmonic manifestation of the Zero dimension, the very heart and mind of God. Love does not depend upon intelligence to be expressed, but it does depend on the ability of a thing, being or entity to match resonance with love's vibrations. If you do not have the resonance of love, you cannot perceive or experience it, yet like a fine instrument, the heart resonates to the tones of that love constantly.

Sadly, however, both language and emotions baffle and muffle the sounding boards of the heart and keep it from being able to resonate properly. When you are told again and again, "You're a loser, you'll never amount to anything," or, "You're a failure, a jerk, stupid, or a waste of space," and so on and so on, your ability to resonate with love's energy is often damaged for lifetimes afterwards. Words with hate in them not only drown out the love hidden in the heart, they put layers and layers of damping on love's vibration so that it loses its impact even when it is presented to the heart again. Feelings and emotional states such as hate, shame, loneliness, depression, despair and misery also dull and dampen the heart's natural resonance and when that happens, you feel deeply lost.

Yes, the heart is still responsive to the love vibration and can be renewed. However, emotional factors such as desperation, wounding, revenge and/or disdain can create the dis-empathy I have mentioned before and can lock the heart into a place beyond love altogether. This takes much healing, some of which can be done only when you are human and some of which can only be accomplished when you are done with your lifetime on Earth and are gently drawn back into the core of the Loving Light again. This healing love of the Core and its pure vibration is communicated in words on Earth and in Heaven.

Language is used to help the heart resonate to love again through words of kindness, appreciation, sympathy, empathy or friendship, because these can break down the dampening layers of emotions based on pain. However, the emotional toll of being bullied and teased or continually challenged and abused emotionally, physically, psychically or spiritually can lead to the horrific situation where there are no good ways, or even any ways at all, left to repair the pain of being rejected. The desire for bitter revenge has an incalculable human cost if the sense of self has been wounded deeply enough, so that there remains only the desperate, non-thinking and non-feeling rage. Being this wounded causes spiritual and emotional desperation. That desperate person may not have any chance of finding his way back to love while on Earth. Yet the only chance he has is through language: using the meaningful words that restore the feeling of being lovable.

Lies, Epithets and Calumny:

Language, your most human ability, can open your inner self's wonder, joy, delight and enlightenment or be perverted into instruments of excruciating pain. It is so closely interwoven with your human identity that abusive language is highly destructive and should be shunned altogether. Everyone recognizes his own name, whether the birth-name or the name chosen deliberately: so aware, in fact, that the sound of your name penetrates even the unconsciousness of deep sleep. Yet almost everyone remembers being made the butt of harmful "jokes" made by abusive versions of your name, much less lied to or made into a fool by someone setting you up. Teasing someone, even in fun, re-names him or her: it can open your identity or strangle it to death.

A name is given power by repetition: when you are praised as being a kind man, a loving person, a thoughtful woman or a generous child, all of these positive images find their resonant places in your personal area of connection to the dimension of Identity. But if you are called stupid, worthless, deceitful, a slut or a whore or a brute or a jerk, these words also carry their own lower-level resonances and can bring you down to that lower level of energy amazingly quickly.

178

Just training a child without praise can cost the child heavily, never mind the parent turning his own frustration at his own inadequacy into blaming a challenging child, to say nothing of the times when children tease one another in order to mask *their* own fears of inadequacy.

Nicknames or names within a group such as a club or a church group can be silly or fun when done in the right spirit: not to judge or diminish the other person, but to unfold possibilities. But any name that is given with negative judgment limits and lessens the ones so named. When the intention of the epithet is neither fun nor even based on discernment it can instead become part of a slow, belittling destruction. There have been complaints about people being "over-sensitive" to epithets and racial slurs, mostly by those who want to use such slurs. Yet when your own value of your self is shaky, a cruel word can distort your human identity and then cement it into a new, damaged shape through the words' resonances. Slurs, insults, slanders and aspersions also create the shock of "frozen" time, weakening those that are targeted. Alas, many groups of people are continually faced with unfair situations, expectations and dictates from society that are aimed at reducing their value, effectiveness, significance and chances of receiving love from and within the whole. This continual erosion of the self through words matters and can cost Humanity heavily.

Sadly, too often you choose to do or, perhaps, cannot do anything about it. Almost as though the dinosaur-parts of your brain look at such harm with the same bland unconcern as a mother bird looks on when the stronger chicks force the weaker ones out from the nest, you take few actions to create real change. This lack of change leads to stagnant, intractable problems that appear to be so much a part of society that it seems that they can never be fixed, though with determination they would change if there were will enough and caring enough to change them by shifting your attitudes and values.

Still, too often your responses are limited to the lowest-energy ones. The epithet "bird-bran" usually means someone of limited intelligence. However, it may also mean a brain that depends on its most primitive coding to make its decisions. In short, this is a brain that cannot see outside of the animal view of "always me first" into the thinking, planning and empathic stratum engineered by the cerebrum. Granted, responding with empathy and foresight by resisting the impulse to blame someone for the negative situation they have been put into takes extra work and extra training. Yet constant misery results when the collective energy drops below a certain level. You have already experienced nearly six thousand years of this since the Iron Age began in 3102 BCE: it is time for a change.

Nevertheless, taking the lower-energy way is common in modern societies. For instance punishment takes less energy than full understanding, so hundreds of thousands more criminals are punished than are helped. Demonstrating caring, responsiveness and responsibility in the course of your daily life often takes so much energy that it is easier to become self-centered instead of centered in Self: there is not yet enough energy in the current Age to support the high level of spiritual awareness for everyone yet. In addition there is so much evolutionary momentum behind putting yourself first because greed, selfishness and even trickery work so well to provide you with what you need in times of uncertainty and scarcity. Thus, it feels far easier to slide into selfishness than to become aware of others. Any naturalist knows that thievery, trickery, dominance and brutality work very, very well in the short run, for animals employ these methods all the time and all of these methods are used to deal with times of scarcity when minimal energy is available from the environment.

The Schism between Love and Emotions:

But what schism between heart and feeling, the core of the human self and human emotions, could cause such a total lack of human feeling and create such toxic harm that abuse and all its corrosive effects is possible in the first place? Are there any words that could ever be said that might heal you, that overcome the pain by recalling your originally clear and transparent feelings that are without toxicity, abuse, or grief?

The gulf that divorces the heart and emotions' expression is most usually the yawning gulf of unhealed grief. Very frequently emotional, physical, mental, psychic or spiritual violations through being taught poorly or incorrectly about your intrinsic value can sometimes cause the soul's evisceration by deep confusion. Unhealed grief does not just mean a child's petulant anger when someone ruins a favorite toy or an opportunity has been disappointed. The grief that breaks your emotional self is the grief of your intentions being thwarted by being continually dismissed, your love being misused or abused and by whatever experiences that may shatter the original Core Self.

When dogma, cultural pressures and even other people's emotional damage denies your value, this perpetuates the gap between what you know yourself to be and what you feel you must become. Originally, you were a shining, loving being that only wanted to play with Time and Space in order to learn and discover what might happen: you wanted to discover your true nature by fathoming what it was not. Yet when you have been presented a Book of Definitions For Your Self by those around you that is torn, stained, miss-paginated and written in several disparate emotional languages, you must of course become confused: the struggle of resolving that confusion separates what you know of yourself with what you are told you must think of yourself.

There are words of healing for all of these situations, though most of these words are silent. The time spent patiently with another in love of that other are not words said aloud, yet it is nevertheless the language of one soul reminding the other of Love's inclusive power in the face of loss. As the Core Tone in your own heart is a silent sound, so also is the silent language of the Self's essential and original pattern that is so needed to re-capture the integrity and wholeness of the violated self. Often there are no words possible except those silent spells of power that create gentleness, peace, nurturance and loving-kindness again.

The steadying effects of silence can sometimes be the only answer when you are so confused by lies that you have been taught, by the maladaptive parts of yourself, that you have hung on to old misconceptions out of loyalty beyond their utility or by wanting to please the paradoxes, contradictions or falsehoods you have been told about yourself. With that speaking silence of the heart you can discern the deceptions and contradictions, thus creating the peace that might make you whole again. Certainly there are spoken words that help: words spoken from love, empathy and caring wisdom. Listening is a language of its own as well: a person that listens with an empathic heart speaks that language eloquently. The schism between the human heart and the emotions is a wide gulf at this present time; this can be seen quite clearly by the rise of desperation in so many. But though the silent words and words of silence are not so easily perceived, they can be created and re-created through caring, bridging that gulf.

The Wounding of the Self and the Desire for Revenge:

Revenge is the desire to hurt the person that harmed you so that the harmer feels what you experienced to the same vicious depth and detail of his harm to you, or even more. Balancing the scales of harm and your own hurt feelings was often the way of the world. As we've mentioned before, the injunction of, "An eye for an eye and a tooth for a tooth," was actually an improvement on the degree to which revenge could be pursued, such as killing all of your family for an affront you alone caused. Bitter revenge that consumes the mind and heart becomes a systemic, implacable sickness of the soul. You are able to see no hurt but your own, no satisfaction but pushing the hurt onto all others, even though this will close you off from Love. Even after death only words of true spiritual power might break this state of bitterness.

Granted, in much the same way a bitter poison can be used for healing, even that bitter desire for revenge can be used by the Divine Mind. Though, when your bitter revenge is combined with arrogance, you create disdain. While it rarely manifests in its full potential degree, disdain is such a corrosive emotional state that it can affect whole communities, states and nations. Disdain is the ultimate projection of your own negative feelings about yourself onto others. This arrogant kind of revenge has created everything from bigotry, pogroms, torture and genocide. Disdain refuses love, creating bullying, name-calling and belittling, negative epithets.

Paradoxically it is disdain's own arrogance that says it must bring people down to its own level by making them more wrong in the hope that it makes the arrogant, bitter person more right. Indeed, both arrogance and disdain are rooted in the anxiety of those that are convinced they are inadequate: they cannot bear to look at that inadequacy lest they discover it to be truth. Revenge can be totally unsubtle but the desire for it is based on the subtle, elusive and too frequently unexamined conviction of God's inadequate justice: that you are or have been judged by the Source of Love as less worthy of love than another. If that Love has rejected you and it is inadequate in the fulfillment of its duties, then you have no recourse. Where else is there to go other than God? For a human being, who is also an expression of Love, this perceived inadequacy is an intolerable agony, driving many of humanity's most vicious and violent acts.

Though it can sometimes be a palliative anesthesia, revenge cannot heal. In the end it is as counter-productive as wounding yourself in order to distract yourself from the way others have wounded you. There is much bewildered grief, sense of violation and lack of self-value when you realize that you, an expression of Love, have been hurt by what should have been another expression of Love and have been deeply wronged by what Love seems to have become: the murderer, betrayer, rapist, abuser or fraud. This is the hardest and most pernicious aspect of reality's fundamental state of illusion: that Love can become un-Love. In the end, perhaps, only the silent words of Love can heal this, in the secret place of the human heart where even God can come only at your invitation.

Love and Other Divine Feelings:

MG: I really believe that human emotion is a language that in my opinion possesses such depth and innocence that it is a gift unlike any other. Why aren't these energies seen as divine counterparts?

NT: I certainly agree that human emotions are a language of depth and innocence: they are immediate, as is the Divine; they are pure, as is the Divine; they are interactive, as is the Divine and their source is in the higher realms, as is the Divine. The innocence that you perceive is the original integrity of the Divine Being, for the power of emotions and feelings reflects the Divine authenticity. And it is this very resonance of human emotions and feelings with the Divine Being that makes the silent languages of love, caring, and healing possible.

It is clear that love can change Reality quite directly: this is seen in the tale of when a young boy cuddled the traumatized rabbits in a cosmetic product testing facility lovingly every night: he was able to help the rabbits withstand the rigors and assaults of the tests enough to skew the test results! This love resonance can also be seen in the countless examples of dying people waiting for a loved one to arrive from far away to have a chance for a last good-bye, perhaps, or of someone even pulling back from the brink of death for the sake of a spouse, friend or children despite severe health problems, only succumbing after the last words are shared. The love in these examples was steeped in both emotion and feelings: joy, courage, longing and compassion. Even anger can be a part of these compassionate actions, for surely the fuel of anger and rage help create the determination to live and the determination to care.

It could be a delightful mental exercise to work out how many parts of anger, sadness and happiness create compassion, what core emotions and complex feelings meld together to become love or perhaps to debate if love is the source of even the core emotions of happiness, anger or sadness. However, the only way to understand a feeling is to feel it; the only way to understand emotions is to experience them. The mind can amuse itself perpetually with codifying, arranging and cataloging things outside of itself, yet in the end this kind of analysis is only glints of light on the surface of the ocean of the Self: this ocean is much, much deeper than the mind could ever be. But many people, being trained out of their emotions at an early age, are afraid of the necessary depths towards which you must go to fathom the Divine Core of your own feelings. It suffices to say that sometimes the deeper the depth of pain the heart and the self can feel, the wider and higher the joy that can be experienced and the more immediate the Divine Being can become.

Cultural Attitudes to Emotions and Feelings:

In my own opinion, if emotions and feelings were more accepted in some cultures there would perhaps be less insanity; there would certainly be a great deal more deep communication. However, emotions would have to be better understood in the first place. This is paradoxically where the mind can be very useful indeed, as long as it is instructed in discernment instead of expecting to define emotions in action. If the shame of being unable to deal with feelings and emotions were removed, then emotions would become on the one hand more transient, as they would no longer need to be stored away as being unworkable; at the same time emotions would become more authentic because they would be allowed pure expression. These purely expressed, transient emotions would clarify things instead of muddling things dangerously the way blocked and damaged emotions and feelings often do now.

This of course demands a different cultural approach for some, perhaps by no longer seeing emotions and their manifestation as a feminine and thus an unacceptable weakness. Culturally and religiously, masculine energies have been emphasized and over-emphasized too often in the last millennia. After all, if you want help from your God to accomplish victories in war or to dominate other tribes, groups, races or peoples in order to the create unhindered promulgation of your religion, then surely He cannot be weak! Nor can such a God be female either, because, to the over-masculine mind, women are subject to dominance by definition. This is true even today, not simply in the warlike tribes that had to battle to live. And this is a human loss because the feminine principle is naturally inclusive.

Today, even though emotions are part of the divine expression in form, particularly in but not exclusively to living things, all human emotion has the reputation of tainting scientific data, as though objectivity was part of the test of verifiability. If you are not objective, you and your data are by definition suspect. However, it is not the emotions, but their mishandling that leads to unwanted effects in scientific studies as well as making human relations difficult. In many ways, emotions are like hormones: they exist because they have global effects within an organism, as well as significant effects within that organism's environment.

Emotions and feelings also operate at a level deeper and thus faster than the conscious mind. Indeed, unexamined, unclaimed, unconscious or misunderstood emotions and feelings do color every part of your actions and reactions regarding your experiences, even if you are a scientist. However, there are times when the only way you can move forward with your life, work or growth, is to examine those deep and perhaps frightening feelings that you have been unable to look at or experience. Even to reach into your own divinity demands that you understand your unconscious emotions: you *cannot* become spiritual without becoming truly human first. If you have any unconscious pain regarding unmet needs, unfair treatment or challenges for which you were not prepared, it is difficult to become any sort of clear spiritual light.

Emotions, the Wisdom of the Heart and the Sacred Power of Language:

MG: Whatever happened to intelligence and emotion going hand-in-hand with the wisdom of the heart? The heart is where the true power lies. Knowing how clear this sacred space of language is, what do you think is missing?

NT: Much as science and religion are, the heart and the mind have been forced into opposing roles. It has been said that the heart is the depth of the mind: where the heart leads, the mind must follow. But if the heart has been damaged and cannot communicate save through its pain, then you avoid the heart to the same degree that you do not or cannot have the courage to face the heart's pain. As the heart has been devalued, dismissed and even disdained as being too emotional, willful, paradoxical and inexplicable, you have also forgotten the paradox that mystery and the unexplained are all doorways into the Divine Presence. Because emotions are actually living energy-fields, you can never solve pain by avoiding it, distracting yourself from it or anesthetizing yourself into unconsciousness of its effect, any more than you can ever entirely remove emotional patterns of trauma and influences that have caused some profound change in your human psyche by using mere distraction.

Emotions remain in patterned form: the energy of an old emotion remains as a vibrational texture interleaved with countless others. Deep changes in your sense of self become "strange attractors" in the dimension of Identity, with the result that the frozen time of emotional, physical, or psychic shock persists. All of these emotions and patterns remain within the greater human identity, because emotions and feelings, as they are sourced in the Divine Core, persist beyond time and space. If you have ever experienced a good past-life regression, you know: the feelings of that past lifetime still remain.

Indeed, these vivid emotions are often the very energies by which a specific past life is found: phobias are an example of such persistent patterns and are often doorways into your past lives. Sometimes viewing such a past life through the eyes and mind of your present lifetime allows these old and damaged emotions to be resolved, because you have gained the necessary detached perspective from the trauma's origin. However, because it has retained these energetic fields and patterns, the heart is also able to reveal the lessons behind them. That is where the heart's wisdom is created and where your intuition actually receives much of its data.

The sacredness of language is a very human thing: as I have said before only human beings can create a sacred space. There are special places for animals, as where a doe gives birth in the forest or the cave where a bear dreams the winter away; there are holy places for the Elves and Faeries or the places where the divine energies of Earth and the Divine influence of the enfolded dimensions mingle. But a sacred place is where words are spoken aloud with sacred intention to invoke the Divine Presence. Speaking to the hearts of those in that place and opening the space to higher-level energy deliberately is a very human thing. Yes, other beings of other realms, planets and planes of existence do the same, yet human beings are some of the few that speak aloud. In the majority of the universe's many worlds, communication is telepathic or uses pure energies of various kinds, such as silent gestures or unusual methods such as scent. There are very few beings in the universe that use radio waves for communicating, though there are some few that use radio waves as a way of sensing their environment as bats do with sonar. This makes human words and speech almost unique and certainly important. Especially sacred song is the most powerful human communication.

In the present time, that is much of what is missing: words said and songs sung sacredly with the deep awareness of giving voice to the Divine Will, whether as a channel as with a prophet or as an ally, as in Co-creation. You know what you are saying is real when you declare or affirm that the prayer will come to pass, because you hear that particular tone of voice resonating directly with the Divine Intention. This distinct timbre of the voice cannot be faked, though many have tried and even appeared to succeed. Words sung with joy or said in a spirit of integrity with all of your human honesty and determination behind them, bridge the gap between the real and the false, the obfuscation of deceiving lies and the sound of truth. When you train your ear to discern the difference much changes in your reality and your experience of it.

The Gap between Emotions and Love:

MG: What is the gap between love and emotion?

NT: It is emotional, psychic, spiritual, mental and even physical pain. Psychic pain is when you finer sensibilities such as clairvoyance, clairaudience, or clairsentience are traumatized by shocks, overwhelming input or even direct attacks by those who are afraid of what you might do or become as a result of your abilities. Spiritual pain is when your aspirations, hopes, life purpose, reason for living or even your perceptions of the Divine are similarly overridden, overwhelmed or deliberately traumatized. Frustration, obfuscation, confusion and contradictions create mental pain, as well as being impoverished in your mental tools of perception, discernment and creativity.

An example of psychic trauma might be living with too much chaos, especially with loud noises, disruptive people, indiscriminate use of profanity, name-calling, or vituperative character assassination; these do not even have to be directed at you but just be in your vicinity. To a sensitive person this perpetual dissonance is as though you were to take a fine scientific instrument or medical tool and start throwing it around the room: if by some miracle it does not

187

break, it will certainly get out of adjustment rapidly. Spiritual trauma can be created by someone that is actually psychic but that is firmly "in the closet" about it: this person can be so terrified of his or her own finer perceptions that every time you demonstrate them, you are shut down by belittling, bullying, or unilateral rejection. This trauma can also be created when someone imposes his very narrow view of God upon you at your expense, either because you are this person's child, or the object of a religious pogrom.

Mental pain is harder to define, because, in much the same way that the brain cells do not feel pain, only the nerves around them do when damaged or pressured, the mind can be incredibly wounded and not feel any of it. Mental wounds are inflicted by lies, confusion, obfuscation, "gas-lighting," or any of a variety of verbal manipulations and the kind of slow, layered confusion that can be deliberately constructed in "confidence games," where you are led to the con man's desired conclusion at the cost of your own. A very deep kind of mental wound is inflicted through neglect; when your mind is not exercised; another deep wound is when you are given low-level mental "food:" vapid, pointless or inane content from whatever sources, many of which serve to merely entertain, not to instruct. You are mentally wounded when you are forced to learn something too far outside your mental abilities, or conversely are allowed to take the easy, slow, and "stupid" way out: dumbing yourself down instead of reaching into your intelligence.

Mental trauma often results in brittle mental rigidity, creating either a perfectionist's exacting attitude that seeks to control everything and everyone around you, including yourself: when this rigidity breaks, it can take your mind with it in a so-called "nervous breakdown." The trauma can reveal itself in obsessive attitudes of prejudice, bigotry and snap judgments or even in disdain; it can also lead the mind to want to take in *everything* without assessment or discernment, trying to learn it all, do it all, conquer or accomplish it all. In short, the mind loses its own internal governance: it lives with too much structure or not nearly enough.

Most human beings are quite conversant with emotional pain, and we discuss that in the article on the Costs of Emotional Pain. However, the traumas caused by emotional damage are generally forms of separation from Love and so have aspects of loss, loneliness, abandonment and rage in all of them. Though human emotions are

188

not as plain as physical injuries, there has been much work done, for psychology can be a rich, fascinating and highly creative field.

And, much as a bad injury might create a blockage of some kind in the body, all of these traumas create frozen time and impede the free flow of the psychic, mental and spiritual energies. You can manage with a little of such mental damage, much as you can still walk when you legs are badly bruised. However, if the damage is persistent enough to actually break you own inner connections the pain becomes so great that it becomes your entire focus. And, similar to the way drinking a sweet drink or taking a vacation will do less than nothing to heal a broken leg, unless you deal with psychic, mental, emotional or spiritual trauma with a psychic, mental, psychic or spiritual methodology, the pain will always remain.

Your heart and your wisdom are part of everything you speak aloud, everything you feel and everything you imagine in your mind, as well as everything you are aware of psychically or spiritually. When the heart hurts too much to function well, then all human aspects are compromised. Yet if the heart can be healed with true Love, then the emotional, mental, spiritual and psychic functions can become sensitive and responsive again. Indeed, this is a great deal of what happens in an NDE: when someone returns with a spiritual mission, a renewed enthusiasm for life, a clearer mind and/or psychic faculties not demonstrated before. This is healing on several levels.

The Human Nature of Healing

Key Points: From the questioner's definition of healing as "A Genesis driven by the soul, not just the physical body, that touches every part of your being," Tesla reveals his own after-life perceptions of what healing is and how it relates to the human soul. Healing is variable because the enfolded dimensions are intricately "layered" together, forming an energetic structure similar to some cross-grained building materials. There are times when a positive emotion can support healing, though there are times when that positivity can support the illness for the soul's reasons, though not for your human ones. Yet when human DNA is fully awakened, much that has been difficult to heal may be changed with surprising ease.

Subheadings:

- Nikola Tesla's Own Definition of Healing

- Multi-dimensional Aspects of Healing

- Overcoming Resistance to Healing

- Using Specific Types and Colors of Light

- Humanity's Healing Potential

Nikola Tesla's Own Definition of Healing:

Question from Melany G.: I believe that healing is not what we're taught it is, but it's something completely different instead. From my own experience, I define healing as "A Genesis driven by the soul, not just the physical body, that touches every part of your being." What is your definition of healing, Mr. Tesla?

NT: I am enchanted by your definition: your are quite right to put healing in the hands of your own soul, for the soul is the source of healing and illness, burdens and miracles and is its own answer to those burdens, illnesses and all potential renewal. As genesis is defined as the source from which something begins, the soul does indeed drive the changes that healing creates. It is, after all, your soul's choice to wander the realms of danger, damage, sickness and systemic disharmony known as the Earth Plane by taking on human form. However, the reasons for accepting and embracing illness and physical dysfunction are not simple, though they are instructive and illuminating. As all marginal factors may, areas of relative stress, disharmony and disparity engender, give form to and impact creativity. From the point of view of the All In All, the One Core Source of Being, fresh creativity is of incalculable value and precious beyond compare. However, minute the differences may be between two methods used for the same healing, in their subtle differences each is unique and reflects the very nature of oneness.

Generally speaking, health is defined as a working system's dynamic stasis: low levels of pain and/or dysfunction, ability to withstand the strains, shocks and damage you might incur because, when healthy, your body can give an able, capable response to all of these shocks. Healing therefore usually means returning to health's dynamic stasis, either naturally or with chemical assistance, so that the body continues without pain or dysfunction after the healing process. My definition of healing is to dynamically re-create and infuse patterns of wellness upon a living system by physical, paraphysical or other-dimensional means in order to replace dysfunction with function, giving that system renewed potential for positive change and sustaining that body through the clarity of its own innate intelligence. The body knows what its own heath is and also knows the Karmic patterns it was created to work out within your human experiences. Consequently, part of physical healing is soul healing: reviewing and clearing past-life traumas, contracts, beliefs and feelings of guilt, shame, self-pity, self-hatred or true Karmic debt. Renewing health thus means working with both unfolded 4-D and the enfolded M-D energetic systems. This involves both the psychic body interacting with Ether as well as the mental body's own deliberate re-structuring.

Multi-dimensional Aspects of Healing:

However, some issues of ill health are easier to clear than others and that aspect of healing frustrates many. Though usually anecdotal at present, some healing is miraculous: from a diseased heart's total renewal to documented bone replacement, removal of cancers, as well as the impossible health improvements that can happen in NDE's, quite without any psychic or mental work at all. Other times, healing work of many types and kinds can be done, again and again, without any positive result. This is because there are several dimensional layers, off-angles of force, hidden enfolded geometries and other indirectness in play. As I have discussed above some of this is inevitably part of the direct and indirect nature of reality, and some is because of the multiple layers of the personal factors and issues involved.

Self-forgiveness can be involved but there are times when you have done all your homework, cleared this and placated that, prayed and worked and tried numerous therapies and the healing process still hasn't worked. Because you are dealing directly with the dimension of Identity, this type of fundamental resistance demands an entirely different methodology: the dimension of Identity is so closely allied with the Zero dimension and the dimension of Primordial Chaos, there is a tremendous amount of inertia in Identity's effect. This inertia assists many processes, from sustaining you when you are injured in any of your bodies, to allowing longevity. Yet at the same time this inertia can become detrimental when your sense of identity *includes* the damage.

When the dimension of Identity shifts its relationship to you and you to it, then injury, illness or disease can become your personal identity and this can be very difficult to change. Because the dimension of Identity works through the Torsion Fields of Formation, Translation, Proportion and the Etheric plasma, these fields' energies can layer upon each other so that their differing "directions" within the enfolded geometries create a stronger pattern when joined that when separate. However frustrating a durable illness can be, this multi-directional, multi-dimensional layering also allows you to have tremendous strength and courage when confronted with disaster, torture, abuse and other shocks, because the Torsion Fields' enfolded energies are necessarily of a higher order than most patterns in 4-D. This is one of the reasons why an implacable, especially congenital, illness burdens you: you learn things about these layered energies through bearing it that you cannot learn in any other way.

Unfortunately, the strength of this energetic layering can work against you and it is very hard on your human self. There are times when the soul feels it must demand some super-heavy, persistent restriction, creating birth defects or chronic illnesses that demand daily care and are certainly embedded in the dimension of Identity. Because, much as Time's continual, unchanging reference point enables forms to relate to one another in space, such maladies create a constant reference point for the soul as well as the human personality. In other words, the Karmic or chosen restrictions from illness actually provide stability in the soul's human experience.

Understandably, as its source is within the Timeless, eternal enfolded dimensions, the soul is a stranger to Time. The soul may use this illness's persistent manifestation as a marker to determine whether or not Karma has been balanced, the chosen lessons learned or whether your heart has comprehended tenderness and empathy through difficulty. Even though it is invariably difficult for your human personality, you can understand their meaning only by doing and experiencing some things in your human person from the perspective of your own inner divinity. So, much healing is soul healing. However, if the original restrictions are sourced in the soul's own intentions, whether in Karmic patterns or momentum from past lives, you may have to consider using payer and to call for miracles. In comparison to the higher-order enfolded geometries, 4-D reality is uncommonly slow and not nearly as malleable.

Overcoming Resistance to Healing:

Oddly enough, positive emotions, especially those sourced in your soul, can provide the greatest resistance to healing, though of course also the greatest support. When you are pulled down with a common cold, you can either accept it as a necessary chance to rest, in which case you can shorten the time of its effects, or you can push on to continue working and generally add to the length of the illness as well as its severity. In another form of positivity, people with chronic diseases will frequently refuse to be defined by, or as, their disease. In some cases this denial results from the original shock at the diagnosis but in many cases it is a deliberate and positive shift of focus towards the greater human self.

As your perspective changes when you realize your body is enclosed in your human experience as a soul rather than your soul being encased in the body's experiences, so also gaining the soul's Timeless perspective regarding your limitations can both help you overcome them, or accept them as the crucible of change they were meant to be. If the soul is able to clear Karma, discharge obligations, contracts or agreements with several people in one life because of the malady, then surely the soul will feel very positively about the illness As the soul's intention is creating a whole, human self that is able to experience the Divine in fourth-dimensional Reality directly, any progress towards that gives the human soul great joy. As the soul is of course rooted in the higher Zero dimension and the dimension of Identity, this deep emotion can override human concerns and actually create a barrier to healing! Not because of punishment or malice, but because what is learned is more true than the process that gives the learning.

To say the least this does not seem fair: the soul, in its timeless unity, cannot feel the direct frustration or tedium of having a chronic illness, for pain is completely ephemeral to it. But the human self feels the whole weight of both pain and burden, suffering the soul's mandates by being forced to allow them. *Of course* there are numerous benefits to the soul: learning patience, forbearance, self-healing, self-control and numerous other things that you can generally only learn by having a physical experience. However, you, the soul's human expression, seems to have all the hard work foisted upon it. The only help seems to be demanding gifts from the soul in return, such as intuition and inspiration that allows you to find physical solutions to the malady or disease. You may demand that your soul finds the medications, corrective surgery or physical and psychic restructuring that opens inner doorways into profound states of meditation that will alter your experience of the disease itself. And with these demands, you can reach into the higher, broader realms of your soul that give you the leverage for change.

In this light it is no surprise that one of the resistances to healing is resentment because of jealousy. Jealousy of others that are whole and think nothing of it; jealousy of those that have the financial means for the medications and treatments they need and think nothing of it; jealousy of the self you once were, carefree and easy without any burden or even jealous of the self you might have been if only your DNA had not betrayed you. But hidden in the resentment of "I can't have the health," is the hidden kernel of "I might have the healing," and within that is the hidden kernel of "I can embrace healing even through the limits."

Again, these limits are important: as the best and fastest racehorses have the heaviest weights added to their saddles, there are times when the most shining souls are the ones that have the extra burdens. And, again, this is where the joy comes in: realizing that you have become a person of such strength and refined power. You have been tested and tried by 4-D physicality for centuries and are such a potent and competent being, that you outstrip the parameters of the age for which you have incarnated and so must be weighted down! That is success: that is triumph worthy of celebration! And even though your burdens might be crafted from Karmic agreements and contracts so that you learn the harm you have caused others by the law that "what is done in the flesh must be paid for in the flesh," that is also joy. Shaped by the cutting tools of your soul's truth and Divine Justice, these particular Karmic bonds create a particular depth of meaning to your human experience: atonement though comprehension.

Using Specific Types and Colors of Light:

MG: Considering that I am a young adult, what do you think about the idea of taking in more light, essentially changing the chemistry of my form?

NT: Yes, of course: this is a fruitful and wise idea. However, as the inner layers of the physical human self depend on the cross-grained, multiply oriented higher-dimensional geometries, obviously you need to work with more than one kind and "direction" of light. If you refer to Volume One, considering the various natures of light and the meditations from the sinusoidal light and luminal intelligence or the "solid" nature of the Para-light at the core of Reality you will see what I mean: there are several aspects of light that can be perceived by human consciousness alone. You can also choose the psychic colors of the light that permeates your body by simply asking, "What colors do my cells need to function properly?" It may be a mixture of colors, such as "pinky blue" or "purple-orange," or the color might not look like anything you have ever seen before. The latter types of colors are those that are "octaves" of light-vibrations that are beyond human vision, such as far ultraviolet or even higher vibrations; these colors may even be the "colors" of Ether.

Ether is the energy plasma that permeates all reality: through Quantum Entangled Inductive Resonance, Ether is the most directly physical manifestation of the Zero dimension because it provides the matrix for the Units of Consciousness to form. Within the Ether there are also "colors" of consciousness that use the primordial Units of Consciousness that are the precursors of all physical forms, energies and fields. There is also the light in your own human aura. Perceived as variants of the visible spectrum, these colors of auric light engage luminal intelligence because they also impart meaning: silver and purple being more spiritual colors, greens being healing and love, red meaning passion, determination or focused physical energy. Granted, the color's description and meaning varies from system to system and from person to person to a degree; however, working with your auric light can be delightfully instructive.

195

So, you need to play with the different kinds of light to create your own "light cocktail," pulling on your body's wisdom to choose the forms. If you want to work with the brain and nerve cells, generally speaking you might combine the "dark" form of the sinusoidal light, a high-energy auric light of silver/light blue or light blue mixed with deep purple, an Etheric "color" of buff (tan brown with white) and a color of light green- blue for the energies of intelligent light. In this way, you are not only drawing on different colors, types, and "directions" of light, you are layering them one on another and within each other. It is perfectly reasonable to draw those colors out into either a mandala or a pattern with each of the different types of light depicted with different patterns, such as the dark sinusoidal light being a swirl or spiral, the auric light drawn as an arc of pure color, the buff color surrounding them both, and the light green-blue of the intelligent light depicted in the center core of the drawing.

This will not be art! Some of the color combinations may not be at all to your taste, but they will be the colors you need. You don't need to stare and stare at them: just allow your gaze to rest on the image once you have drawn it, perhaps for a few minutes before meditating, allowing the colors to work. The colors will change over time in any event, sometimes subtly and sometimes profoundly, such as the Etheric light-color needing to be vivid red-orange and the auric color a bright clear yellow: these changes will be automatic, though you will need to pay attention. Usually a week of one set of colors is enough, and then you re-draw your color pattern. And although you can think of healing as you gaze at the colors, it is not necessary: by asking the brain cells or the nerve cells to tell you what color they need, you are working with them quite directly.

Humanity's Healing Potential:

MG: What is there to know about Humanity's true potential to stretch its limits and create miracles beyond imagining?

NT: Realizing that miracles are possible is surely the beginning! On a practical, human level, becoming aware of the increasing energy and comprehension within your DNA and promoting it through prayer, meditation and imagery is the next step. Contemplating what the masters and saints in the world could do is another door into the further limits of healing and imagination. Also, accepting the responsibility for breaking down your own barriers to healing, whether past-life issues, genetic patterns, soul-agreements and even subconscious pay-offs allows you to break through your barriers to health. Spending time each day to listen to your intuition, asking for healing energies in dreams and learning to trust in the Divine Presence gives you yet more keys.

But the thing that most needs to be known about the true potential for healing is that for miracles to be enfolded within Time in the four dimensions of physical experience, they must be given a way to relate to Time, paradoxically through Timelessness. And your DNA is the human point of translation between Timelessness and Time. The pineal gland works with the "space" of the enfolded dimensional geometries. Yet the DNA quite properly uses the Torsion Field of Translation to intersect human consciousness with all the aspects of Time I have mentioned before, such as the "colors" of Time and the temporal haloclines, as well as more that I have not discussed. When you are able to open into your DNA, when more of it is activated and "awake," then first of all you can relate to Time differently. Healing will be accomplished more rapidly; your body will age more slowly; "frozen" time will be cleared with much more ease and Karmic patterns will be comprehended, given Grace and removed or enhanced, elegantly.

And this is only the beginning. Positive habits will be learned more readily, and negative habits including addictions will have less allure and thus less effect. Your emotions will be more balanced and your outlook far more benign and positive. You will be able to program your sleep, increase your lucid dreams and be able to remember things more fully and accurately, even to the point of having a selectively eidetic memory. In addition, you can choose which abilities and skills you want to enhance, increasing and refining any and all of your physical senses.

When your DNA is activated, your may speak to it directly and be sure of its response. You may work directly with your genome and paragenome, changing everything from congenital birth defects to your eye or hair color, though as these changes would all take about the same amount of time and energy, it would be far more efficient to use your focus for more important things. Moreover, you would already know this because, with a surer sense of yourself, you would not need outer recognition for your own sense of value.

Genius, exalted creativity, physical prowess and deep compassion will all be possible when your DNA becomes open to communicating with you again. Greater control of your hormones will be possible, resulting in anything from a much more even response to the angst of adolescence to renewed fertility and self-control of that fertility, as well as easier pregnancy and birth. In a very real way the body will be able to automatically take the place of pharmaceuticals through its innate wisdom; as we said above, there will be far less addiction or any need to pursue addictive substances. Allergies will be managed quickly, whether in the beginning of life or at the time of exposure until they become a thing of the past. Psychosomatic issues such as eating disorders, body dysmorphic disorder, IBS or and even Alzheimer's may be removed through the agency of an awakened DNA. In addition, many forms of psychosis, sociopathic tendencies or schizophrenia will be more readily recognized and at least ameliorated if not entirely cured. Issues resulting from strokes, brain damage through accidents or toxins will be corrected much more quickly as well as epilepsy, MS, cerebral palsy and Parkinson's. Cancer will not only be detected more quickly it will be healed readily.

And when all these things have changed, when all these things are possible and accomplished, when your body no longer seems to be a prison but becomes instead a willing and responsive friend, what will you choose to do? Granted, for a long while healing will still take time, though as you become more proficient in working with your awakened and responsive DNA it will need less and less time. Granted, accidents may still happen, but they will be fewer and fewer because emotional, Karmic or issues of misperception will become fewer as well. You will at last feel a part of the Earth and its many environments, being able to live in more climates with far less impact on the Earth's resources; as a side bonus, you will able to understand other living things more freely and completely as well.

In short, what would you choose to do if you found yourself in Earth's Paradise?

Living Within and Creating with the Natural Self
(As Explained to Nikola Tesla by Carl Jung)

Key Points: Not simply a static collection of your attributes, the Natural Self shifts constantly from the enfolded to the unfolded realms of Reality, responding to what you have discovered and experienced. Much of your True Self shone out from you when you were a baby, yet you became human to learn fully human maturity. When the human self gets damaged, healing is not straightforward, partly because of emotions' lingering effects. Blame is something given, but taking responsibility is to acknowledge your actions: taking responsibility actually keeps the human self suppler, because you do not remain stuck in old hurts or emotional confusion, but rather take charge of yourself. You can recapture much of your original Natural Self through creativity, dreams and welcoming "unofficial" information. Your own True and Natural Selves are not alien to you, and both are expressions of joy.

Subheadings:

- The Identity of the Natural Self

- The Innocent Nature of the True Self

- Emotions and the Challenge of Healing the Damaged Self

- Innocence: Ending Blame, Cultivating Imagination and Accepting Unofficial Inputs

- Beauty, Splendor and Guarding Your Self

- Lessons about the Natural Self

- The True Self

- Experiencing the Natural Self and the True Self

The Identity of the Natural Self:

The Natural Self is an agile acrobat: living simultaneously in the enfolded and unfolded dimensions, it scintillates in the ever-changing fields of the Collective Unconscious, the genetic/Akashic data in your human body as well as the psychically transferred fields and forms of emotions, memories and purposes received from everyone around you. As changeable as the dancing patterns of shadows in the forest, the Natural Self flickers constantly, yet is blithely constant: it changes its area of impact continually and yet expresses itself with a steady, resonant effect. This Self retains its identity through all the infinite possibilities of alternate realities, constantly shifting that identity in response to its manifested conditions, yet rarely losing its sense of "I."

The Natural Self is intelligent, creative, adaptable, mystical and spiritual. Precocious, inventive, intuitive, determined and full of purpose, this Self has joy and curiosity, empathy and courage at its core. Strong and sensitive, the Natural Self re-creates its connections to and relationships with living things and Life's own love of its Self with free self-confidence. Scrupulously honest and as fair as circumstances demand, the Natural Self is eager to look for humor and joy in all things, retaining its integrity. It is the Self you wake up to each morning before you start thinking, worrying or planning. It is the Self that regards the world with a sense of grace. Its root is the True Self, which represents the amalgam between your human being and the infinite, divine Becoming through the ethereal substance of your soul.

The true Guides and Spiritual Masters for humanity were all presenting the Natural Self and the True Self, particularly those Masters and Saints that expressed Divine Love. That is one way you can tell a true Master from a false prophet: is the message of any prophet, self-proclaimed or otherwise, one of love with respect, love with empathy, love with strength and the love that shows its true power in peace? Then it is Divine Love, and not the kind of selfish love that a damaged human being will represent. Damaged love shows itself in draconian rules, emotional extortion, rigid hierarchy and exclusions. The conundrum that human unnaturalness and the inhumanity of perversion, vice, cruelty and malicious violence can spring from the sweet ground of the Natural Self's innocence and trust has been a puzzle for countless centuries. However, any child born clearly it has its past-life memories and habits, its wounds and terrors: these always will have an effect, especially if something was not resolved before incarnation. Thus, healing the human self means to heal the Natural Self and recover the True Self.

You might think that going back Home to the Heavenly Source and being held in the tremendous Love with which every soul is bathed, should cleanse all your human Selves and make them new again. Surely Divine Love is obliged to wipe away all stains with its purity and all hurts by healing them, is it not? Surely the perfect Integrity of the Whole *must* re-integrate and refresh even the most battered soul? If we come from Heaven, mayn't our self be renewed? And the answer is that of course it may. And yet at the same time, the damage that was done in manifestation as an incarnate being on Earth represents an enigma that can best be solved on the ground upon which it was created. Even though much can be done in the enfolded dimensions to heal what has happened to it, the soul can only completely solve the problems of the Earth on the Earth, within 4-D manifestation. That is part of the reason why your Natural Self has the agility it has.

The Innocent Nature of the True Self:

The essential nature of the True Self is innocence, but I must define that here. You are not more innocent if you are more childish: you touch innocence when you become more child-like. There is already too much childishness in the world today as it is, because there are so few adults in the world today. The strains of raising a child have been so heavy, unremitting and unsupported for so long, that you do indeed have children raising children: with tiny, nuclear families, there are few wise ones available anymore and immaturity is too often presented as a standard for life's choices.

Indeed, if you have a child "so that it will love me totally," you are in for a heartbreaking shock: the baby is, and must be, limited in its ability to express, act, and communicate, much less understand a young adult's longing need for kindness and caring. The fact that the baby's memory of its heavenly Source shines all around it does not mean that the child automatically knows how to give that light to you. You should never expect that love from a child, whether it is a child in body or just in emotional age: every child must be self-referent, self-centered and even oblivious to others until it remembers its own Natural Self in its own time. You may understand where I am going: the True Self I describe is the divinity within the Self that can understand, value, and train the physically-based impulses of "Me and mine!" into maturity. Whereas the childish Self manipulates others for what it needs because it must, the True Self considers others because it is able to do so.

When you mature the Natural Self into the True Self, then you can have empathy, because you are sufficiently aware of your Self to

201

know what your true feelings are *and* that there are others that might feel as you do under the same circumstances. With the True Self you find it easy to be honest: in fact you are quite surprised that anyone would need or want to lie, prevaricate, shade the truth or play confidence games. The idea simply does not occur to your True Self and confuses the Natural Self profoundly. Remembering your source in Truth, you are often puzzled and mystified by anything other than truth, honesty, integrity and character. You remember what you have learned from the mistakes you have done before, recalling that action creates reaction as inevitably as gravity: not in judgment but because there is a real boundary between right and wrong, for boundaries are the genuine nature of reality.

When you are in the True Self you feel it is silly enough to do something stupid the first time, even though that might lead to learning what *not* to do by the foolish action's result. You feel it is even sillier to do the same wrong or incorrect thing the second time, because certainly you could have learned from it the first time? But the notion that you keep doing the incorrect thing out of defiance is quite hard for the True Self to understand. That you could keep on doing the wrong things: the cruel, unkind, thoughtless, vicious or harmful things, not only once for the sake of learning but numerous and continual times, seems entirely absurd. What would be the point of causing pain to others in the first place, much less again? What would be the point in harming yourself again and again? Of course the reason is because of the totally mistaken idea learned from others: that hurting others will make you feel better.

In your innocence, you are shocked when others hate you on sight or even just because of your name or family. You are astonished that others would lie to you and to others, simply in order to hurt you. Your True Self does not realize how easy it is to be persuaded into thinking that a lie is truth or even that you could learn to lie to yourself. Innocence's clarity believes only what it knows: truth, integrity, honesty and compassion. When those qualities are lost or made into lies, truth becomes damaged and so also does your Natural Self, your True Self's representative on Earth. The Natural Self is the sense of who you are and why you act as you do; the Natural Self holds what moves you and changes you as well as what motivates you and where you feel "at home." In some respects this Natural Self is as hard to define as Consciousness, but at the same time it is a recognizable part of your identity. Certainly, it can feel hurt, as well as joy, quite distinctly.

Emotions and the Challenge of Healing the Damaged Self:

When your inner self, the Natural part of who you feel yourself to be, is injured, the main challenge is to regain your poise and stability. You do this by realizing what your True Self is and what the lie is. Your True Self can only be found through your own self-honesty, your attitude of integrity and reaching into your courage, for all of these are intrinsic aspects of the True Self upon which the Natural Self is formed. Your True Self is where your strength lives, for your True Self is your better nature, the angel within you.

It is valid to say that human beings are the angels of the Earth: strong, bright angels that have learned, loved and dared so much that they have willingly stepped forward to walk the shadowy halls of 4-D reality's hologram. You have become physical in order to reveal the true nature and perfect stillness of the Divine Mind within the tumult of vibrations, forces and forms. You had the courage to step forward into blurry dimness: the places where confusion, misunderstanding, miscommunication and perplexity may burden you every day. You had love enough to seek and reach for the truth of your own nature and to reach for the true natures of those around you. You have enough trust in the Divine Intention to deal with lack, fear, loss and misery. And thus many of you illustrate the truth that the Divine Nature can be distilled into true comprehension only within this phantasmagoria of physical reality.

Anyone who has studied the subject of memories, emotions and feelings as a profession or in the patterns of his or her own life understands that emotions, however strong or slight, are incredibly durable despite the passage of time. As shocks to the physical system create little bits of "frozen" time in the cellular memory, those minute superconducting loops of emotional Time also blur your temporal engagement in Time because they, too, are actually outside of Time. Physical, emotional, mental or spiritual abuse can also cause "cankers" of emotion and feeling: little scars in the soul where the Self is unable to move freely, either within Time or apart from it. Your inner Natural and True Selves are multi-dimensionally wide and deep, strong and powerful, but the costs of living on the Earth in the particularly low-level, semi-conducting edges of four-dimensional expression can be incredibly high. If you want to return to any natural innocence, you need to release the emotional scars first through honest self-discovery and the balm of kindness.

You generally keep an old pain with you because it is not resolved: you have not understood it and thus have not been able to return it to a state of healing through your own divine self's Grace. For some, this Grace manifests as comfort, as with a therapist or healer, though perhaps it may manifest as rigorous self-searching. For others, you simply need to understand what your parents went through in their own lives to realize that the harm caused by incompetent parenting was not engineered in order to harm you specifically, nor do your friends and enemies hurt you without the cause of their own pain. Granted, it is similar to understanding why someone let the horse into your living room: even though you still have to clean up the dung, the other person and the horse might become blameless. Yet if there is past-life Karma in contracts, agreements or vendettas, you might spend lifetimes trading pain back and forth, until one of you stops the blame.

Innocence: Ending Blame, Cultivating Imagination and Accepting Unofficial Inputs:

For that is one of the essential things that may help you to reclaim your original innocence: you can cease to blame others and work instead with the results to reconcile and change them. Blame diverts the mind from the task at hand and wastes energy, breeding defensiveness and arguments, even shame and humiliation: none of those things help to heal or change anything. Granted, if you find someone responsible for some trouble, you usually feel he is the one that "must" clean it up: you don't want to clean it up for him or her. However, responsibility differs from blame in this essential way: blame is something given but responsibility is something owned. If you have done something wrong: something illegal, immoral, unkind or negligent and you realize what the action has cost you and others then you have taken responsibility and can respond to the need that your actions have created. However, if you are blamed for something, whether or not you have done it, you immediately get defensive and too often shut down any healing process. For surely defensiveness is never healing in much the same way as being right is never the same thing as being healed.

Indeed, when you have been blamed too often you can refuse to take responsibility for anything: you are too afraid to "own up" because all "responsibility" has come with blame and the pain of being punished, sometimes unjustly. And punishment itself is an assault. Dealing with assaults takes energy, yet this energy could be used to solve the problem and move on. Like the old Buddhist story of the two monks, when they meet a woman on the road and they see she cannot cross the ford. The master takes her up, carries her across and goes on. But the student frets and worries for miles afterwards until they make camp and then protests, "Master! I am so surprised you did that: Our Order is not supposed to touch women." The master said, "Then why have you been carrying her all this time? I left her there on the other side of the ford." If action can become clean and clear again because blame is let go, this re-opens your innocence: the ability to respond to present conditions and move forward feely within your integrity and your clear sense of responsibility. When you do not need to blame others to ease your pain, you can let the hurts go: you don't need to hang onto them in order to throw them back into a miscreant's face.

Another way to re-open your innocence is to be open to wonder, mystery and astonishment through imagination. This requires that you give yourself time to be aware of things in unexpected ways. If you are already imaginative and creative, it is much easier: you might practice picking up three normal, everyday objects: a bowl, a pillow, a shoe, and put them together in unusual ways. Make up stories about how the three of them might converse with one another or what a creature from another planet might think of finding the three objects or how that creature might find them and when. As it has been said elsewhere: "Imagination is the Master Key to the Inner Worlds," and so it is: scientists have that Key as much as artists; parents have that Key as much as prophets.

The purpose of imagination is not necessarily to produce, to create objects or works of art: the reason for imagination and creativity is to shake your mind away from its static, well-worn channels. If you are not used to "making things up," this will seem stiff, silly and artificial at first. But if you take every opportunity, every chance to approach your daily life in new ways, your soul will expand a little more and engage with you more readily. And the soul, of which your True Self is a part, is the real source of your innocence: the innocence that can hold several lifetimes of experience and still see things with refreshed vision, with hope and Grace again. With this innocence you can live in the moment and see each person as just that one person, each thing as just that one thing, neither as a group nor as the past has colored it but new each time instead.

A third way to recover your original innocence is to be willing to open to, receive, and perhaps embrace "unofficial" inputs: dreams, daydreams, imagination, outré impressions, unexpected impulses and "uncorrelated" data. You will not only literally add new dimensions of information to your human experience you also will be more able to understand which aspects of Divinity you have used to make your True and Natural Selves. Realizing the divine Core of your Humanity eases helplessness and fear; touching the core of Love within you frees your own love enough to change the meaning of everything, because you become the Actor, not the one who is acted upon. You even become more aware of your intrinsic Magic.

Beauty, Splendor and Guarding Your Self:

And when you have a source of beauty and splendor inside yourself, you are far less likely to be tempted to look for your sense of autonomy in the darker and more dangerous places of your psyche: the impulses that lead to abuse, arrogance and tyranny. You will no longer have an empty place inside of you that needs to be perpetually, impossibly, infinitely filled with things, control, entitled demands or abusing others. When you firmly embrace your angelic nature again and truly own it as yours, this will create a profound internal shift in your sense of self. You will feel far freer to let yourself be real.

And if, in addition to feeling sure of the presence of angels, you can also begin to welcome the Earth-sourced, numinous spirits: elves, fairies, sylphs, kobolds, brownies or other non-physical spirits and entities that would willingly work with you without harming you, then your loneliness for the higher-energy realms can ease even more. Most of these numinous ones, being parts of the direct Intelligence of the Goddess, are responsive to many subtle aspects of the real conditions of the physical world of the Earth. As we discuss below, when you can tell you which element is your native place of comfort: Air, Water, Fire, Earth or Ether, it is easier to discover which of these you wish to perceive and can perceive, as well as those you can work with joyfully.

In Lemuria, every child was told which element he or she worked with naturally: this can be determined in these days by looking for elemental trines in your astrological chart, as well as other methods. But in Lemuria, there was far more connection between Humanity and the Elemental Spirits: indeed, the intelligences within those Goddess-sourced spirits would assist the child and then the adult in all his endeavors. As was described in Appendix Three of Volume Two, creative people may work with the Helper-elves. These are positive entities that are able to work with human beings and do so because, the less strained and fraught with unmet needs and frustration human beings are, the more likely you will be empathic, considerate and kind to other living things and to your own self. In addition, to create beauty exalts the human being and soul, changing the world into a new pattern of positive energy. Positivity is indeed the genuine desire of the Core Source of Being: to shine its wonder, power, light and love into its own edges and beyond, even into the dimmest of manifested worlds.

However, you must be the guardian of your own gateway at the same time you approach the universe with innocence's utter trust. Innocence is quite a different thing than being unable to learn from experience! Your psychic, emotional, mental and spiritual gates need practicality and openness together, guarding your Self's boundaries like the two pillars of Mercy and Severity, though certainly these pillars must be balanced. Much as you cannot walk far if you look back and check every step you have taken forward, you cannot explore the unknown if you distrustfully demand continual proofs, guarantees, sureties and explanations at every venture into the unknown by demanding that Mystery explain its nature in the terms of the known.

On the other hand, if you take in all inputs without discernment, you allow a chaotic mixture of energies and identities that cannot be evaluated properly: these can confuse or harm you. If you use no discernment in your search, it creates a monochromatic mass that can be worth less than nothing. For nothing, at least, has potential. Everything cannot move forward: it's everything and thus there is no space through which to move *towards* anything. If every experience is taken in without assessment, all spaces in the heart and mind are filled: there is no longer any room for wonder, mystery or even innocence itself, which, of course, was the original purpose of the exercise. Facile, flexible, lithe and impressionable in its integrity, the Natural Self is wisest about this balance of trusting and learning, discovering and integrating, because it can be relied upon for guidance to the degree that it recognizes its divine origins.

Lessons about the Natural Self:

You can learn many things both gracious and ungracious about both the Natural and True Selves from children, but it is wise to take care that these children's needs do not remind you too sharply of your own. When incompetent parenting, social bias and disenfranchisement, abusive family members or neighbors mar your intrinsic Natural Self, you must fight to free that Self from the damage that has been passed on to you. The deceptions with which the Divine Being has enclosed its infinite, monadic Self have the power of the dimension of Identity within them: they must. And so these deceptions seek to augment their own "lives," feeding on the light, strength and love of other living things, because they must expand their own existence much as would any other living creatures, from mice to microbes.

So to be human is to be at once a deceiver and to be deceived, to be a thief and to be stolen from, to create fear and to be afraid and to forget that these shadows are not your Self but rather what has happened to you. If you are able, it is far better to search for innocence inside of yourself. Choose to live in the moment with your full adult mind and your emotions. Perceive each experience you encounter as though for the first time. Trust the wordless inputs of intuition, psychic awareness, otherworldly guidance and instructions; finally, choose to be continually aware of your own divinity and its challenge of discerning truth from illusion.

In situations of stress, abuse, danger or terror, children naturally do everything they can to reduce if not regulate the inputs that are beyond their ability to understand. While that early lesson can become so ingrained that it becomes dysfunctional avoidance, you can retain that power to choose your focus as an adult. In other words, you can take your childhood experiences and learn from them, instead of being directed by them. For this reason alone the child-self is not synonymous with the Natural Self: the Natural Self must be at once crafted from your human experiences and also be received from the Intelligence of the higher dimensions. Healing is found in these dimensions, as are comprehension and understanding. Thus, to not only conceive of these higher dimensions but to perceive them as well, you need enough clarity of mind, integrity of purpose and ability to train yourself. However, except for astonishing examples of psychic and emotional prodigies, few children have the breadth and depth of mind, feeling and experience necessary to do this kind of focused work.

The True Self:

Searching for your True Self may be done at any time in your life, though some children know of its existence from an early age, realizing the difference between right and wrong intuitively. Some of these children might even be a trial to their parents, reminding the father to come to a full stop at the stop sign or the mother to finish something she had promised to do. The best time to begin to seek out your True Self is actually in your early teens, say eleven or twelve. However, you can do this search when you become an adult, at eighteen, forty or any time when circumstances allow and you are inspired to do so.

When properly approached, the True Self needs no religion, philosophy, ideology or social strictures to form it or through which to discover it: it is your natural possession and is thus unique to you and the currents within your soul. The True Self expresses itself in graciousness, aplomb, kindness, empathy and selflessness. The great, inspired teachers of humanity lived in both the True and Natural Selves simultaneously.

The essential point here is that your True Self and your Natural Self is not at all foreign to you, though these selves have often been put aside for the purposes of society and those that wish to control others within that society. The reasons for wanting to belittle, encumber and debilitate the Natural Self's individuality and strength or the True Self's natural honesty and compassion are legion, thus are too vast for this article to address. Suffice to say that someone that is like a hollow reed can be blown down by the wind of someone's will and used all too readily. But even a sapling takes more effort to break, much less a fully mature tree. The True Self is your soul's own strength, giving you the courage and wisdom you need.

Experiencing the Natural Self and the True Self:

And your Natural Self is not at all hard to find when you look for it. This Self easily works with templates, archetypes and all human patterns. Your Natural Self knows what it means to be any type of human being, from infant to Wise Elder, from rebellious adolescent to Caring Parent. When allowed its personal scope it can empathize with and understand all Humanity because this Self recognizes its

209

true origins within the human experience. Given its natural scope, this Self can be child-like when it's needful and responsible when necessary; it can be wise when needed and foolish when it chooses. When you live from your Natural Self you allow your human ego to ask for help when it is needed as well as knowing when to rely on your own strength. Sensitive and receptive to Wonder and Mystery, you will most frequently have a surer sense of purpose with this Self.

You are most aware of your Natural Self when you are most aware of your own humanity. When you are most aware of your impact upon Humanity and your own purposes, you touch the edge of your True Self within the Natural Self. It is natural to live in the present; it is true to live in Time's infinite integrity, with each moment riding on eternity like bubbles on the surface of a stream. It is natural to love, have joy, create pleasure and create with pleasure; it is truthful to love with respect, have joy with grace, create pleasure with wisdom and to create when you are totally absorbed with Divine Intention. Stillness is natural; peace is true. Joy in movement is natural; gracious actions are true.

When you are in your True Self the most common sensation is joy: not only the delight in being alive, but the delight of seeing your origin, the Divine Being, shining out in the everyday things of your world. The sun glinting off a window, a bird singing through the mists of a spring morning, someone's laugh you overhear or a story of someone's honest courage, can be enough to open the bright center in your heart: the center of your own Divine Compass, the lodestone of Who You Are. When you are in your True Self, you cannot help but feel others' pain; you cannot help but comprehend why hurting someone is unwise at least and ultimately counter-productive, because every harm you deliberately do another cuts away another part of your own soul. When you touch the core of this True Self, you will touch your own wisdom and knowing; you will be at ease in your own skin and you will never feel quite abandoned, for you will always have the sense that you are rooted in something deeper than you can see.

Training Children the Lemurian Way
(As Explained to Nikola Tesla by Carl Jung)

Key Points: Being so recently arrived from the heavenly Source, children take time to understand Earth's strictures and limitations. However, misfortune, chronic illness and other tragedies can train the child's soul in compassion and courage. The hardest part of incarnate life is grief and loss. Grief can be particularly heavy for the children who were Lemurians and are burdened with numerous past-life memories, but it can also be a most transformative experience. However, blurring, silencing or anesthetizing grief keeps the soul from the presence of Divine Compassion. In Lemuria, children were given at least three essential pieces of information from the wise in the community: their elemental nature, their important past lives and a talisman representing their purpose in life. You could reproduce the Lemurian methods of childrearing today, but you have already improved upon them: over the centuries, you have learned to withstand more grief and loss with more courage and strength than most original Lemurians ever had to experience.

Subheadings:

- Your Heavenly Origins

- Poverty, Misfortune and Betrayal

- Grief and Loss

- Grief and the Divine Being

- Working with Grief the Lemurian Way

- The Lemurians Now

- The Soul's Palimpsest of Past Lives

- "Why Don't Children Come with Instruction Manuals?"

- Parenting in Modern Times

- The Lemurian Method

Your Heavenly Origins:

As we said above, in order to begin to understand children it is important to consider whence they came: a place where everything is the way you want it to be when you desire it and precisely how you wish it. There is no cold, heat, sickness, discomfort or pain. There is no loss, loneliness, judgment or castigation. There are no shocks or surprises that you do not plan for, nor is there betrayal, disappointment, duplicity or any kind of abuse. You can live simply or in circumstances that your broadest imaginings could not begin to encompass. You are always with those you love and you know that you are always loved fully without having to earn it.

Because there are no irritations, there is no reason to learn forbearance. There is no need to be attentive, empathic or even aware of anyone else if you do not wish. You are always remembered, never forgotten, nor do you need to worry about forgetting anyone else. There is neither impatience nor unmet needs there; there is no confusion, implacable demands or any kind of misunderstanding. Because there is nothing but truth there, you need never quite know what honesty is. You are always treated with especial kindness: the Divine Attention and Regard bathe you continually in specialness, simply because it is God's true nature to love you unconditionally. In short, you are never frustrated in anything you wish to see, do, or experience. In physical life, your mother's body gives heavily of its self to allow your soul to take incarnate form, but any child's true womb is Heaven and its soul. Indeed, generally speaking, the soul only brushes against this tiny body as it forms and may not even enter it until the breath does.

Because there is no fear in Heaven there is neither need nor chance for courage. Because there is no confusion, there is no need for understanding. Because there is no frustration and all whims are gratified in the time it takes to think of them, there is no possibility of patient, careful work towards creating something unique. Nor is there any need to build something painstakingly over time so that you can understand it with full elegance and at depth. You always live how you choose: thus you never learn how to live with discomfort or poverty, cold or heat or sleeping in the rain.

You are never judged, so you cannot understand being judged; you are never put down, so you never need build yourself up with self-confidence, determination and persistence. Because you are

212

never abused, disappointed or shocked, you cannot really know your soul's true resilience. Because you are always special there, you do not learn how to *become* special: special in whom you are, how you act, what you do, how you do it or because of how much you love. Because you are continually accepted and understood, you do not need to understand anyone else. You cannot learn how to see things as another person sees them because you do not need to learn to value their insight as much as your own.

Poverty, Misfortune and Betrayal:

Many say poverty is such a terrible, unkind and unfair thing: surely it makes living in this planet most difficult. It takes away your health, your value in your community and too often your own self-respect very much too soon. Poverty is a loss that replicates itself blindly and does not scruple at beggaring any part of your human self, including your heart. However, poverty can act as an exacting focus by which you can determine what really matters to you, what is worth working and fighting for, what is truly needful and what is merely raiment for the ego: a show of false light and not genuine love. It can reveal the true nature of kindness; it can reveal the price of loss.

Many say that misfortune is unfair: terrible accidents, children whose bodies are damaged by genetic codes gone wrong or through a parent's addictions; betrayals that cost fortunes, lives and love as well as causing cascades of misery; wars, famines, plagues; being born the "wrong" color, nationality, religion or family so that you can never get an even break and are continually under suspicion no matter what the color of your heart: all of these excoriate the soul and sometimes lead to lifetimes of misery that haunt the soul's dreams. And yet in the crucibles of misfortune your soul can find its steel, the determination that keeps you from yielding to anger, depression, rage or the phantasms promised by alcohol, drugs or other addictions. Your soul can find its gold: the beauty, kindness, courage and forgiveness that can be found nowhere else in all the heavenly universes. You discover your strength this way; you discover your patience.

The Earth can be a cruel place. Many agree that betrayal, be it through a confidence game, callous use, misuse, abuse or some heartless, utter rejection of who you are or what you have done, can be the epitome of injustice. Those that have been slaughtered for no other reason than insanity or one man's mad vision; those that have

213

been raped, savaged, used as an example for political purposes or forced to bear impossible burdens from the spiritual debts foisted upon them, have all been treated with excessive cruelty. It is the agony of injustice that particularly causes you to demand: "How can a loving God *permit* this?" Many, so many, reject or betray God when faced with such injustices, repudiating even the chance of trusting the Divine, much less believing in it. For how could a God that permits atrocities, villainies, desperate insanity and cold-hearted cruelties deserve any trust? You are told, "God is Love." Why would Love permit these things?

To say that you can understand the light better for having seen the darkness may be somewhat true, but it seems such a poor thing with which to counterbalance the agony. To say that this is God's Own Experiment with His Inner Knowing, that only through driving us away from Him can He know how far His Love can reach, hardly seems to offer any solace. Surely, could not courage and heroism be more easily bought? Surely, could not kindness be an easy thing, instead of something limned with suffering and anguish?

Yes, the answer is certainly yes: courage and kindness can be found in the simple, little things and do not need to be depicted in broad canvases of blood, terror or pain. But the unfailing power of true forgiveness needs the challenge of such heinous crimes, abuse and despicable actions in order to fathom its true depth, strength, value and cost to the soul. It needs to overcome the challenges of the implacable craving for revenge, the bitter hatred rising from the harms done. It needs the utter strength of accepting the unacceptable: not because what was done could be *made* acceptable but because you realize that you are greater than the harm that has been done to you. This kind of forgiveness needs to know that judgment is not the answer: rather, the human answer is that there is true healing for all of the pain.

Grief and Loss:

Loss surely seems the cruelest price for having life. It is hard enough to leave the pleasant comfort of Heaven, missing the love and loved ones remaining there and losing the clear sense of God's constant, beneficent support. To find love on Earth, to craft it, nurture it in spite of the heavy difficulties, frailties or strains that love on Earth demands and to keep your integrity in the search, is challenging enough. But then, *must* you also have to withstand seeing your own capacity for love or a loved one on Earth dashed away in some stupid instant, for some idiotic mischance, much less because of malice, injustice or rage? How can you endure doing without the love of Heaven and then also surrendering the fragments of love that you do find here?

And worse is the sundering that leaves you lost and unknowing, hung between fear and hope, despair and joy: when you do not know what has happened to your loved ones, you must live in an agony of mystery and fear. Such pain cuts a jagged wound into the soul and leaves it bleeding. There is no grief deep or wide enough to hold the pain. Sometimes the only thing that keeps you alive is the fact that your body is particularly used to breathing. In the face of this, should there be any wonder that the angels are in awe of your courage? Is there any wonder that human beings are considered so special by so many? Yet, still: whatever could be the Divine Purpose behind loss and grief?

The price of this pain is terrible. However, you have allowed it to create something full of meaning because loss deepens the human soul. And the deeper the soul, the more it can contain the Divine Being in a living form that can be aware of and recognize its Self. By experiencing loss in all its piercing brutality you may re-create your soul as one of the Hearts of God. Not as a fragment or sliver of that Awareness but as one of the most loving, responsive and sensitive parts of that paradoxically separate Unity of Singularities, becoming a truly responsive part that can open wonders even deeper than pure creativity. Without these living, deeply responsive parts of its Self, the Divine Being could not expand or grow properly into its vast Becoming. Grief does more than give focus to significance: it allows things to become specifically precious so that they are not blurred by the infinite infinities of sameness. Loss, when healed, is like any pain: its significance is remembered, given value and meaning, yet pain itself is let go.

And loss, like pain, is not without purpose, even though your human mind may be opaque to its value: loss is the dearly bought gift of the Infinite Self's love for its Self. Grief lives deep in the cells of all living things, manifesting in all species, because it is so important. Grief is not an emotion: it is a portent of significance and a poignant reconnection to the touch of the true Divine Awareness and Love. Hidden in every grief is this Divine exaltation: that when a loving, responsive being experiences loss, that searing agony actually

215

increases aspects of Love that cannot be magnified in any other way. And because Love is magnified, healing becomes more complete. The value and meaning of your life and the life or lives of your loved one become more vivid, more real, calling up deeper parts of yourself in order to deal with the shock.

Grief and the Divine Being:

We do understand how cruel grief can be and how hard it is to bear; anyone human understands. But the ability to withstand grief, to face it, work through it and allow it to create new space in the mind, soul and heart is one of the countless reasons why sentient creatures have evolved. Yet deeper than any reason for grief's meaning is to uncover the love that overleaps separation, by which all souls may return. Loss was not crafted, allowed or permitted because of the pain it created, not even for as worthy a purpose as expanding the divine Knowing. And even though loss gives Time different meanings and shapes it in countless ways, Time is not why grief was created. Loss was created in order to fashion bridges from the finite to the infinite though emotional honesty's purity: the purity of the moment when there is nowhere else to look for truth or solace but the Loving Presence of God.

This is why you must beware the dangers of damping, blurring or silencing grief. Not only does unfelt, unmet grief become a wound that cannot heal, like the wound of the Grail legend's Fisher-King, it saps the human energies of soul-strength, emotional strength, mental acuity and spiritual evolution. Indeed, a soul that has not grieved properly can no longer be supple and responsive to the Divine Intention: it calcifies instead, becoming by degrees mulish, uncommunicative, resentful, jealous and vicious with rage. All advice for damping the effects of grief: being told to "Just get over it," or "It has been long enough," or, "Keep busy, and find someone or something new," cannot allow grief its growth, maturation and fruition. Grief must find its way through and past the pain, for only then can it give you the strength and understanding of Grace.

Unhealed grief freezes the time within your human makeup as certainly as shock: because feelings of grief are rooted in your higher-dimensional aspects, whatever is not let go remains and thus has much more leverage than your mind or thoughts. If you heal too quickly, it is like allowing the skin to seal over a puncture wound: if any infection remains, it increases until the body is threatened. To blur your grief by using any type of chemical means beggars both the body and the soul, because the body can turn the unexpressed emotional burden directly into illness and the soul never learns the lesson that grief might have taught.

Whatever pain the psyche has not felt must be revisited fully, else it becomes a psychic apport: a part of the self, once divorced, that must and will express its self at whatever cost and by whatever means necessary. This unhealed pain can even change your reality though its intrinsic, inner Magic: in order to force you to confront those unhealed parts of yourself the hidden, subtle weight of unhealed grief can turn Reality inside out by creating challenges in your environment. Indeed, the grief loses its own humanity by projecting the grieving aspects of your soul into your physical reality as disasters, causing hurt to yourself or others or harm to countless ones unknown. For when you silence grief by flinging it aside from yourself, then you must necessarily fling it towards others, re-visiting the harm you have not dealt with in yourself upon those others, too often your loved ones. In short, if anything keeps grief from its full growth to the fruition that re-opens Grace and Love, grief withers and becomes poisonous, even toxic.

Working with Grief the Lemurian Way:

Grief must be given time and clarity so that you can find your strength within the misery and the gift within the pain. This takes a spiritual sense of will, determination, self-love and pliability as well as the strength to let go and to be vulnerable. Teaching all of these strengths are very much part of raising a child by Lemurian methods: self-resilience paired with self-reliance and at the same time, trust in the wisdom of others and the innate Grace of Reality may all be promoted and uncovered in the child's development. When the child is young, simple instructive stories will serve; when the child is older, examples from both your own experience and your actions will serve. When a child is older still, it may be best to ask him or her to show or describe to you what other way he or she would use to solve the problem of dealing with grief and other heavy emotions.

Ideally, you can allow that child to find his or her own way through loss or grief only when a child is old enough to understand consequences, to think ahead and able to respectfully take into account the possible outcomes leading from a chosen action. For some old-soul children this may be as young as four or five. For others

217

perhaps young in soul-experience that are still wedded to avoiding lessons, blaming others for the outcomes of their creation and being right rather than real, it may take most of a lifetime for them to be mature enough. Maturity can be forced, as when a child must take on more than it should in order to deal with some exigent, demanding or tragic situation, but the best maturity is evolved through deep understanding of the child himself.

If you don't know whether you are dealing with a child that is not only immature but is also attached to avoiding growth, you have a more difficult situation. Children that easily find maturity are those that have had enough human experience to learn why immaturity does not work, for these children also have no vested interest in hanging onto immaturity. They have learned how to identify themselves with their souls and spirits, their creative intention and their own native wisdom, instead of wanting revenge for past wrongs or being so full of leftover rage that they cannot forgive.

The Lemurians Now:

A great many old children of Lemuria have returned and are alive again. You will see them everywhere now: in the grocery checkout line, in offices, hospitals, art colonies and bookstores. These are the ones that "cut to the chase" and do not need the tedium of being shown 1,000 times how not to harm someone: they already know that surely the harm would return to them forthwith. These are the children that watch, consider, learn from others' mistakes and then act; they even ask others' advice before moving ahead. It seems wishy-washy to your current culture that grabs on to instant gratification, instant knowing and "instant" wisdom within some blithe phrase put out for all to see. Patience is not often rewarded in these days. However, introverts will realize that giving proper consideration to action is the way they work naturally.

If you are a Lemurian child, you may or may not be an introvert, but there will be times when you find most people amazingly tedious, frequently bewildering, and sometimes frightening. Dominance games may puzzle and distress you, especially where others do not strive to heal situations or solve them but rather become the brute that attempts to control the situation through intimidation and arrogation. You may be puzzled why so many others seem dedicated to making things more and more difficult for themselves by escalating unworkable situations instead of standing back, getting out of the way of the temporarily insane person and perhaps finding a way to heal the situation in some quiet corner later.

You, true sons and daughters of Lemuria, have empathy, patience and vigorous creativity, yet often you feel tremendous melancholy if not outright depression. The main reason for this is that you often feel profoundly alone, if not abandoned: not necessarily dismissed by your families but rather because you are used to a much deeper sense of community than is generally presented to you in the modern world. As in Carson McCullers' Member of the Wedding, you are looking for the "we of me:" those that are quick to understand what you mean when you say the world frustrates you. You look for people that can think the way you do without hours and hours of explanation.

Unfortunately, some of you, alas, can become so desperate to find a supportive group that you will leap into any group that calls itself a community, even though it is a gang of thugs, drug-users, despots of intolerance and bias or even a religious cult that truly has little of God in it and even less spirituality. Or, seeing the dangers in these things, you might work at building your own eclectic and eccentric group, with greater or lesser success.

For many expatriate Lemurians, the adage that "friends are the family you choose" can be of tremendous help, especially if you are unlucky enough to be born to parents that are less experienced or less mature than you are. You do not do well in chaotic, hyper-rigid, dictatorial or "infantile" families, situations, or countries. You also do not usually do well in families, work or other situations where you have too many demands, particularly conflicting demands that are presented simultaneously. When you look for others of your stripe, look for people that are intelligent mentally and/or emotionally, empathic, naturally considerate, creative, thoughtful and kind.

The Soul's Palimpsest of Past Lives:

The reason why we spent so much time on grief, loss, betrayal and other shocks to the soul is because those shocks last over several lifetimes, particularly in Lemurians. This is partly because so many of you have stepped into numerous difficult lifetimes in order to keep the light alive and it has cost you heavily. But when you discover your past lives, they can reveal what you trust and what you distrust; what you long for and what you reject; what you love and what you fear. As has been pointed out elsewhere: if you dislike a particular country,

219

it may well be because of a horrific life lived there or a life in which you betrayed the innocent. Similarly the countries where you love their artwork, foods, costumes, mores and culture are often places where your lives worked out well. If you are allergic to a certain food or group of foods, this often has a past-life origin; although the DNA of your body appears to cause allergic reactions, your DNA also has the records of your past lives.

So close to the Shift, incoming souls sometimes took on bodies with specific genetic lineages in order to achieve a specific purpose and they may have simply accepted the allergies that were within that particular lineage. So some reactions are just part of the body you have chosen, instead of because of your soul's Karmic patterns. Your past lives are coded in your DNA, certainly, but so are the lives of your ancestors. Thus, there have been times lately when you would take on burdens that were not your own in order to capture the specific DNA pattern that allowed you to excel in music or healing, teaching or emotional intelligence, because that is what you needed to do now. Or you may even have chosen heavy physical or mental trials and burdens so that you would be reminded of compassion and empathy from your direct experience. Your likes and dislikes, skills and preferences, your disabilities and superlative abilities are all clues to the paths your soul has traveled.

Though, especially recently, new issues have been added. Ideally, the X or Y chromosome are as determinative to the body's abilities as is the additional copy of chromosome 21 in Down's syndrome caused by rubella's genetic damage, much less the genes from parents that cause cystic fibrosis or color blindness. In an unobstructed, unadulterated environment, there are true genetic differences between the way a male or a female brain translates and codifies information. However, too many recently added chemical influences have shifted what might have been a clear dichotomy into a shifting, though potentially highly creative, physical expression. The major difficulty with these chemical and hormonal additions is that they are cumulative: the effects increase and become more significant over generations, until the chemicals re-write how the human body grows and expresses itself.

So to speak, the brain is the hardware that allows the soul to express itself on Earth, but outer influences can alter the way the hardware functions. Many toxins, hormones, antibiotics, pesticides and other powerful chemical agents added to your food have created deep physical confusion. These chemical factors have been flooding your living system through many and various agricultural methods, industrial runoff into the water, to say nothing of even the synergistic combinations of separately benign chemicals that have created totally unexpected side effects. So, originally an unusual circumstance that provided a unique opportunity for learning compassion, the ambiguity between the sexes now is a very physical issue.

Yet, even though it must speak through the cells the body has, the human soul speaks quite loudly. This is a challenge for many being born now: they have so many past lives pressing against them in their unconscious memories that they have chosen bodies profoundly altered by the environment, bodies that have been changed without any conscious intention of the persons so affected. Such conundrums deserve compassion and respect: hormones in particular are very powerful substances in themselves and there are many in the environment now. When toxins and chemicals with unknown effects are added, there can seem to be no way to find balance. But of course the answer is compassion: the care and nurturance of a loving family that recognizes the child's intrinsic value as a human being, an expression of a human soul, and wisely embraces the child's differences.

In a responsively evolving society, girls and boys would not be automatically presented with a role they must live within without any effort given to understand their souls' intentions, much less their body's physical aspects. Especially now, when so many old souls are reincarnating, Lemurians among them, nearly all of you remember lives of being male or female, gay, lesbian, bisexual and even asexual: in many there is a deep desire to re-structure your selves and the expectations of your own culture. Life grows by adapting to challenges: this new challenge of unexpected and even undesirable chemical and hormonal influences can be met with expanded compassion and creativity, allowing new wisdom, instead of with fear or blame, that lead only to devaluation and misery. Guided by compassion and wisdom, a life of heavy limitations, confusion or ambiguity can open the soul's courage, transforming human society much for the better.

To quote the Sufi Master Hazrat Inayat Khan, founder of the International Sufi Movement, "Unity, not uniformity." As in our reference to the wall made from irregular, differently-shaped stones, although it takes more time, you can build a better wall with stones that are not uniform. Similarly, a society that understands how the whole can work with amorphous, shifting and highly adaptive methods can become much stronger, more vital and much more responsive. And certainly when you are raising children, whether ancient Lemurians returned or newcomers to the Human experience, none of them are precisely the same, and all of them demand different responses.

"Why Don't Children Come With Instruction Manuals?":

In Lemuria, the wise ones gave three gifts to you and your parents when you were born: your elemental makeup, a psychic reading of your past lives and a description of your purpose in the life you were beginning. These things were deemed essential; along with the child-rearing wisdom the elders had, these all represented your instruction manual. You could always go to the temple to receive updates, have things explained, see whether or not some Karmic arrangements might be changed and seek even more information, especially when your child was growing up enough to consider a trade, vocation or calling.

But the most important gift to the child was the cultural attitude of Lemurian parents towards their children: "This is a soul that has its own history, desires and purposes. This child has chosen to have its purposes and desires fulfilled in the most respectful, caring and elegant way possible by choosing us as his or her parents. This soul may be a former friend or a former enemy: nevertheless it has chosen us to be the ones to launch it successfully." In short, when you were a Lemurian child you were not seen as a reflection of your parents; certainly your were not seen as a reflection of the parents' un-met needs, since the mother and father had already worked with themselves enough to be ready for this priceless opportunity. When you were a parent, you knew that you would not only reflect the child's strengths back to him but also help him to balance or overcome his weaknesses. You sought to learn from the child: how she worked, what she wanted to learn, what he needed to learn; you discovered not only who the child had been but who he might become.

Receiving a workup of your elemental nature determined such things as whether your body might be a Fire type, but your mind might be Air and your emotions Earth. Generally speaking, your parents already knew their own personal elements and this was part of how they knew how to work with you. If your mind's main element was Air, you might respond more readily to logical arguments as reasons for doing what was needed in the family, instead of the demonstrations and examples that might help a child with an Earth mind. If your body was a Fire type, they might know that you were physically more a sprinter than a marathon runner; if your body was a Water type, they might know that you would love to express emotions in movements and that you would tend to be emotionally empathic.

A great deal of this kind of information survived in East Indian Vedic (sidereal) astrology but has been refined somewhat in modern Western (tropical) astrology, especially since so many new aspects such as asteroids have been discovered. Nevertheless, a good elemental practitioner would be able to discern how well your native energy would work in specific situations and which situations you would find difficult to manage. Were you naturally active or contemplative? Were you creative in a fiery way, a flowing, emotional way or did your more Earthlike creativity need long periods of incubation and refinement before it would manifest? Were you particularly mental, curious and mercurial; would you prefer to consider things at length or would you prefer to respond emotionally to solving the creative challenges in your world instead?

As I said, the second reading you would be given was of your past and in some cases future lives. This would help your parents to find out which propensities, desires, skills, lessons or fears from other lives were strong enough to frame the inner structural latticework of your personality. Would you flinch at unkind words or even sudden noises? Or would you thrive on sudden shocks and changes and feel exhilarated by them? In what ways would these past lives and past-life impressions limit or open your inner gifts?

Indeed, if the wise guides and your parents thought it necessary, they would request information directly from your Akashic Field to determine whether or not there were specific agreements, contracts, spiritual, emotional or psychic debts already in place between you and your family members or with someone in the community: in short, they would study your Karma. What healing could be done at this early age was done. Very often methods of training were worked out in advance for the benefit of all, often custom-fit to your elemental type and internal Karmic patterns. This certainly kept several kinds of difficulties and misunderstandings from developing later! Because they knew how you would work best, learn best and thrive best, they

223

would know how easy or difficult it would be for them to work with you freely, even with their differing elemental aspects or their own Karmic patterns.

The third gift you would be given at your birth by those who could discern it would be a talisman or totem that would represent and remind you of your life's purpose: not what was imposed upon you but what you had incarnated to accomplish. Were you a builder, a healer, a creator of beauty, a teacher, or a natural parent? Were you a challenger: someone that could perceive weaknesses in systems and societies, personalities or beliefs so that they could be pointed out and corrected? Was the dearest thing to your soul a sense of justice, joy, inspiration or discovery? Which type of work would nourish your sense of accomplishment mentally and emotionally; which type of work would leave you drained, uncomfortable or confused?

Undoubtedly you can discern much of this information in modern times as well, with astrology, personality tests, psychic readings and even past-life regressions, for yourself and your children. Certainly, much friction can be eased this way. Although, quite frankly, so much more emotional calcification has developed over the centuries of time since Lemuria, that your inner selves have more stalactites of rigid thoughts and more stalagmites of rigid feelings that you had in the beginning. And the current cultures that consider children chattel, possessions, extensions and vindicators of the parents or the parental family lines still cost you heavily: these demands refuse to perceive the child as she or he is. In short, without understanding, there is too much grief and pain for both children and parents.

Parenting in Modern Times:

But this kind of Lemurian upbringing can return quite readily once you decide: "This child is not my child: this child is his or her own being and I need to understand that first. I need to train this child instead of possessing him, using him and then hoping he gets the training he needs out of the atmosphere around him." You need to do everything you can to make sure you are not too busy to take the extra work needed. Children are relatively easy when you start teaching and training from the beginning; adolescents are increasingly difficult though they can still be persuaded. But a poorly trained adult can be totally impossible to change: by then it is frequently far too late.

I do understand that cultures all over the world are geared to a strange mixture of raising children with a sense of their utility instead of their capacity for discovery; where problems are only solved through immediacy instead of patience; child-rearing and guidelines are cobbled together because of expediency, so that parents and children both are given "fix-its" rather than respect and purpose. But all that can change with a modification of your *attitude* and every parent may begin where he or she stands. Alas, I also understand the real price in the present demands of a monetarily skewed culture, where teachers earn almost nothing compared to sports stars and even doctors earn less than politicians, where schools must rely on volunteers simply to function, instead of corporate CEO's depending on charity just in order to find a place to live.

I feel that the first things that must be altered are: the attitude that compels you to fix things *after the fact* rather than at the beginning: that supports roundabout accusations of blame instead of true cooperative problem solving. For both children and parents to thrive, the notion that creating a child with a moment of sexual pleasure is equal to knowing how to raise the child needs to be let go, as well as the notion that if the parents are damaged or incompetent, children are still able to raise themselves well. Other ways in which calcified ideology replaces wisdom need to be reviewed and understood.

Parents deserve not only support but also understanding: children take a tremendous amount of energy, money, time and consistency. But if you, as a parent, have been poorly raised by parents who have themselves been poorly raised, you have to work three times as hard to decipher the instruction manual you were given. Far too often your instructions for life passed on automatically through your own family are a cobbled-together mass of contradictory suggestions, edicts, general data and anachronistic traditions, with sections in ancient emotional languages, very personalized ciphers; hidden secrets and old diary entries that may have nothing whatsoever to do with you. And all of these parts are held together with rubber bands, mixed-in upside down and sideways, presented to you in a frequently quite indigestible whole. It can take a lifetime of diligent work simply to *sort* the mess, much less decipher it!

That so many parents succeed as well as they do is phenomenal in the best of conditions. And if you also have the pure tragedy of being an "undesirable" race, religion, culture or gender, that adds yet another weight to everything you do. If in addition your children or you are afflicted by autism or any other congenital disorder, the load you must carry is increased several times on top of that. Adding

225

inappropriate drug use breaks everything down into hellish misery where the children are blown away like chaff, society becomes strained to the limits of its endurance and beyond: lifetimes of healing may be needed just to begin to recover.

That enough children survive all of this; that enough adults manage in spite of this; that enough families remain whole in the midst of this, shows the amount of stamina that you possess in order to have the courage, strength, patience and determination to succeed in those conditions. The love that succeeds despite all of these burdens will shine out from Earth as brightly as a supernova: your faith, hope and love alter the very nature of the universe and quite frankly exalt the hidden secrets of the Divine Being itself. In the exhaustion, tedium, frustration and despair of the day-to-day, this can sometimes be forgotten. Distracted by the dramas of wounded people, despots and criminals grabbing the attention of the media, too many parts of your modern society forget that in order to raise children of joy, in joy how necessary allowing concern, care, love and patience must be.

The Lemurian Method:

With this in mind, it should not be surprising that several modern methods that parents have crafted themselves are not only a recapitulation of the ancient Lemurian ways, but are an improvement upon them. Certainly the shocks and strains of the last 24,000 years have given you a more meticulous and detailed canvas upon which to work. You know so much about how people can be shortchanged, traumatized and damaged, that you can not only work out ways for healing the situations after the fact, but also how to prevent them. The fact that there is so much cultural interference that removes the support that parents need is a travesty and a tragedy.

As has been pointed out elsewhere, you need far more documentation, training, peer reviews and so on to lay claim to almost any other trade than for becoming a parent, for parenting is thought to be automatic, instinctive and easy. It certainly seems so for animals, but you must remember that the animals that were raised poorly also managed poorly and were usually the first thing a predator would catch. Even the practiced mothers have to yield their offspring to predation, so it is indeed true that the ones that survived did because they knew how to survive particularly well. Human kindness is a superlative quality indeed. However, if kindness is not bolstered and supported by wisdom, the results can be very uneven, from adult children still living at home, gangs of young thugs that seem to provide the young men with the only identity they can find or even those that keep 50 animals in one small house because they are still trying to capture some vanished comfort they were denied long ago.

Rather than the current attention in school as to who has the prettiest or "coolest" things, clothes, electronic devices or hairstyle, it would be far better to pay attention to who has the most patience, forbearance, graciousness, emotional intelligence or courage. Rather than focusing on statistics derived from tests, it would be far better to focus on understanding the child in such a way that you can work with his or her own tendencies for success, thus not rewarding that child with pleasing the teacher, but rather with pleasing his soul. Rather than presenting children with drudgery by rote, training them with discovery through wonder would work so very much better.

A Lemurian child might come to school prepared by already knowing how she worked best, whether in solitary or with groups, instead of the naturally solitary forced to adapt to groups at every turn or the gregarious forced to work alone. Coming to school, a child would already know what his tasks in life were and how he intended to accomplish them. Coming to school, a child would already know how his creativity or her intelligence worked, the skills he came into life with or what kind of training would give her the best ground for her life's purpose. Rather than an extension of the parents, each child would be seen as her own noble self; rather than fulfilling the will of the family, each child would fulfill the will of his own divine spirit. All of these things would be known in advance once the three gifts were given: the child's elemental makeup, past-life history and the talisman of purpose that provided a touchstone upon which the child and her parents could build a life of success and joy.

This is possible now: you do not have to re-create the past of Lemuria, because you have learned so much more in the centuries that have followed. Yet this does demand a choice to re-examine the systems you have now, so that you may change them in accord with your best human abilities.

More on Subconscious and Unconscious Forms of Magic

Key Points: Magic interpenetrates all aspects of human consciousness and your conscious work with Magic is thus affected by the subconscious and unconscious. This creates enmeshed waveguides for both your human and Magical energy, which can have unexpected effects and some of those effects can be manipulated intentionally, for good or for ill. Magic, as it is sourced in higher-energy, enfolded dimensions, can sometimes create insurmountable problems when tainted with unconscious or even subconscious drives. Finding your real, inner self through the subconscious and unconscious can allow you to take Divine Energy in, stabilizing your whole personality. The process of restoring your Magic from within the tangles of the unconscious demands both self-honesty and courage. Both human beings and animals have their own Magic, though this Magic overlaps to a degree. Using the higher-order energies of Grace and Para-light, you can nullify or remove Toxic Magic.

Subheadings:

- Magic and Human Consciousness
- Magic Enmeshed With the Human Sub- and Unconscious
- Meditation #1: Using Positive Primordial Chaos to Heal Your Inner Magic
- Working with Your Subconscious Wave-guides Regarding Magic
- Opening to Mystery to Uncover Your Authenticity
- Encountering Light and Goodness
- Meditation #2: Aligning Your Self With Your Own Core of Truth
- Magic and Animals, Elementals and Other Expressions of Divinity
- Interactive Geometries of Magic
- Using Grace to Re-structure Toxic Magic

• Working with Para-light to Enhance Magical Effects

Magic and Human Consciousness:

Magic is sourced in the Zero dimension, allied to the dimension of Primordial Chaos and focused through the dimension of Identity, in much the same way as your human consciousness. Therefore, Magic deeply interpenetrates the human body, mind, psyche, emotions and spirit. Although it is not human, Magic is a conscious field: it can interpenetrate human consciousness to the point that they affect each other constantly. When Magic becomes entangled with your human unconscious and subconscious mind, in addition to or in spite of your conscious mind's beliefs or intentions, the results may be costly or unexpectedly beneficial.

In experience, a fair number of happy synchronicities are helped by Magic's slope within the enfolded dimensions, as well as your own unconscious intuition. The obverse is true and particularly so when there is a disjunction between your conscious and your unconscious beliefs and ideas about yourself and your intentions, motivations and Magical aptitudes. In this case, when you have a fair Magical aptitude but could never believe in Magic's existence, your Magic follows your unconscious, frequently unexamined, motives and engages your will without your being aware of it. This allows Magic to act out blindly, often quite negatively or at the least very selfishly.

There are even times when Magic is so restricted by your unconscious beliefs that it can actually turn on you: it will help your conflicted unconscious to arrange things so that the *one thing* you desire, work or hope for is precisely the one thing that keeps getting thwarted, trashed or ruined. Yet the little things that do not matter much to you are the only things that work, open up and happen gracefully. This is a situation where Magic itself has become so enwrapped within your unconscious field that it has become enmeshed with quite toxic subconscious and unconscious factors such as hatred, revenge, arrogance, narcissism and domination; or with emotional structures like martyrdom, jealousy, self-pity, bias, bigotry and toxic guilt. Similarly to what happens with addiction, this warped and Toxic Magic can become quite sly, quite frequently disguising its true nature from you and others.

Magic Enmeshed With the Human Sub- and Unconscious:

The difficulty is that when Magic is enmeshed with any of these unconscious factors or structures, this forces it to act in human ways. As being human is not its purpose, Magic becomes in a very real sense insane. Responding to your unexamined human needs, it mingles its own identity with your hidden and unexamined drives, actually altering its purpose and nature in order to adapt to your human passions. As Magic and human consciousness is already linked within the dimension of Primordial Chaos, this enmeshed Magic can become a negatively chaotic force. In its confusion, Magic develops a ghost-identity, patterned after your own unconscious mind, especially the unexamined parts of your rage, anger, despair, despondency or loss. Thus Magic adds its own misshapen energies to your human actions, sometimes super-charging their effects.

The obverse, thankfully, can also be true: even though your conscious mind might be filled with despair, grief, frustration or depression, the positive ghost-form of Magic would underlay this. In this way Magic's M-D slope from the higher dimensions could create anything from an inexplicable optimism in the face of impossible trials, to a life that really works very well despite your grievous complaints, to say nothing of the happy synchronicities mentioned above. Shaped through Primordial Chaos, these positive aspects would frequently either seem to happen inexplicably or appear to be random chance. Random chance certainly exists, as does the Heisenberg Uncertainty principle. But although Magic's simultaneously enfolded and unfolded field cannot command or control random chance any more or less than human consciousness can, positively enfolded Magic can shift *you* in relationship to random chance and its effects.

Even when it is semi-conscious in the sense of being semi-human because of enmeshment, Magic can align itself with both Grace and blessing. This alignment can augment your intuition by guiding your dreams, timing and sense of synchronicity, essentially resonating so closely with the Divine Intention that you can act as an agent of blessing quite unbeknownst to yourself. Granted, this demands a delicate balance, as often feelings of frustration and despair have subconscious and unconscious causes, though oddly enough, this is where the enfolded, interior M-D geometries of the dimension of Identity and Primordial Chaos may work together. There are several geometries in both dimensions that encompass divine Mystery within them, allowing contradiction and paradox to be combined quite effectively. Examples of this magical mingling of paradoxes sourced in the dimension of Primordial Chaos are things like the strange joy or courage you discover even when you might be persuaded that everything is hopeless.

Meditation #1: Using Positive Primordial Chaos to Heal Your Inner Magic:

In this meditation, feel yourself in your house. Everything is ordered and spotless because yesterday you did a lot of Spring Cleaning; today you just want to sit back and read the morning paper. You go outside to get the morning edition of the paper and suddenly it seems as though the weather has gone distinctly weird: there is sunshine on the walk, but there are heavy rain clouds overhead and evidence of hail on the walk but not on the street. You step forward cautiously: all of a sudden it's raining, with thunder and at the same time the wind is blowing quite hard, mixed with dry dust! Stepping back as you shake off the rain, you step into some new snow and then in the next step everything becomes dry and hot. Not at all sure you want to go on, you suddenly see something bright up ahead on the path: it's a shining silver box.

Putting your head down against the wind, you press forward, getting wet, then dry, then listless in the humid heat or chilled to the bone. Yet you press on and are able to reach the box in a few steps. The box is larger than you thought at first. It starts to snow gently as you pick it up and open it. It has three horizontal compartments in it: a large bright one lined with blue felt, one in the middle lined with gray felt and the last compartment lined with black felt. Each compartment has a gem inside: a blue sapphire in the first compartment with the blue felt, a diamond in the middle part with the gray felt and in the compartment with the black felt is a dark fire opal, large and brilliant.

Pick up the three gems one by one and as you hold each one in your hand, say to it, "You are Magic! You are the Magic that knows me, but you are not I: you are your own self. You are Magic!" You kiss each stone one by one, repeating, "You are Magic!" And then you toss each stone up into the air. A swirl of snow, a gust of rain, or a dry, desert wind catches each stone and swirls it up into the sky. Shining brightly and expanding in size, each stone flashes its own brilliant color. When you see this, you say, "You are free again! Return to the Source that knows you, remembering what you are."

The moment you throw the last stone into the air, the weather turns nice again: the sky has soft clouds in it, the sun is shining brightly and the wind is gentle. If you already know how to work with Magic, invite it back and feel it embrace you as you say to it, "Dear Magic, be my ally now. Help me create the best and most positive things for my life and the lives of others." You will feel the Magic respond with happy excitement. If you have not had much experience with Magic, you can end the meditation at the moment the three stones have all been released when the weather turns sweet.

Working with Your Subconscious Wave-guides Regarding Magic:

Needless to say, whatever your attitude, aptitude, and agreement regarding being a Magical practitioner [See Volume Two], you will work better with Magic when you have discerned and understood the subconscious and unconscious parts of yourself that would enmesh with it, determining to clear these parts as needed. One way to do this is to actually listen to what you say aloud and tell yourself during the day, especially things you say when a certain situation repeats itself yet again. If, when you try to accomplish some action and something else always interrupts, takes precedence or interferes outright for what seems to be the thousandth time, watch what you think and what you say!

If you say, "Oh, of course: this always happens!" or you tell yourself, "I can never get what I want no matter how hard I try," you are not only dealing with a set of limited and limiting beliefs that would be good to change: alas, you have likely also created an over-emphasized, self-reinforcing sub-harmonic geometry, a wave-guide paired with your own Magic in your subconscious and/or unconscious self regarding this belief, that allows it to perpetuate its own expression through your human identity. It is this kind of unfolded and enfolded geometry within the human mind and psyche that can entrap Magic's more enfolded, higher-dimensional field and cause many difficulties because of Magic's higher-energy, M-D slope.

Subconscious waveguides also account for the tremendous difficulty you can have with changing a bad habit, such as changing your identity from an angry person to a kind one, a super-thin person to a healthy one or a person that always feels a victim to a person of Grace and courage. Once again, since both you and Magic are expressed through the dimensions of Identity and Chaos, your constellations of inner thoughts and your unconscious Magic become octaves of each other. Indeed, Magic can work in very human ways even by itself in its own consciousness, as you can work in very magical ways when being your most human, especially when you learn how to attune to the Mystery that is the bridge between the Zero dimension and the dimension of Primordial Chaos.

Spiritual training, discerning and studying your own human nature at depth, life-altering experiences and simple actions of Grace can open you to Mystery. Sometimes this Grace can challenge your sense of self to the point that you have to go through Mystery in order to regain your equilibrium and adapt to your new reality: obviously there are times when it is not an easy road. As I have mentioned before, Divine Mystery can actually terrify you to the point that you reach for the most rigid structures you can find to hide in, from a fundamentalist religion to the truly rigid constraints of obsessions or addictions. This is regrettable, because it tends to harden and constrain the Magic already within your human field. Because of Magic's higher-energy slope it can sometimes lead to what seems to be insurmountable problems, for yourself and others.

Opening to Mystery to Uncover Your Authenticity:

Paradoxically, the best way to determine how you are affecting Magic and how Magic is affecting you is to open up into Mystery as much as possible, by deliberate, conscious action or through a spiritual state of surrender. This can be done in simple ways, such as just noticing the odd things around you and in your life: the sudden changes, unusual arrangements of things, incidents or circumstances. These can be shifts and changes in your moods that seem to have nothing to do with your current experiences; the sudden odd clarity of your dreams or even persistent daydreams. Just noticing what is going on around and within you may be enough to invite Magic and Mystery into your experience. So often, you can become trapped in old patterns: you find certain ways that work and stick to them, ceasing to think about or consider them.

When you travel somewhere for the first time, because you are learning the route you will notice every tree, house, person, road sign, building or open space. But once you have learned the route, you no longer pay any attention to it. As in to the practice we have described of becoming aware of Space to extend your sense of Time so that you have the wider sense of Time that you used to when you were a child, you need to become aware of the time you use to traverse through space in order to catch the hints of Mystery that you need in order to keep a fresh sense of your Magic. When you are more aware of Magic in your own energy-field and outer life, you will of course be more able to sense what you are doing with that energy. You will also be more able to sense Mystery, engaging more parts of your own unconscious and subconscious wave-guide formations intentionally instead of inadvertently. This process, however, could be a challenge as you may encounter more of your own unconscious and subconscious content than for which you are prepared.

Like Chaos, the sub- and unconscious contain a tremendous number of aspects: your dreams and desires, your more primitive shadow-emotions and your exalted but sometimes terrifying impulses and motivations of the Light. Make no mistake: your intentions towards and of the Light may be quite unsettling to your sense of yourself for many reasons. If you have, so to speak, an angel of goodness inside of you, you may fear its excruciating sense of fairness and balance, as well as its inexorable and perhaps implacable alignment with Truth. It may demand that you confront your irresponsibility, lack of authenticity, prevarications or self-delusions: you may have used many of these as cloaks to hide yourself from self-confrontation in the first place. When it rises to the level of your conscious mind, you may wonder what your own inner goodness will cost you or your ego: what will it demand that you change?

Encountering Light and Goodness:

In a culture that asks, "What's wrong with you?" far, far more frequently than it ever asks, "What is right with you?" you may simply feel unprepared to deal with your own goodness. Additionally, good has been presented as the antithesis, the enemy, of evil, and evil as the anti-matter of goodness rather than what it is far more likely to be: a warped, confused or narcissistic copy of Goodness itself. So when you feel you have been evil, must you become an enemy of your own self? And to have this war potentially fought deep inside of your unconscious can create a real sense of dread: the unconscious is deeper than the subconscious self that may be able to speak in dreams, intuition or inspiration. However will you know what is happening there in the black depths of your unknowing? How will you know what is real?

234

The best way to understand the depth of your own real self is to encounter that self at a level even deeper than the sub- and unconscious: in the depths of meditation, by listening to your soul's Core Tone or when you come to a point in your own life where the true depth of honesty is the only way forward. This may happen when you have lost everything because of disaster, misfortune, addictions or your own careless actions. Sometimes gamblers come to this point and sometimes widows. Sometimes drinkers come to this point or sometimes men whose wives have left them. This depth can be opened with loss or great joy, with death or birth, because in all of these things the deeper self must rise so that you may live.

These times of great strain and change happen when the dimensions that form your human identity intersect with Primordial Chaos, shifting even the steady-state formations of the dimension of Identity, wrenching them open in order to reveal the presence and realness of the Core of the Zero dimension: the self of the Divine Whole Being. When you touch that Essential Being within the Zero dimension in the wordless, magnificent silence of deep meditation, your alignment with that divine Core changes what needs to be changed in your human self in order for that self to align with truth.

However, you can reach those depths more easily through your Core Tone, for this Tone is always in resonance with that deep and living Knowing. You do not need to deluge your human self with this Divine Reality as though you stood under a breaking dam: you can simply sip the water gratefully or even just breathe in the mist. Like a plant might absorb droplets of fog through its leaves, you can absorb the deep truth and goodness of the Divine Being slowly, in balance, never having to confront the terror of the changes that Mystery might demand.

Meditation #2: Aligning Your Self with Your Own Core of Truth:

Imagine meditatively that you have been walking a long, long time. Footsore and weary, filthy with dust and mud, hungry and parched, you are carrying a heavy backpack, a suitcase in one hand and a large sack in the other hand. You even have something slung on your neck that hangs down, impeding your balance and your breathing. You have been struggling for so long you have almost forgotten that you are looking for the Path of Remembering. This is a path you have heard so much about: a path that leads you to joy, healing and never feeling alone, ever again. Such a path does not seem at all likely. However, it is as though this path were drawing you forward, even when the road under your feet is stony, slippery, dangerous and terrible with heat or cold. The allure of this hidden Path has drawn you forward for miles.

At last, you see something different about the ground up ahead. You can't quite decide what that difference is. Is it brighter up there? No, not really. Are there perhaps more flowers there, or is the path smoother? Yet as you wonder, you keep moving forward and the path gets steeper and harder to climb. Breathing heavily, you decide to take off the heavy thing around your neck and put it down by the side of the path: it's too much work to carry it now! Besides, you are beginning to smell something wonderful: fresh, sweet water up ahead. You keep going, but by the time you begin to hear the roar of a distant waterfall or a great river, you realize the path has become even steeper. So you let go of the heavy sack you are carrying in one hand, laying it gently down as you listen to the birds, smelling the flowers and wet earth on the path ahead. Soon, though, you have to use both hands to balance yourself on the steep, rocky way. You let the suitcase go and hardly notice where it falls. In a little while, you are frankly climbing, but the water sounds so strong and lovely: you can begin to taste the mist in the air. You keep climbing until you come to a place that is so steep that you have to let go of the backpack as well, using your hands and feet to climb.

You make it through and see the most magnificent, shining waterfall you have ever imagined, shimmering with light and rainbows, thundering with delight! Free of everything that has encumbered you, realize that the path is smooth and level, full with flowers and dewy grass on the edges. The waterfall ahead of you is so huge, so loud and full of sound you can hardly think. But you laugh aloud: just breathing in the mist from the waterfall quenches your thirst, while the water on the path heals your sore feet.

You run forward joyfully so fast than you run right into a cascade, an arc of water leaping off from the main waterfall. Shocked at first, you stand there, feeling the water wash away all the rest of the mud and dust and hurts from the journey. You smile suddenly, because you know this is the waterfall of your personal Core Truth: your own Core of your realest Self. It is not alien to you at all: it caresses you and holds you in a gentle, warm embrace. Your long journey got you here, so this place is your own now. This is the truth of your own Mystery and the place where you are most magic.

You may think it impossible and strange that your soul and Magic are so closely aligned, especially if your life feels anything *but* magic. However, this resonance is a very real thing and is one of the several things that put Humanity into a different type of energy and expression than the animals: not a superior type as much as a state of being with certain specific potentials. Animals have their own versions of Identity, Mystery, Magic and alignments with Divinity. Indeed, when acting as familiars with your Magic, they also work with Magic's own conscious field: in some ways they can understand it better because of animals' own class of inner alignments. This is also a factor in trees and other plants, as well as the five elements: Earth, Water, Fire, Air and Ether because their specific alignments allow their field potentials to switch, balancing combinations and re-combinations of elements. As we discussed in Volume Two, the true source of Magic is Love and Life: certainly, Magic is one of Love's major expressions.

Animals use Magic to communicate, especially when there are few opportunities to find mates: to sense each other in difficult situations such as very dense forests, very bad weather or when encountering human cities. Granted, those lost from a herd or animal family do not always find each other and animals have of course been driven to extinction pair by pair. But this has as much to do with the choices of the animals' Over-soul as with the occasionally quirky intersections of the enfolded geometries of animal Magic with 4-D reality. But the interesting thing is actually, now that human beings are beginning to come into deeper awareness of their own souls, some of the human levels of Magic are "rubbing off" on the animals' inner magical geometries, frequently for the better. This happens each time someone is kind to an animal, rescues it and cares for it wisely, without over-caring by feeding it too much or with the wrong food. This interplay of human and animal Magic is also why human beings benefit so much *from* animals, resulting anything from having better health to having more hope to live, to say nothing of the superlative gifts from service animals.

Generally speaking, though, this kind of mingling of different forms of Magic is not the same thing as Magic being trapped in the human sub- and unconscious: the two fields are just different enough. Much as the different haloclines of Time allow different aspects of Time, Space and alternate Realities to keep their discrete identities and thus their own temporal orientations, the differing enfolded geometries involved between human and animal Magic retain their level of separation. There is overlap, though there is not an energetic restructuring as when both the geometries and the inner dimensions of human consciousness and Magic resonate too closely. This is another reason why animals can be very good for human beings to work with and vice versa: like the shallow roots of two redwoods helping each other withstand storms, the present degrees of manifested Magic for both human beings and animals are assisted and augmented by intersecting each other within these specific, open geometries.

Elementals, however, are a different story yet: they keep their coherent pattern beneath and within each of the five elements and are more like geometries of conscious structure than any kind of soul or being. I must stress that they *are* conscious: they can be communicated with and will respond to both human emotion and human intention. The whole project of working with Elementals themselves is too lengthy a subject to go into here; indeed there are already several discussions of the proper methods to be found in other books. But I bring them up here because, as their Magic is different again from the Magic of human beings or animals, there is a strong potential for different synergistic combinations when the human Magic and Elemental Magic find ways to overlap that can add greater leverage to any Magical work.

Interactive Geometries of Magic:

As is suggested by the magical tradition of familiars, both human and animals' magical fields may be combined additively through their interactive geometries. Sympathetic Magic makes use of these geometries constantly, though often empirically because few practitioners can see into the higher dimensional, enfolded geometries that allow Magic to have the energy-slope it does. Sensitive ones that see auras could be trained to see Magic or at least perceive it to a degree, as clairaudients could "hear" the silent sound of Magic's field when they came near it or clairsentients could feel where Magic was operative. Yet Magic, as a field, is similar to Ether in that it engages reality differently under different conditions. As in our example in Volume One where we point out that an apple can be several things simultaneously and not cease being an apple, so Magic is an inter-dimensional energy-slope as well as a field, an aspect of human consciousness within the dimension of Identity and a conscious, intentional field of its own as well.

All of the rituals, implements and procedures of Magic work with Magic's geometries and of course, since your human field of intelligence and your own human will create their own multi-dimensional geometric structures, this leads to very individualized methods and experiences with Magic and its effects. However, as you can accept someone's training and change your own internal geometries thereby, so you can allow Magic to entrain your own inner being in more than the simple empiricism of, "This works, but this doesn't." In other words, you can interact with Magic itself as a conscious field; you could even give it the form of an entity should you wish: in much the same way as you create gods, sacred places and numens, you can pour Magic into any shape.

Some of this is done unconsciously or subconsciously: there are tales of children that are healed when they are given their special, plush bear to hold or are told that a talisman of some kind will help then live. A belief in angels does indeed allow the angels to attune to you and you to them, thus engaging their positive energy: when you accept their existence they are able to help you to focus your own intuitive impulses into comprehension, so that you may receive and act upon your own inner Divine Guidance.

Similarly, perceiving and relating to Magic as an entity can be of inestimable value, particularly when you are faced with a conundrum that your conscious mind is too anxious or frustrated to solve. Moreover, when you work with Magic as an entity in itself you can learn how it interacts with Humanity specifically: you can open up new avenues for human expression and thus re-structure Humanity's inner geometries as well. This will create a steadily additive effect, opening its own positive nature until those darker, coercive or even toxic remnants of Magic are no longer part of human experience, because the enfolded, higher-dimensional geometries have been permanently changed through human will and human action.

Using Grace to Re-structure Toxic Magic:

You cannot counter Toxic Magic in the realm in which it operates, any more than you can solve a child's argument by becoming childish. Indeed, if you were to descend into the child's name-calling, tantrums or acting out, you would know you have already lost: the child has pulled you down into a state too similar to his or hers. Now, you can no longer act with grace, wisdom, intelligence or even parental authority. Similarly, if you try to meet Toxic Magic on its own level through using its tactics, you may win several battles and win them well, yet the war may have overrun you completely before you realize it. There are enough tales and tragedies concerning the notion that you have to become like your enemy in order to defeat him, especially in war, where the tortured become the torturers and the ethical become unethical. For that is one of Toxic Magic's most dangerous lures: the belief that because you act with good intentions and for a good reason you will remain good even though your methods may be evil. Yet as with unconscious Magic that acts with its own blind intentions, Toxic Magic's field can entrain the human mind, will and intentions as surely and inexorably as a magnet's field aligns iron filings.

It is for that reason alone at least, if not for many others, that you need Grace, which is receiving the higher-order energy from the Divine Source. Grace not only has more leverage from its higher energy state: based upon the Divine Intention, Grace naturally has the higher perspective necessary to see even the most complex internal geometries within Toxic Magic. This allows your conscious mind to perceive the necessary structures within its fields to shift those geometries. And, as you are employing Grace, you are far more protected that if you were to attempt to dismantle Toxic Magic on your own. Grace is, of course, also engaged through prayer, blessing and deep spiritual meditation, yet when you practice Grace together with the conscious field of Magic you are given another point and angle of leverage for positive change. When you are trying to shift Toxic Magic, you are wisest to engage the intelligent field of Magic together with Grace.

If you are dealing with some of the effects of Toxic Magic, the first way to counterbalance its effects is to center into all the places of the Zero dimension that touch your inner dimension of Identity: your truest, realest self that resonates with the perfect stillness of Para-sound and Para-light. Instead of diverting your energy towards the source or the instigator of the toxicity, clarify and crystallize the truest, innermost version of your Self that you are able to discern. You may spend extra time in your Core Tone; you may deliberately do something that you truly enjoy, particularly if it is something creative.

Then, removing all extraneous thoughts of that toxicity, wait until you feel the touch of the Divine Regard and become aware of that moment when you know that you are known and you catch a glimpse of the One that knows you. From this vantage point, discern what your own inner Magic shows you about what may be the natural counter to that particular Toxic Magic. Is it a song, a prayer, an affirmation or a shout of joy? Could it be a memory, a glimpse of an alternate future? Or could it be seeing that the practitioner of that Toxic Magic is after all just a scared little boy or a deeply injured little girl that needs nothing more or less than pure healing? The answer will be within and *not* in the field of the toxic magician.

This is again where Grace enters into your work: Grace, and trust. Trust is often difficult for human beings because trust has too often been used, misused and abused, but you may always begin with trusting yourself: trusting that you will do as you say, live within your ethical standards and determine to remain pliable and able to learn. Trust yourself to recognize when you have made a mistake or deceived yourself; trust yourself to realize when you are living in your honesty and when you have chosen to slip into temporary expedience. The great teachers and masters of humanity all trusted themselves even though they realized they could not see every part of themselves: they knew they could be blind at times.

Yet their trust was so clear that it led to their deep self-confidence of faith. They knew that they knew what they knew and yet that the Source of Knowing always knew more. Similarly, you need to trust yourself with Magic: knowing that you do indeed sense what you sense as far as your senses allow but that Magic is always something to be learned again and again. The more you hold to your own strength of self in this way, the less you will be seduced by the easy ways, the careless ways or the ways that lead you into dark usages of Magic. When you keep in your mind and heart that Grace is the touch of the Presence of the All, you will treasure Magic's wisdom.

Working with Para-light to Enhance Magical Effects:

To review: Para-light is the solid core of light, the motionless, essential Idea of light that the Zero dimension, as expressed through the dimension of Identity, uses as a steady reference point, much as 4-D existence uses Time. As we said above, Time and the dimension of Identity are also closely related. However, asking Magic to step outside of Time is very easy once you have a sense of Para-light's stillness: you can work with Magic to use Para-light as a fulcrum to reach into the future, back into the past and even into alternate

241

realities. If you have practiced with Magic enough to get a sense of its identity and individual consciousness, working through the temporal lattices is particularly easy. And if you also call upon another higher-level Being such as an archangel, a fully realized avatar or some other numinous spirit from within the enfolded dimensions, because you have three intentional consciousnesses working in relationship to one another, your leverage does not only double: it is cubed.

Although as we have said, Magic is not prayer, prayer can have much Magic within it; moreover, Magic itself benefits from being combined with prayer. For some, Magic is already an instinct, automatically called upon whenever prayer or any other Lightwork is done. For some it is easy to go into or be aware of that stillness at any moment. Yet the more intentional your actions are, the more focused they will be. It is best to create a ritual that calls in Magic, Para-light and a higher-order entity from the enfolded dimensions so that the "slope" of Magic, the fulcrum of Para-light and the added wisdom and perspective of the higher being synergizes into an amalgam or alloy of intention. This becomes a tremendously positive tool for change, enhancing healing, shifts in your personal reality and in the inner structures of the world, giving voice to the inner resonance of the Zero dimension.

Indeed, versions of the ritual for calling Magic, Para-light and the enfolded multi-dimensional Being may be used to work with other things, particularly the inner structures of Reality: the energy grids, inner arrays of crystalline intelligence or even the Collective Unconscious to a degree. Certainly, these rituals can be used for your own subconscious and unconscious issues regarding Magic and within Magic. When used in harmony with a higher-order Being, Para-light becomes a reference point, a caliper with which to re-calibrate your own purposes in the world for yourself and others. Working in this way has the potential to create astonishing changes and should not be approached lightly. However, Para-light will always provide a stable center around which you can engineer intentional shifts that will add positive energy to Reality.

How Torsion Fields Affect Units of Consciousness through Matter

Key Points: The tiniest aspects of manifestation, the Units of Consciousness, are neither particles nor waves, but might be considered foci of the divine intention. As the triangle is much more stable and less fragile than a cube, they form intricate, multi-connected geometries of tetrahedrons, creating space and the relativity of forms within space. As several fields work with the Units of Consciousness directly, the Torsion Fields from Volume Two are reviewed below. The Torsion Field of Magnetism actually creates a "tone" as it flutters in relationship to Timespace. The Torsion Field of Translation opens up communication between living and non-living things through the tetrahedron-shaped Units of Consciousness that give form to physical matter and fields. Human beings exist in both the enfolded and unfolded dimensions: you are in Heaven's own matrix now and are uniquely responsive to the Formless God and the Form of Goddess. Psychic abilities work directly with the Units of Consciousness through the Ether. The meditation offered uses Para-light to open the filaments of all of your human experiences.

Subheadings:

- Units of Consciousness

- The "Photons" of Reality-Construction and Their Geometries

- A Note on Pyramids

- A Review of the Torsion Fields

- How Torsion Fields Interact with Matter and Each Other

- The "Tone" of Magnetism

- Perceiving Living and Non-living Systems with the Torsion Field of Translation

- Living and Non-living Systems and Units of Consciousness

- Monotheistic Animism, Cyborgs and Communication

- Psychic Perception and Units of Consciousness

243

- Meditation: Opening Your Own Units of Consciousness' Inner Arrays

Units of Consciousness:

We are necessarily indebted to Jane Roberts and her colleague Seth for discerning the minute bits of identity they called "consciousness units" that we have called Units of Consciousness: these Units are the first forms created from the infinite Whole Center's infinitely dense, infinitely minute, vibrationless Para-light Core. I know that what I have said here is absurd, yet to a degree I mean it to be so: when contemplating this Source the mind must extend to the edge of its limits of comprehension in order to realize that Source's nature.

As your human mind is a reflection and hologram of the Divine Mind, it has the same "form," but is not and cannot have the same "substance" as its Source: although you are comprised of multi-dimensional information from the enfolded structures of Reality, you cannot be the dimensions themselves. God is incomprehensible to the human mind: even though you can reflect God in form, your human mind is not its Source, much the same way as the reflection of a house cannot be the house. There are moments of comprehension, certainly, as though the reflection realizes that it reflects something that gives it a particular shape, yet is not the reflection's self.

The "Photons" of Reality-Construction and Their Geometries:

The Units of Consciousness are the "photons," the minute foci that are the means by which and through which the reflection of Divinity is created on the surface of Reality. These "photons" of the Units of Consciousness simultaneously create vibration and relativity. Because they are the first separate form of the Oneness, Units of Consciousness are one of the most miraculous and essential Ideas of the One Source. And because they are first manifested as a trinity, not a singularity or a duality, they have created everything else: unity, disunity, multi-dimensional geometries and thus relative positions, movement and form. I must necessarily say trinity because Divinity's first expression was not one or two, but three, six, and then nine. Duality is far too limited to encompass the transition from Formless into Form and a quartet of particles would be at once too stable and too fragile.

The corners of a triangle act as pivot-points, receiving and engaging leverage without being affected adversely, whereas the square or cube is static in its oppositional arrangement of two and two, two and two... It cannot accept or engage leverage, but must be levered itself, while, indeed, the lever is part of a triangle by its very definition. The flat side of the square or cube offers too much contact with its local area because of surface adhesion and it does not move from that contact. A cube also has no clear axis, no clear line of force around which it can move. However, a triangle automatically allows dynamic change, particularly in the form of an equilateral triangle or tripod: the triangle or tetrahedron shifts and turns easily, creating multiple reconfigurations while still retaining its form. And, ironically, the pyramid shape, the combination of triangular sides with a square base, is the most stable form in nature: it is an "easy" form like a sphere or circle, because both manifested shapes are the closest to their higher-dimensional forms. Even more important, instead of having the cube's six sides, the tetrahedron has only four. This paradoxically allows this triune principle to evolve into more forms!

In addition, cubes arrange together to create solids; tetrahedrons create forms while giving direction for energy to follow. When the tetrahedrons or cones joined tip-to-tip or base-to-base and iterated, they create lines. And when the triangle's sides change in length, creating isosceles and scalene triangles, all forms are possible while the original triune aspect is continually retained. And as isosceles triangles contain the right angles of the cube this makes the arrangements needed to allow the Infinite to be enfolded within the Finite possible. So the Finite is a reflection of the Infinite because the cube-like right angles of both isosceles and some scalene triangles create space by addition, while the equilateral triangle creates form, direction and movement. In addition, the triangular leverage allows and enables all the Torsion Fields.

A Note on Pyramids:

As we said above, the triangular solid combines with the cube to create even more stability while retaining its potential plasticity, particularly when it is a pyramid with its four-sided base and the triangular sides rising to its axis point. Yet of course within that stability is an energy focus: the pyre-amid, the fire within, as several have discovered with varying degrees of success. Certainly the "sarcophagus" in what is called the King's chamber seems placed suspiciously close to the geometrical center of the Great Pyramid, while what is called the Queen's Chamber is more directly centered,

245

though lower. I put the term sarcophagus in quotes because my own experiences with that aspect of the Great Pyramid resembles that of a Sufi Master who was asked to settle impartially once and for all whether reincarnation was a fact or not. He replied, "Well, I can't give you an impartial answer: I remember all of my past lives…"

In this case too, I and many others, remember and know that the sarcophagus had a far more powerful ritual purpose than entombment; any reader is encouraged to pursue the question of such an experience in their or other's memories of ancient Egyptian lifetimes. In the case of the ritual I remember, the fire in the pyramid's center was the light of God, the near-death experience. So another purpose for the combined form of the pyramid is a focus for the divine energy in a way that a cube could never become.

Two tetrahedrons joined base-to-base, as well as two pyramids joined base-to-base or point-to-point, are actually of the first solid or solid-like forms ever created by the Units of Consciousness, functioning as a seed crystal upon which every other form could grow and every possible geometry be extracted. Most imagine the particles from which atoms are made to be either points or perhaps vibrating "strings," but from my vantage point those points are double tetrahedrons. However, as they are formed of the Units of Consciousness, they are more like principles or actions of geometries than forms.

A Review of the Torsion Fields:

The Torsion Fields I listed in Volume Two are: Numeration (enfolded fields creating discrete "compartments" for numbers), Proportion (an enfolded field that provides templates for proportion in form and numbers) and Para-gravity (the enfolded aspects of gravity). More readily known and understood, though as yet in a mostly empirical way, the Magnetic and Electric Torsion Fields are unfolded and enfolded fields that regulate spin; the Magnetic field's enfolded aspects explain the absence of monopoles. Para-Sound (the silent "essence" of sound), Para-light (the "solid," vibrationless light at the core of reality) and the Ether (the field that works as a plasma-like matrix for all energy) are readily apprehended and engaged by the human psychic body/mind.

The Torsion Fields of Formation (unfolded aspects of the Dimension of Identity) and Translation Fields (deeply enfolded fields that allow communication between the Divine Mind and Reality) create permanent connections between the Divine Being and its Manifestation. Aspects of the dimension of Identity act as Torsion Fields to create pulse (periodicity and vibration). It also creates comprehension, creating specificity's stability in the roiling shifts of fields, forces and matter that is 4-D Reality and thus providing consistent scope to express the Divine and Human Intentions. There are other Torsion Fields, some having to do with Time, some with Space, but the fields I have listed here are at least perceptible to the human mind, imagination and the psychic faculty, thus are more comprehensible.

The most profound thing about the Torsion Fields is that the Units of Consciousness, being so infinitesimal, are not only the "substance" of Ether's Torsion-field effects, these Units act as the "stem cells" of physical matter to give form to Time and Space. Neither particle nor wave, these primordial shapes of the Divine Focus may be described as the locations where the enfolded and unfolded dimensions and Torsion Fields merge in order to spin reality out from the core of the Zero dimension.

As said above, these Units of Consciousness generally arrange themselves first into triangles, tetrahedrons and double tetrahedrons in the process of creating form and then "string" or spin themselves out from the placeless focus of the Divine Intention; this is of course another way of approaching the original String Theory. However, these Units of Consciousness are very unlikely to be discovered mechanically: it needs the human mental/psychic perceptions plus a good dose of imagination to actually perceive the hyper-fine, fundamental aspects of reality of those Units of Consciousness. Indeed, they will not be perceived by any other method for some time: atom smashing sometimes acts as letting an entire herd of bulls loose in the shop where these Units might be found...

How Torsion Fields Interact with Matter and Each Other:

But another thing to remember about Torsion Fields is that they have a very strong effect over a very limited area; the only exceptions are the dimension of Identity and Ether. Although it acts as a Torsion Field, Identity is a dimension, the only dimension that limits other dimensions' expression. Because Ether acts as a matrix generally and creates its own subtle side-effects, Ether is the other exception. The Torsion fields are generally limited to their areas of focus, as well as their physical conditions.

Magnetism in particular may change its shape and move when it is part of a dynamic system such as the molten metallic core of the Earth but it does not wander off to the moon: it stays with the planet. The Fields of Translation, Formation and Numeration also tend to stick where they are found: they are both such an intrinsic part of 4-D manifestation that they cannot be separated from it nor can it be separated from them. These three Torsion Fields are very focused on living systems and do not tend to be as global in their reach as the three inner dimensions of Identity, Primordial Chaos and the Zero dimension. Even though Numeration, Formation and Translation are a global phenomenon, they remain static within the Etheric matrix and do not shift.

The "Tone" of Magnetism:

Magnetism's Torsion Field and its right-angled manifestation of electricity necessarily work with the dimension of Identity, both as itself and as its Torsion Field of Formation within living systems of all kinds. Magnetism also works with Ether and thus the human psychic faculty. The Translation Field that links the unfolded and enfolded dimensions works for and within your psychic abilities as well. As we have discussed earlier, the body's magnetic and electrical fields help set up the minute potentials in each cell's quantum signatures such that they can shift to receive the unofficial information presented from "outside" of time.

This is another reason why magnetism is so important to life: it "flutters" Timespace at a quantum level, keeping stable in terms of "tone" and dynamic in terms of shift. I have not brought up the "Tone" of Magnetism before, but it is created through a combination of the way magnetism affects matter and why it affects certain specific parts of matter such as hydrogen atoms and ferrous materials, though not others: there are enfolded resonant geometries at work. Particularly as regards your psychic faculty, this Magnetic "Tone" is indeed related to your soul's Core Tone. But the magnetic quantum fluctuations function more like a sound box for the inter-dimensional vibrational geometries, providing a supportive matrix for the Tone so that it can be perceived by your human awareness.

Another aspect of Magnetism's "Tone" is how it creates resonance with gravity, creating "locked" planets such as Mercury and the Moon, the odd nature of galactic spin, and living systems' stable magnetism that does not get degaussed readily. Yet at the same time, magnetic fields shift their orientation to each other, so that the Earth's magnetic field responds to the sun's magnetic field and meanwhile, the human being's magnetic field shifts with the Earth's.

This dynamic response of stability and shift created by the interplay of magnetism and gravity has profound quantum effects. For instance these effects allow the dimension of Primordial Chaos to find the "holes" in Timespace it needs to bridge unpredictable and unexpected information into 4-D reality. But these gaps in the quantum geometries created by these shifts also allow higher-level information from the Zero dimension to impose its patterns into the cellular level as well as the quantum. In this case, Magnetism's "Tone" acts a bit like a carrier wave within which the enfolded, higher-dimensional information can be contained.

Perceiving Living and Non-Living Systems with the Torsion Field of Translation:

The Torsion Field of Translation conveys information, intention and Para-temporal connections between the enfolded and unfolded dimensions; in its engagement to Reality it is as peculiar as Ether or some aspects of Magnetism. Strongly linked to the dimension of Identity, the Field of Translation works quite singularly and particularly with each identity as well as all identities. Within the points of focus through its natural quantum factors that are enabled by the Units of Consciousness , this field is in fact the means by which the Divine Mind and Presence remain aware through the Translation Field's omnipresent loci of each and every separate thing, being, process, entity, intelligence and form, living and non-living. The Translation Field's profoundly individualized perspective actually allows every living thing to be comprehended by any other living thing.

To the degree the Units of Consciousness are arrayed in the proper internal geometries, non-living things may be comprehended through the Torsion Field of Translation as well, though it takes a precise mind that can combine the needed stillness, imagination, flexibility and ability to receive "alien" data from an object, material substance or machine. But with practice, you may perhaps even be able to fathom such processes as tectonic shifts, floods, shifts in air pressure and the like. Granted, the Earth has Her own Consciousness, not to mention the consciousness within magnetic entities such as the channeled entity Kryon. However, it is good to remember to that to communicate with living and non-living things, your own psyche can work with Ether, Magnetism and the quantum information within the Units of Consciousness. Indeed, with either magical rituals or prayer, you are engaging all of these factors at once when you call upon the intelligent field of Magic to engage the field of Translation directly.

Living and Non-living Systems and Units of Consciousness:

Living systems receive information from other living systems regularly and although a lot of the data are ignored, living creatures of all kinds are aware of tipping points regarding everything from their own extinction to years of plenty or famine. Granted, the sense-data of scent, hearing, sight and other input such as perceiving magnetic fields are acted upon first: the first lesson any animal or plant learns is immediacy, whether that sense is a part of genetic instinct or direct experience. But subtle things like the predator-to-prey ratio and the hierarchies of herds and other groups are refined through the group's psychic gestalt. The sum intentions of the physical forms as interpreted though the Units of Consciousness and directed by the Translation Field's involution create the patterns from the higher-level enfolded dimensions. Because you are both connected with and operating from several enfolded and unfolded dimensions a once, human beings have a particular mandate: to continually become more and more aware of how that higher-level information interacts with and augments the entire living system.

As has been said elsewhere, you can be the stewards of the life on this planet. Yet the more aware and spiritual you become, the more humble you become too and the more readily you can allow yourself to be taught to perceive other living systems from their point of view as well as your own. For the spiritual awareness you have been striving for does not only have to do with God the Formless Creator of Form, but also with Goddess, the Form of the Formless Creative. That same Divine Spirit is within form as surely as it is outside of form. Shamans and workers of Magic know this; so do animals in their own way. When you put yourself into physical form, the Formless would not abandon you outside its Love into a place without the divine Presence! Do not doubt it: Form is a direct expression of Divinity.

But so many of you, still shocked by the self-deception that the Edgeless and Formless needed in order to create the Mystery of Form and Separation, have railed against that decision to create the illusion of Separation into Form by blaming Form. But through the Units of Consciousness, Form retains its divine origin and its divine intelligence: there is ultimately nothing else. You are in Heaven now as much as you will ever be, though your body often gets in the way. But that does not mean that Form is Heaven, for Form does confuse the soul temporarily when you are focused upon it, distracting your inner vision and awareness quite effectively. But then again: you say it's a good movie when you forget that you are in a theater while you are watching it.

Monotheistic Animism, Cyborgs and Communication:

Once you become aware of the Divine in Form, you cannot go back to the old perception. In this way animism can become monotheism and there is less and less separation between Form and Formless and this makes subtle awareness, psychic perceptions and receiving pure information much more likely. Although you are not aware of it, you communicate with "non-living" things all the time, receiving some communication through the physical senses and some through the psychic channels of Ether. But as everything is based on structures formed from Units of Consciousness, there is a point where the distinction between Form and Formless ceases to have much if any meaning.

In any event, you have the capacity for communication in terms of the quantum layers within your brain, especially if you have been trained empirically or specifically to perceive the subtle intelligence within the Units of Consciousness: thus you can approach a non-living thing through the Field of Translation in order to understand its nature. As I mentioned earlier, there are those who seem to understand mechanical objects so well that they appear to have a magical "fix-it" aura or field around them; this field is a combination of Magic's own intelligent energy field and the subtle geometries of the Units of Consciousness' communication through the Field of Translation. When you open yourself to the idea of communicating with "non-living" objects, you may be surprised at the conversations you can perceive. An untrained person may be able to repair a complex piece of equipment this way, simply by listening to what is needed in order to ensure its best possible configuration.

These subtle geometries are why it is easier to connect to and even communicate with non-living objects that you or other people have made, particularly organized mechanisms such as cars, clocks, or electronic creations such as computers, copiers and even medical devices. When these things are created through human conscious action, they automatically retain a similar resonance through Quantum Entangled Inductive Resonance with the inner lattices of the Units of Consciousness. Various types of augmentation devices, from the computer chips that enable the blind to see again or pacemakers that remind the heart to beat steadily, are already designed to receive the brain's electrical impulses and focus them into action or to restrain inappropriate responses such as bradycardia.

However, at present these types of devices only have limited one-way communication: the purpose of designing such objects is meant to over-ride any other communication and in most cases that is exactly what is needed. In at least this sense, human cyborgs have already been created. But when you get more used to speaking with these devices through your shared links within the Units of Consciousness, the solutions offered will be more elegant and responsive. I cannot extrapolate on the ramifications of creating cyborgs for purposes other than healing at this time, save to say that you always have the choice of becoming more human or less human through myriads of decisions and methods.

Psychic Perception and Units of Consciousness:

Nevertheless psychometry, to some degree augury and other forms of psychic perception works because of the Units of Consciousness' ability to align with the human psychic perception and consciousness through Ether and the Fields of Translation. The Torsion Fields used are Para-sound, Para-light to a degree, as well as the dimension of Identity in its aspect as Formation. Para-sound and the Units of Consciousness also enable the human psychic ability to reach into alternate universes, as well as alternate worlds in your local universe: i.e., different haloclines of time, different realms as in the Faerie Realm, and so on, such as past lives and other minds.

Yet it is interesting that the Units of Consciousness align themselves with the dimension of Identity in such a way that you always recognize aspects of your experience that are a part of you, even though that recognition might immediately lead to rejection, rendering the memory opaque again. But in a very real sense, your human soul has scattered itself across all the universes, times, spaces and expressions of the Divine because you realize that you are a finite, particular part of that Oneness with which it is contemplating its Self.

Understandably, you want to succeed in opening what cannot be opened easily: enlightenment, which is the pure reflection of the Whole. And your identity-resonance within your personal array of these Units of Consciousness allows you to know who you are now, have been and will be.

What you are striving for in every life is pure harmonic resonance with the Divine Intention, because that clarity allows the Infinite to increase. The hologram of reality becomes refreshed with each re-perception so that the colors seemed brighter, the crystalline arrays of particles seemed clearer, the Divine Awareness is able to reach further and creativity is remade from its own substance again. Each moment of enlightenment re-anchors the Whole: these moments of perfect harmony with the Divine Mind help form the inner structure of this field of awareness.

Interestingly, this interplay of physical fields and forces is part of what has caused Spacetime's uneven distribution: certainly it has caused an uneven distribution of Healing, Grace and Peace in human history. There have been several shining times in history where places of learning, human dignity and zeal for creative discovery have added profoundly to human meaning. And there have been times when the brutish, cruel, selfish and thoughtless impulses of humanity have strangled possibilities and ruined lives in the pursuit of shortsighted gains.

Meditation: Opening Your Own Units of Consciousness' Inner Arrays:

You can begin by imagining an ancient, primordial sea: somewhat shallow and calm, it is still very clear. Imagine the sunlight glancing through the water as though it wanted to touch the dark depths and add life to them, infusing the water with brilliance and beauty. Imagine that you are a tiny, tiny form of life: a diatom, protozoa or rotifer, one that is perfectly at home in this still, clear sea. Feel yourself float in the water as lightly as a bubble, perfectly balanced in the water, sensing the light and the tiny currents that nudge you from here to there. Imagine you feel drawn to something far away from you: you swim toward it, moving silently in the clear, shining water.

As you swim closer, you feel minute, hair-like filaments brush against you, sliding gently over your tiny body without harming it. On a sudden impulse, you look for the place where all those filaments originate: where are their roots? It's odd: the further you go the smaller you become, so that the filaments you are hunting become

253

shining, shifting strands that catch the light like glass. And as you go further you get even smaller, small enough so that the tiny filaments seem to be huge cables, until they become immense, gently moving shining shapes overshadowing you.

Continue forward. As you move you become so small that you start bumping into the water molecules themselves: they seem to be gleaming, triplicate shapes that flicker and change more quickly than thought. And still you search for the filament's root, until you see a bright, still place from which all the sinuous glassy shapes originate, now so huge you can hardly see them. But you continue until you touch the light at their base: a warm, vibrant light that hums without sound and quivers without movement.

When you have reached the filament's root, you look up and see all the patterns and paths those lovely, glassine fibers create in the still, silent place that is smaller than even the inner parts of molecules. With an abrupt sense of wonder, you realize that these are your threads that you have used to weave your lifetimes into being! Spend a long moment watching them, feeling something of your own intention as a human soul. Know that everything you have done in your lives was done for the sake of discovery: the discovery of the Divine Being in the human self, and the Human Self in the divine.

Finally, return, floating gently back to the top of the sea. Know that, now you have gotten to the roots of your lives, you will begin to have dreams and memories of them, for you have touched the core of your own Identity at the level of your Units of Consciousness, reclaiming some of your original intentions, decisions, and discoveries. As you work with this meditation again, know that can re-set your life-paths, changing them so they are more in accord with your soul's true intention of revealing the Divine to Its Self.

Meditations to Open the Lemurians'
Inter-dimensional Sense

Key Points: Opening up your mind through meditations in order to start receiving "unofficial" information will help to re-train your mind/brain to learn and in some cases re-learn the Lemurians' awareness of the enfolded, higher-order dimensions. Contemplating triune instead of dualistic energy is another part of this increased inner sight. Becoming more aware of your own subtler bodies will help you to perceive how your brain is working. The meditations below build on some of what was presented in Volume One, using three points of focus to open up your multi-dimensional awareness.

Subheadings:

- Opening Dimensions of Perception

- Triune Perceptions

- Becoming Aware of the Subtler Bodies

- Reclaiming the Lemurian Feeling/Sight

- Meditation #1: Nerve/Brain Warm-up

- Meditation#2: Evolving the Multi-dimensional Focus, Part 1 & 2

Opening Dimensions of Perception:

In Volume One we gave a meditation to limber up the mind's dimensional perceptions by using the point, line, sphere and hypersphere: begin by imagining a point and then turning itself around itself until it becomes a line. Then use your original point as a pivot so that the line turns around the point to become a two-dimensional circle. Turn that circle around the original line like flipping a circle on a strung: it becomes a sphere. Then turn the sphere around the original circle to create a hyper-sphere.

If you work with that progression of dimensions diligently, you will find that your mind will become more used to thinking in other than the usual channels and with more than the usual methods. The other interesting thing that will happen is that you will automatically see some of the unofficial information contained in things. You might begin to see that a particular building on a particular piece of land looks very well built on its surface, but there will be something awry with it inside: it is badly placed for the energies in the land beneath it, or it was built in a mad hurry and was not built with integrity. You might look at a flower, seeing the other colors inside it or see its hidden colors as though you could suddenly perceive it in ultraviolet the way bees can.

There is no particular route of discovery: your mind will open up as its own multi-dimensional structure dictates, for your mind will always follow its native interests: beauty or utility, love or control. And it may be as tiring to open these changes in your perception as it would be to train for a marathon: it is wiser to do only a little at first. Your precise conscious focus was evolved over time as the best general focus for dealing with 4-D reality: it is foolish to step outside of this reality you're living in without making sure you are unlikely to get into an argument with that reality that you would certainly lose.

Triune Perceptions:

Another way to add dimensions to your thinking and perception is to consider, not duality, but triune energy: not the polarization of duality, because as long as you see things in dualistic terms, the most exciting combination you're ever going to get between black and white is gray, which is too frequently only confusion. In a very real sense you can learn how to see the *colors* of things: what is their inner meaning, energetic structure or intention? If you must see in opposites, make an effort to add a third factor each time. Think of up and down and sideways. Imagine good and evil and creativity, or hot and cold and loved. This will quite literally add dimensions to your thinking.

This may seem silly or artificial at first: how could you think of the inner meaning of the desk that you are working on? But you do it all the time with objects, realizing the meaning of anything from a precious family keepsake, a medal for bravery or an AA pin commemorating 15 years of sobriety. All of these things mean something far more than the materials they are made from or how new or worn they are. You will begin to evolve a tremendous sense of the *presence* of things: how their meaning through time gives them exquisitely particular and precious shapes inside of them: shapes of light and love. More than wanting to have some piece of someone's

256

magical life, such as an article of clothing from your favorite singer or the baseball someone threw in the winning game, you may realize that every separate thing, every object, has its own inner meaning, its inner "color," that keeps reality out of duality's trap.

We have also discussed perceiving "polarized" Time in the sense of being aware of Time's haloclines: the slightly different types of time in alternate and disparate times, as with alternate realities or the temporal perceptions in other species, material and immaterial Time and Magical Time. These haloclines may be considered offset temporal dimensions that need a specific parallax to be perceived.

As an example: if you were born significantly myopic visually and you took a trip in a car or a train, you would only be able to comprehend the things that were within your field of vision: the interior of the car and the people in it. You would not be able to understand the colors blurring past: the green blurs of trees, the gray of buildings or the yellow of prairies. People might even tell you about these, but you would have no referent points to understand how these colored shapes might be the things described, not even were someone to show you a book of pictures put right up to your nose.

It is similar with Time's haloclines: so many parts of Time sweep past your perceptions like the green blurs of the trees. If you were asked about trees when you finished your trip, you might be able to say, "Well, there were some nice colors, and some I liked better than others." But if someone were to ask you about the poplars, oaks or cottonwoods, you would likely stare at them in consternation. And again, even were they to show you pictures, you would never be able to tell that those green blurs were poplars or the gray blurs were office buildings: certainly not that one was a department store and the other was an apartment complex. What you could not see clearly, you could never comprehend. For most, 4-D reality is enough of a challenge that you need the steady reference-point that Time provides through its Möbius strip of enfolded temporal structure, so reaching out into other types of Time is often difficult.

Becoming Aware of the Subtler Bodies:

Another way to approach further dimensions of Reality is to become aware of the bodies inside your body: your dream or etheric body, your emotional body, your mental and spiritual bodies simultaneously with your physical form. Some of you are already

257

quite adept at doing this, already feeling comfortable enough with handling multiple inputs to be aware of several bodies at once. But simply imagining what your emotional body might look like after you have had an argument with someone or after you have greeted an old friend that you have missed, will add to your direct human experience.

Though, if your imagination is *too* vivid, viewing your emotional body could be a grisly experience: some people are quite capable of eviscerating and dismembering you emotionally; even self-castigation can leave deep scars. But to see your emotional body *as* a body may actually give you a reference point for change. If you can imagine or even see the deep, bloody furrows of self-harm or the bruises and broken "bones" resulting from emotional abuse from anyone including yourself, you might take greater care with guarding your emotions from such rough handling.

If you could see how mental issues such as loss of integrity, prevarication, bigotry or obsessive thinking damages and cripples your mental body, you might literally review your position on such careless and sloppy ways of thinking: if you could *see* how healthy, strong and supple your mental body became when you lived honestly with mental integrity, clarity and tolerance, you might be a little more interested in changing your mental attitudes. Such training was standard for several human societies, including the Lemurian, Atlantean and to some degree ancient Egyptian society as well. But when the tumult of clashing cultures, immense natural disasters or plagues forced your attention onto the immediate panic, such refinements as being aware of your subtle bodies were put aside, ignored and forgotten. Eventually even integrity, clarity and honesty had been forgotten as well.

Reclaiming the Lemurian Feeling/Sight:

Your physical senses are the brain's interpretation of the data that comes though the nerves into specific areas of sensitivity such as taste processed originally in the nose and tongue because smell is part of taste. Touch is a part of your kinesthetic sense, the sense of where your body is in space, so that you know that the soft sensation on your back is the pillow you're leaning against and not something you're holding in your hands. Sight is not simply interpreting vibrations of light: there is a tremendous amount of extra processing that goes on, such as correcting for the retina's blind spot automatically, to say nothing of the fact that, as all other lenses do, the lenses in your eyes put images of the world upside down on the retina.

As anyone listening to very loud music knows, hearing is again nerve impulses as interpreted through the brain, not simply receiving sound waves via the eardrum: not only can you hear throughout your body, but also your mind is busy editing, cataloging and correlating sounds constantly so that you can hear your friend's voice in the midst of the cacophony. And although tinnitus is most often caused by nerve damage, it is the brain that gets confused enough to keep "playing" that whine, hum or buzz long after the nerve damage may have been healed.

Most Lemurians had another form of perception; you might call it sight, you might call it comprehension or perhaps an exalted kinesthesia. Each Lemurian was trained from a very young age in a type of quantum perception that allowed him or her to discover and determine the inner nature of other people, things, places and situations. The present perceptions of good psychics reflect this other sense; however, even though this Lemurian sense engaged Para-sound as psychics do now, most Lemurians perceived the higher dimensional data contained in the Para-sound through a different physical form of brain/neuron communication.

This inner sense was part of their brain structure and had to be trained as much as sight, hearing, taste and touch are: you are told, "That's hot!" or, "That's cold" when as far as your brain is concerned it's just data from the nerves in your skin. Similarly, you are told, "No one can see ghosts/auras/angels: they're not real!" as much as you're told, "See that color? It's red-orange." The proof of this is when you have a clairvoyant family that quite cheerfully trains its children to see auras, shadows of the past, ghosts and angels: these children generally retain that sense if they are born equipped with it.

Now: Lemurians were indeed human beings, as you are, but because they were used to the "language" of this feeling/sight, they trained their children in it intentionally. Much as there are some shibboleths in language that you cannot pronounce unless you are raised with the sounds, this feeling/sight is potential in your brains even now, but it is neither natural nor automatic: it must be learned again. However, because of the human brain's adaptive plasticity, all children, barring congenital birth defects, are born with the ability to speak any human sound and, indeed, could mimic any other human language if they wished, as well as nearly any animal call. So, although you would have a distinct psychic "accent," you could learn at least the easier stages of this Lemurian feeling/sight.

The little meditations above are actually a first step: like a baby's babble that allows the mind/brain to get used to connecting the intention of speaking with the sounds produced, they help train you to perceive when you are working in the deeper realms of Para-sound. Unfortunately, it is likely that only the relatively gifted will break through into feeling/sight. Oddly enough, already being psychic might be as much a hindrance as a benefit: rather like your mind trying to reach for the Italian you have already learned in order to understand Swedish when your original language is English: your mind will try to look into the box labeled "the other language" to find the new Swedish word in that box that contains only Italian. However, your mind/brain will benefit from the exercises below, even though you may not have immediate results.

Meditation #1: Nerve/Brain Warm –up:

You do this meditation with your eyes open and unfocused, in a situation with some ambient noise: the wind in the leaves, a CD with rainfall playing or the sound of the clothes dryer in the background. Begin by trying to discern which part of your brain is processing the information: you may already know that sight is decoded in the back of the brain in the visual cortex and the sense of hearing is decoded in the left temporal lobe primarily. But knowing that is not necessary: you are learning how to trust your own feelings, without distress concerning how correct those perceptions may be. This is *your* mind/brain and you need to become comfortable with it, not worry about whether or not you perceive data according to any standard model.

If you haven't already had too much practice multitasking, at the very least this meditation helps you to think in three dimensions and starts getting you used to doing two things at once. But it also helps you realize something about the part of yourself that watches yourself while it is *being* itself, rather like the infinity created by two mirrors facing each other and reflecting your image into an infinite curve. This helps you get the sense of where you are "placed" in relationship to that infinity and helps you remember that your essential Core of Self is timeless, spaceless and infinite.

260

When you have a sense of your mind/brain and how it works, it is essential to shift your intention into your heart, because the heart is where the Torsion Field of Translation operates, allowing the "solid" core of reality to express itself through you. Metaphorically, the mind is a telescope's lens, but the heart is the telescope with its internal mirrors and its tripod stand. Without the heart, the mind cannot perceive things well or completely. Certainly the mind cannot see as it was designed to see, no matter how clear or accurately focused.

It may take a little practice to think of the mind and heart at once, especially if you feel that they are opposed in substance or intention. But actually expanding your sense of self may make it easier: you may enlarge your areas of perception until you feel as though you are outside and inside of your body simultaneously. If this is done correctly, you will feel more centered and at ease, because you actually begin to touch your Core Self that is beyond space and time, within the infinite Now that changes infinitely without losing its essential identity or its sense of purpose.

Meditation #2: Evolving the Multi-dimensional Focus, Part 1 & 2:

Part One:

Once you have done the above warm-up, sit for a moment with your eyes closed and center your attention on your heart. Become more than unusually aware of your body: how the nerves and muscles keep the skeleton in place, working through the constant communication between the brain, mind and body. Feel your body's particular consciousness that has nothing to do with the brain: the basic kinesthesia that helps you know you are in the chair this particular way, and how your breathing shifts your position slightly in the chair. Imagine for a moment that you were used to perceiving the world through your body instead of through your sense of sight and the conscious focus of your brain. You may actually feel some little shivers of excitement from your body's cells because you are appreciating their input, not as background noise but as of at least equal importance to your mind/brain's perceptions.

Use this same kinesthetic/cellular perception to focus on the back of the skull, where it curves down to meet the neck vertebrae. In other words, don't *think* of the back of your brain: *feel* it and feel *through* it, being aware of how it is able to feel itself without thought. Feel the natural connection between this part of the brain and the heart: there is a constant subtle flow of energy between the two. Add your heart into your awareness.

Finally, allow these two points of consciousness in these two places of your body, the heart and the back of the skull, to create a third point of consciousness outside of the body in front of you. This point can be in front of your third eye, your nose or your throat; however, it will be the apex of a triangle, with the line of energy between your heart and the back of your brain creating the triangle's base. It is best if you don't focus your attention too strongly: you are not trying to focus your thoughts or *mind* in front of you, but instead are opening up the focus of your body's own consciousness through your conscious awareness, with much the same attention you have been giving your body.

Part Two:

Still keeping aware of your heart, the back of your brain and the point of focus, breathe gently, putting yourself in a state of gentle receptivity. Simply receive information from this apex point in front of you by allowing it to communicate to you. If you are doing this exercise with receptivity and focus properly balanced, you will start receiving dream-like information: images or thoughts that are a little chaotic or at least unexpected, with a peculiar sense of knowing and understanding something that would make no sense to your mind. In any event it will be at least paradoxical: a small point that contains an ocean of data or a point that seems incredibly far away even though it might be only 18 inches in front of your nose.

At this time you may need to exercise self-control in order not to push your thoughts forward to analyze the data: you need to remain as receptive as possible. Much as you do not force your eyes to see, the more you can allow this point to simply perceive the information and communicate it to you, the better. If you start to feel a headache or tension in your neck or shoulders, you're over-working the exercise and should close it.

When you feel balanced and receptive, use your kinesthesia to "gaze" at the multi-dimensional point in front of you as though you were looking into water, hoping to see a fish coming up to the surface. As said above, you will see dream-like flickers of things, with small touches of feeling that may be so fleeting that you cannot discern what emotions those feelings represent. But do not be alarmed: as the eyespot on flatworms and some unicellular animals can only perceive gradations of light and dark, this new focus point can only handle certain types of M-D information at first. But by opening this point of perception you will have added to your functional awareness of Reality.

Unfortunately, here are very few trainers available now that could teach you to see further and help you get used to perceiving the sometimes wildly unofficial and chaotic data from the higher-level enfolded dimensions, for in a very real sense you would be learning how to see all over again. Much as someone that has been blind from birth and receives an operation that allows him or her to see again, learning to interpret what he or she sees uses the same trial and error that a child must use. You have to allow the new sight to grow and allow your brain to interpret it properly. However, watching Reality through that third point of focus will help you become constantly aware of the higher dimensions and that alone is beneficial.

Appendix One: Meditation to Uncover Your Core Tone

To uncover your spiritual self's Core Tone, focus on the heart chakra. As the pituitary has been called the "master gland" for the physical endocrine system, the heart chakra affects the other chakras in much the same way. If you are practiced in sensing the chakras' subtle energies, you may simply focus on the heart chakra as though searching or inquiring for a known voice in the hubbub of a crowd. Simply ask yourself to "hear" the silent tone of your Self, the tone that is really only your own. When you hear its silent note, you feel a gentle, welcoming elation, and/or a sense of peace. This Core Tone is silent: so complex and refined a sound that the physical body cannot perceive it directly.

Although similar to spiritual centering, finding your Core Tone does not contract your awareness to a single point: rather, because it is dimensionally unfolded and enfolded simultaneously, it is the ability to be aware of your own multi-dimensional perspective. You can add to your perception of these higher-level dimensional characteristics of your silent Core Tone by taking its energy and compressing its apparent "size," making it tinier and tinier until, as with the Chakra Energy Re-set we presented in Volume One, the silent sound's point of focus turns "inside out" becoming as immeasurably vast as the Zero dimension itself, while still retained within the sonic "shape" of your inner Tone.

You may find yourself suddenly breathing deeply, or yawning: this inward breath is literally inspiration, aligning your subtle bodies beautifully. Just touching your Core Tone in the course of the day or in your spiritual practices can in itself have very good effects, helping to regulate and harmonize your 4-D and M-D relationships. "Hearing" this silent sound is much like feeling emotionally touched by someone's kindness, remembering a quiet, secret joy you once had, some special news or a present from a beloved friend.

If you have not had much practice with subtle energies, the second method is to sit somewhere peaceful where you can breathe. Fold your hands over your heart and breathe gently for five to ten breaths. These intentional breaths are sufficient to engage the silent, super-refined Core Tone. You may not feel any difference at all, but if you persist, you will gradually have a sense of: "It's all right now," or, "I remember more of who I am now." You will very likely feel, "Things are going right for me at last," or, "I have something I can work with."

This is certainly one meditation you can do any time you have a moment.

Appendix Two: Questions About the Afterlife from D. Lopez: Tesla and Heaven

Introduction from Francesca:

FT: As far as I know, Heaven is a place of comfort and comforting; love and peace. *Heaven is whatever version of Earth that will make you feel most loved.* After death you can go anywhere, instantly and take as much "time" as you wish with anything. Heaven is Timeless and whatever you want it to be or whatever you need: a place of beauty or worship; a place of solitude, peace or healing. There are protective Heavens, where people that have been abused can find lovely places of fields and flowers with nothing but quiet places: no people. Someone that has been in great pain or fear might be brought straight to a Heavenly hospital, where they go through procedures until they realize they don't hurt any more. The one exception I have heard is that people that are addicted can remain addicted even after they leave their bodies, because the habit is so strong, even stronger than the "habit" of having a body.

Heaven is like 4-D reality, but all the uncomfortable places, the rough edges and demands have all been removed. In addition, you can see anyone you wish, connecting up with people that you lost track of from your past life. You can visit any place you like, not only in Heaven, where everything is constructed of thought-forms but, with practice, also see anyone on Earth. Because they feel so much the same as their usual selves, a great many people that have died don't even know it: they still feel they have a body, they see people they know and they can stay in the place where they died. We so are *used* to having a body that we remember it and don't always notice that it is acting differently. If you have been in pain, you certainly notice when the pain is gone! But because even in Heaven you can still remember being hungry enough to eat, you can eat anything you wish, so it's hard to notice you're not still on Earth.

This also means that, if you want a Heaven that has your old dead gang members around you, you will find them; this is where the Tibetan concept of the Bardo comes in also. If your idea of Heaven is a 5-star hotel where you get all the attention you crave, that will be the Heaven you create. If your idea of Heaven is a cruise ship, or a cattle ranch, or an extended adventure, that will be created for and with you.

Everything is possible, including, sadly enough, Hell. For the people that have died in dangerous or frightening circumstances, staying where they died can make their experience like Hell and worse. If they feel guilty enough, they may create a Heaven full of God's disdain so that He acts as Judge, Punisher and even Torturer in the Hell their terror creates. But these are all *thought-forms*: like true things spun out of dreams, they can feel as real as you need them to feel or that you fear them to be. Yet there *are* guides, Ministers and Angels to assist! By becoming part of the dream and changing it powerfully, these beings can enter the nightmare and sometimes quite quickly help the deceased soul find a way out of the Hells they have created.

D Lopez: Where is Tesla living now?

Nikola Tesla: Thank you for asking, Mr. Lopez: In a way I am in many places at once. I am helping several children on Earth right now, so I focus on the Earth plane a fair amount. I won't tell you who they are because they need not to be hounded by the press or quizzed by those that do not respect them. They are not I: they are their own selves.

I also spend what are to me extended periods of time simply communing with the Universe in its own Nature: I allow its secrets to permeate me within the attentive care of the Divine Mind. Of course I have time with Francesca, but she is hardly my largest project and she knows that. As I said in my first article to her, I spend time in realms of pure Creativity, visiting old friends, new teachers, exploring possibilities for myself and for the Earth. I study the ramifications of what I have done in this last life and examine alternate possibilities.

You ask about several teachers, below: I have seen several of them already and may look up the others that you have mentioned. As to where I am living: when I want it, I have a "home," but it changes depending on my mood. At times I re-create my old workshop; at times I visit my old New York apartment and my pigeons. At times I join symposiums where I give lectures. But the real home I experience is the Presence of the Mind that is Within the Supernal Light: the divine, loving Being of God.

DL: Are you in Telos?

NT: I have been there: my vibration is similar to its now. That is a true thing: you can never reach to a higher place within Heaven than your own vibration dictates: this may be one of the real reasons why a spiritual life should be cultivated. Not only do you raise your vibration enough to see, learn, do and experience so much more and of such greater value when you leave your body, when you have lived a spiritual life your Heaven is wide and full, rich with wonders and discovery.

DL: In what dimension are you?

NT: You might say that I am in the dimension of the soul or perhaps the dimension of the heart. If you like you may say that I am in the n-dimension: the dimension of all dimensions. I have as much of the 4-D experience as I wish: length, breadth, height and Time because this dimension contains all of them. If I want to climb a high mountain I will climb it indeed, though generally I am more aware of ideas, concepts, beings, physical Reality's process of manifestation and several aspects of my own self and soul. I did need some healing when I arrived and I still go back to aspects of my precious life from which I can learn.

DL: What is the best way to contact Tesla directly and learn more about the universes?

NT: Undoubtedly you must first determine whether or not you have any mediumistic ability... And you need to know how to test the spirit you speak with, including me. Francesca uses the method of asking me, "Do you come of God?" and if I am a true spirit I can and must say, "Yes, I come of God." If the spirit cannot say that, it is not a good spirit. This removes the potential for malicious or manipulative souls to interfere; it also removes confusion in the sense that you will know that you are speaking to another, real being and not your own subconscious fantasies regarding that being. (If someone purports to be me and is not, then you banish that spirit. If it is I, and we merely did not connect well, I will communicate again.)

Dear Mr. Lopez, you already know much of this, but if you do not mind a review: Contemplate communicating with me and sit quietly centered in your heart with a receptive mind. If you see/hear/sense a spirit then test it; when the tests are complete then start by seeing, hearing or feeling the information. Sometimes it is easier to write down the information longhand, though some type it into a computer and others tape it.

Comment from Francesca: It also helps if you are aware of your most natural psychic abilities: clairvoyance, clairaudience, clairsentience or pure inspiration, as generally everyone has one major talent, a good second talent but rarely do you have all three or four, unless you are a true Master.

DL: Is there really a Karmic Board, a group of heavenly beings that judge your acts on Earth?

NT: Yes and no, and also yes. There are beings that weigh and measure the dross in your soul as though they were assaying ore, so that is my first "yes." But no, they do not determine your punishment: they merely assess, for the true judge is your own soul, spirit and your own kernel of the Wisdom of God. And yes, sooner or later *every* soul will receive a life-review: you will re-experience your life in its entirety, not only in terms of your own experience but in terms of how you have affected others and how those effects cascade and reach throughout Humanity. Certainly, if you have had a painful, frustrating and miserable life, this experience of review is made as gentle as possible or is even delayed until you have had enough rest; the same care is taken if your mind was compromised somehow, whether through illness or drug abuse.

If you have been a cruel and vicious person, say, a terrorist, your circumstances will differ. So many of these are so truly convinced that their deaths *must* guarantee them the Heaven of their dreams, they will encounter that Heaven first and only later see the cost of cutting short the lives of those they have murdered. Some will spend relative centuries just dealing with their own impacts! Others can willfully move on quickly and hurtle back to Earth without taking any time to face themselves. These must be treated differently, for it usually takes several Archangels to heal them of their blindness.

Comment from Francesca: I have also experienced standing before a group of beings, Karmic Lords perhaps, that I call the Tribunal. This was for a situation where I lacked empathy and didn't "get it" about my impact on other people: my mind was so sure of itself and so divorced from compassion or understanding that it took the great spirits of that Tribunal to catch me up short and *show* me what I had done. This was done in utter love, compassion and understanding: their purpose was not torture or to cause me pain but rather to open my *comprehension*.

DL: Does everyone need to go to the Underworld to pay his/her Karma?

NT: Karma generated on the Earth is generally cleared on the Earth plane. You may not have to repay your mistakes to the exact same person you harmed but you will be brought back again and again to the lesson you did not learn the first time. You will eventually balance the scales of action and reaction. You can, if you choose, work on your Karma in Heaven, but it is rather like trying to work as though you were in your place of business when you are actually on vacation on a remote island: the ease, comfort, pleasure and peace of Heaven is far, far easier to remain with than the lessons that you did not learn. The Earth plane can be terrible, hard, and unforgiving, but it does help you learn things quickly and well.

DL: What does Tesla eat where he is?

NT: I eat in Heaven as I did on Earth: only if I feel like it! But I must laugh a little. Because I was so enchanted with my visions and working them into reality I hardly ate on Earth: the visions took nearly all of my attention. I haven't changed that much, so I am still only eating when someone invites me to dinner, perhaps...

DL: Are there houses? How do they compare with the ones on Earth?

NT: Yes, there are houses: some are very similar to whatever house you lived in last, though some are incredible mansions spun out of the dreams you had while you were on Earth. Some are hovels, if that is all you feel you deserve. One of the main gifts of a spiritual life is concentration and that helps the afterlife tremendously: what you create with your mind and feelings here can shift and change very quickly depending on your thoughts and emotions, reflecting your own mercurial state of being. For young souls, there are helpers to keep this shifting landscape from overwhelming them. It is easier when you have more experience: when things change you can very well imagine you are traveling from one place to another. But generally, only those who truly wish to live in palaces of crystal or temples of clouds do so.

DL: Are there plants, flowers and animals where Tesla is? Are there mosquitoes there?

NT: Any form that is on Earth will be found in one Heaven or another: *any* form. And honestly, if swatting mosquitoes was something that would give you great joy and pleasure, there are plenty here. However, as every person is infinite within his self, that self's expression is also infinite and based in Love. This means that Heaven has all forms, especially those that bring comfort and healing: this includes animals, particularly loved pets and companions. There are also creative realms where new animal-forms and ecosystems are created: those reams are highly interesting!

DL: What do the animals eat? Do they eat each other as on Earth?

NT: There are Animal-Heavens made for animals, where all that was on Earth is continued to one degree or another: the predator finds its prey, the prey runs and escapes or yields and is consumed, though you must remember that these are images created from the habits of memory and dreams. The blood in Heaven is truly only the memory of blood; the fear is the memory of fear, for each Animal Heaven gives the animal what pleasure and solace it needs. Especially when with their human friends, pets can eat their favorite foods again, play their favorite games, spend time with their human family; they can move back into more primitive experiences or on into another life. They do not have as strong a sense of individuality as human beings, though of course those that are remembered and loved specifically retain that specificity. You can have an old pet reincarnate into a new body.

DL: Do plants emit light in Heaven, and if so, what colors?

NT: The colors on Earth are shadows of those in Heaven: there are more colors here, and they are richer, deeper and reflect the divine Mind and its Creativity more accurately. There are lovely, enchanted "fairy-gardens" here with gleaming flowers and mystical colors that several people have created together. You can visit such a garden or you can create one for yourself. Yet, in a very real sense the trees, flowers and other plants here also become lenses through which the Light, Comprehension, Beauty and Creativity of the Divine Mind shines, so that they, too, capture the divine Presence in their forms.

DL: Is there rain and rainbows as on Earth?

NT: Of course: if they give you joy, they are in your Heaven. And if you delight in fireworks or drag races, horse racing or beekeeping, you will find them here and enjoy them.

DL: Are there books as known in the Earth? What type of books: only spiritual books?

NT: There are the *forms* of books, the memories acted upon by thought: they feel and seem every bit as solid as you remember them. And there are "books" of Wisdom, patterns and areas of focus that reveal spiritual information: you may feel as though you were *inside* these books, swept up in their knowledge or their particular story in order to truly understand what is presented. If spiritual books give you joy, of course they will be there; if a thriller, romance, or how-to book pleases you more, that is what you would find.

Needless to say, there are countless writers here! Some of them keep working, writing or re-writing their stories; others ask permission to speak with people they find interesting and from whom they might learn. There are enclaves of numerous sorts: any group of similarly minded individuals may gather as long as their vibrations are much the same, though there are exceptions, as when someone of any skill becomes broad enough in his comprehension and compassion that he or she can work with many different types of people. There are lecture halls were famous people speak; the audiences may include people of limited vibration or experience, so that they may learn new things. There are classrooms where scientists demonstrate and debate their discoveries with hopeful students; there are gatherings where Archangels speak and are even churches where Jesus joins the congregation.

DL: Are there books stored in crystalline quartz or in paper?

NT: All knowledge is stored within the Mind of God: changed, expanded upon, and enriched by that Being's countless experiences within manifestation, deepened and widened in Heaven. There are all forms of this Divine Knowledge in Heaven, because there are some amazing forms of books in physical manifestation on other planets: crystal tablets, sheets of metal, knotted strings and patterns of beads; the shells of invertebrates that have been altered to grow with the words created by their color-patterns; arrangements of colored stones and patterns created by woven fur. I have even heard of one place where they "write" their knowledge in forms of solid air and I will certainly pursue that demonstration to see how that may be done.

DL: About technology: Do they have more advanced technology compared with what we have of Earth?

NT: In Heaven, all things are conceived in principle, whereas on Earth, all things are proved in action: in the human mind and being, all things that are created change both Heaven and Earth. There are also numerous *planes* or levels of manifested existence where more advanced technology exist, both on Earth as in Telos and other hidden places, as well as on other worlds. New technological ideas do indeed exist in Heaven, as well as the results of that technology in the sense of the memories of those that have experienced its effects, because they create Heaven from their own experiences. In alternate realities there are any numbers of Earths that have followed an entirely different path, so there are times when that information bleeds through from one creative mind to another and reaches a Heaven I can visit.

DL: Are the beings visible and invisible as they request: In other words, do they create their own reality with their thoughts and feelings?

NT: Yes: that is the true nature of Heaven: you are seen, if you wish and held privately in the Mind of God if you wish. Even on Earth, many human beings have crowds of people, entities, Principles and angels around them that are all invisible and unless you are clairvoyant you will not see them. Yet in Heaven, these beings are far more visible: as when you fly in an airplane, you can surely see so much more in Heaven than the one upon the ground on Earth.

DL: Do the people in Heaven practice the five main human values: Righteousness, Truth, Peace, Love and Non-Violence?

NT: If they do not practice them naturally in Heaven where all is peace, comfort and Joy in the Presence, they are shown the consequences of not practicing those values: not in punishment or retribution but in love. It is easy to follow these values when the Grace and Peace of Divine Love surround you. The true miracle is when, even trammeled and burdened by anxious concerns and trying challenges, so many human beings do follow these precepts when incarnate.

DL: What are the beings like where Tesla is? What are their faces like?

NT: When I want to see a beloved face of any person or being I can certainly see it. There are many who do not have a form at all, yet the clear sense of their presence is so strong that they are instantly

273

recognizable and their emotions are unmistakable. I have seen some beings from other planets: some of their faces are strange indeed, though some of them are very human in their forms and manner. However, that is a subject for another discussion.

DL: How do they procreate? Are they masculine and feminine as on Earth?

NT: To the best of my awareness, no one procreates in Heaven as they do on Earth. There are mutual pleasures as intense as human sexuality, though when the bodies are made of light-energy this pleasure is certainly of a different nature. In Heavens where their inhabitants feel that sexual pleasure is the widest, deepest and best Heaven they can comprehend, that is indeed given to them, but that is merely their will and desire, clothed in darkling light, engaging thought-forms.

This aside, most people in Heaven or the Other Side, are neither male nor female, nor are they confused in their gender: they are human beings, with human personalities, wills and the desire to create. There are those that create more than thought-forms: i.e., they are wise and experienced enough to work directly with soul-stuff and help God create new souls and other energies to inhabit new forms, as in times of mass extinction on a planet when new selves must be created to inhabit the novel forms of life. That is as close to procreation as I have discovered.

DL: Do people in heaven meditate, pray, do japa, and love in God all the time?

NT: Those who wish and will to do so can and do, of course. There are those that spend eons in meditation and prayer, but in this timeless existence, those eons may seem as one perfect instant in *darshan* (communion through the glance) with God.

DL: Are they in the top or highest level of consciousness?

NT: Those I described in the answer above are very high in consciousness, indeed, but the only highest level is the level of the All, the All that shifts constantly and joyfully into new and more brilliant forms within the multiverse of infinite infinities. In short, there is no end to prayer or advancement unless a fragment of that divine Consciousness chooses to stop, pausing its forward momentum.

DL: Are the people in Heaven constantly studying to evolve to other more advanced levels of consciousness?

NT: Again, this is determined by each one's preference, but yes, everyone advances and everyone evolves, no matter how slowly, imperfectly or sometimes reluctantly.

DL: Do people fight each other as on Earth because of their egos?

NT: No, fights concerning ego biases are not generally tolerated: usually a person's guides or angels step in. And indeed, most people do change a bit after death, and sometimes more than a bit, so that their souls shine through a little more. (If a boxer's idea of his best Heaven is to fight a worthy opponent, of course that is another thing.) There are times when those who were bitter enemies see each other on the other side and realize they were such good friends that they chose to challenge each other in order to grow. Generally, you can totally avoid your enemies and challengers. This is one of the reasons why soul development can be very slow in Heaven for many: they have no need or method by which to learn tolerance, forbearance, forgiveness, self-determination or empathy in quite the same way human beings may.

DL: Does marriage exist there as on Earth?

NT: The short answer is no. However, dreams may be realized in Heaven, including the perfect wedding in all its panoply: there may be those who wish to re-celebrate the wedding they knew or reaffirm their commitment to each other with a special ceremony and in this case the wedding bells ring indeed. However, the general ramifications of Earthly marriage are not there, such as wife as property, husband as sole provider or marriage as a way of creating children for the sake of the dynasty, family or religion.

DL: What is Tesla doing there: on which projects is he working? Can Tesla tell us about them?

NT: I am working on understanding human beings, including my own human self, as the human condition often perplexed me in my life as Nikola Tesla. I am working, with the Essential Divine Creativity again, if indeed I have ever stopped. I am excited about the increasing light within the Earth as well as the transitional aspects of the Shift that can be said to have already happened and has not yet occurred: there are varying degrees of readiness in human experience now. I am working to help shift some of the ideas regarding

275

technology itself: there are several unforeseen limitations and complications that would be created if certain potential futures are pursued, among them the unnecessary melding of man and machine, or the careless creation of machine "intelligence."

DL: Who works with him on his projects?

NT: I have actually been working with Carl Jung in this Volume Three: I find him a man of great compassion and intelligence. His wisdom is based on his own courage, because he searches for things within the human psyche that are as powerful and real as any fields or energies in physics. Pursuing some of the information for Healing in Volume Two, I consulted with several physicians: Dr. Jonas Salk; Pierre and Madame Curie; Rosalind Franklin, co-discoverer of the double helix of DNA. I have also worked with several others regarding the immune system particularly, as that system in the body works most directly with the dimension of Identity. When we were working on the issues of the Hypnosis of the Media and the Marketplace for this volume, I had the great pleasure to meet Erik Erikson and had long talks with him about human motivations.

You see I cannot list everyone: there are several I have worked with just recently for the channeled material and several others that I have sought out for my own reasons. I have not had much to do with Edison or Westinghouse: they are pursuing other issues. Westinghouse is actually one of those that are trying to help the financial world find a new stability, along with several other financiers, Dale Carnegie amongst them. But lest you believe that "we famous folk" simply gather in each other's company in rarified circles, please know that I have also consulted several herb-wives, shamans, witches and "witch doctors" as well as many other people unknown to history. I cannot always view whomever I wish, but if there is someone with an answer I seek I may speak with that one only if his or her state of soul-energy resonates with or matches with mine.

DL: Does he have family over there with him?

NT: Yes. I have particularly spent time with my mother Duka, my brother Dane and my sisters Angelina and Milka. I was most pleased to find Dane waiting for me: his death affected me a great deal. My father Milutin and I have not been much in each other's company, but that is because he has already reincarnated and I must catch him when he is dreaming; my other sister Marica is also quite engaged elsewhere.

DL: Does Tesla do other projects not based in science?

NT: But of course I do, such as numerous searches and inquiries: psychology, spirituality, mediumship and other psychic practices; occasionally business and finances, though I confess I still tire of the minutiae; I have also studied harmonics and music and had long, if somewhat unexpected, talks with several artists, Albrecht Durer among them.

DL: Has Tesla seen God? Can he describe Him?

NT: I could not say I have seen God: that Being is too vast, too huge. But I have felt the love of His Divine Glance and have received much joy in His presence. The Divine Being's understanding is so wide and yet so perfect, that each man or woman is given just the right amount of caring, just the right amount of understanding to feel at home, to feel surely at peace. I have certainly seen my own guides: some of them have been with me for all of my lifetimes, including my Akashic Record Keepers, but also those beings that provided inspiration, blessing and wisdom throughout my life.

DL: Has he seen Jesus, mother Mary, any Angels or Archangels?

NT: I have seen several Archangels, numerous angels and have indeed spoken with Mary and Jesus, more the former than the latter. Most of the Archangels and many of the angels are not human: i.e., they are the organizing and embodying principles of substances, fields, forces and divine intentions. In respect of this I don't generally ask them to look as they are depicted in current artistic convention, with wings and flowing robes. Remembering the comfort my pigeons gave me, I have also seen the angels that work with animals: that can be a very interesting experience indeed.

DL: Does he talk to people there verbally, or communicate using telepathy?

NT: All communication is telepathic, but those especially recently arrived (or at times simply stubborn!) do use the appearance of speaking language. However, there is no language barrier here: meaning is communicated directly.

DL: Does he use his senses there, his mind or only his intellect? Does he use Divine Consciousness?

NT: If I choose to have senses to use, of course they are there. I have no need for food, but I can still smell a wonderful dish a friend has created or the delicate scent of a rose. If I wish for a Heaven with cold, bitter winds, such a place can be created for me; if I wish halcyon days and a swim in a river, then that is my experience. Heaven reflects our own joys, you see. However, although it is at one time vaster and richer than Earth, the Earth experience is unique and therefore quite precious. Our Heavens are created from our Earthly experiences, and our Earthly experiences may indeed reflect Heaven. As to the Divine Consciousness, it is as logical to say that this Consciousness uses me for its perceptions on Earth and in Heaven both.

DL: Is there any secret information of the universe where he is?

NT: The answer is yes, of course, there is much secret information: there are hidden methods for accomplishing countless things; there are Mysteries beyond description; there are countless hidden places where you may experience complete privacy when you speak with the Divine within yourself: that is a secret indeed. But you do realize it is not my place to tell these Mysteries or secrets until the proper time: physical Reality is balanced on such a sharp edge that only the most judicious hand may change the factors that comprise it. Despite the political, economic and social difficulties in the present, there is more hope for Humanity's creative flowering in the coming years than might be supposed. Though yes, of course there are treasures of mysteries in Heaven, anything from curing all diseases to creating peace: these mysteries and secrets are drawn upon as needed and as granted through Grace.

DL: Has Tesla been able to visit another planet, galaxy or universe?

NT: Yes: I have been given leave to attend a number of symposiums where the presenters spoke of the physics of other worlds and then, at my request, encountering the societies on the planets where this wisdom was evolved. I found it all quite fascinating, though there were times when I felt that could not comprehend more than a portion of what was presented. I have certainly *seen* other planets, galaxies and universes: their splendor can hardly be described. But I have not embodied in any of these places: I remain within the higher-level vibrations of Heaven. I am at present like any other guide or voice of inspiration: invisible and inaudible to most and while I can perceive Earth, I cannot participate save in special circumstances.

DL: Can he expand on the subject of traveling to other planets in Heaven?

NT: The Knowledge and Presence of the Divine Mind reflects upon all of our minds here in Heaven, so we can be given the gift of perceiving another plane of existence, as in the fairy realm or the realm of Telos: an area of coherent vibration that is able to interpenetrate an already existing place in a "polarized" fashion that makes it invisible to most forms of light and clear to see in other forms of light. I have seen other planets and star systems, other galaxies and alternate universes simply because the Divine, Loving Mind knew it would bring me delight. There is very little sense of time here, as we are in the Infinite Now; Jane Roberts (whom as I mentioned I have met) described it best as the ever-changing infinite Creativity that seeks to express itself in all forms, all possibilities within the bounds of time and space.

DL: Does he have to travel through a black hole to get to other planets and galaxies?

NT: No, though I could have that experience if I were to wish it.

DL: Can he comment on beings and technologies from Venus, especially Sanat Kumara, founder of the Great White Brotherhood?

NT: I have studied Venus, yes, visiting its sphere of influence. Venus is for many the premier locus for Love: the place where Love is discerned, comprehended and given depth and breadth. In a very real sense there are no technologies as such on this side: there are few "gizmos," and there are instead more enlightened structures of healing words. There is work being done there to help prevent suicides and wars, prejudice, bigotry and racial and class hatred; work is being done for children: foster children, orphans, runaways, slaves of all kinds and more.

Any place where more love would assist healing or any kind of true betterment that could be created is promoted there, and yes, by many beings including the Great White Brotherhood. I have not yet visited with Sanat Kumara, but that is simply because I have not felt the need to speak with that being in the course of my own work and studies. I may choose to work with the Brotherhood at some point, for they are beings of great love and dedication to the empowerment of Humanity but so far I haven't made a point of it.

DL: Does Tesla have any comments on the sages and rishis from India?

NT: Yes: it has been quite fine seeing some of their lives "from the inside," so to speak. I have had the privilege of engaging with the living points of view of several spiritual people: rishis, sanyasi and also monks, shamans and others. In a way rather similar to a virtual reality movie, I have been given permission to see things as they have seen them, learning the rhythms of their lives, thoughts and divine experiences.

DL: Has he seen such spiritual people as:

Swami Sai Baba? Yes, briefly: he was giving a lecture regarding kindness. *The god Shiva?* Yes, in the sense of some of His least human aspects: the tremendous forces within the dimension or Primordial Chaos. *And Krishna?* Yes. He has a wickedly keen sense of humor, in addition to His natural grace. *Ramana Mahashi?* Yes, though only briefly as well. We spent some time talking about pigeons and other birds. *Paramahansa Yogananda?* Oh, yes: he is quite interested in the present situation for the world and not simply concerned with India.

DL: Has Tesla seen any other Masters or sages?

NT: Yes, those I have described above and others. I have seen several people that are unknown because they have understood some point or aspect of Reality that I needed at the time and could refine my description of it. As a rule, unless that is part of the Heaven that feeds our needs for love and comfort, we do not venerate other people or beings here: we are all expressions of the Divine Being that this Being values everyone qually.

DL: Has Tesla visited Brahmaloka or Visnuloka?

NT: Certainly, if you understand Brahmaloka to be the place where you contemplate the Divine Creative Being/Force and where that Divine Being contemplates you. Every soul entering the Afterlife is given that opportunity, though not all take advantage. Some do not because of fear: if they have been taught to fear God their entire lives, they do not want to meet Him: the Judge, Punisher and stern Assessor of Souls that they have been taught Him to be. Even some that believe God is Love are uncertain about being seen by Love: they fear what Love will demand of them, or fear how they have failed Love. However, the Divine Regard can be as subtle and unthreatening as the scent of roses on the breeze or the quite sound of surf. Some even see the Divine through the filter of a person they once knew that was kind to them. It is so individual!

DL: What other sciences does Tesla work with in his projects?

NT: I have been pursuing several aspects of psychology, certainly: that is reflected in our books. I have been learning a good deal more about astrophysics as well, though I can only hint at the fact that there are some exciting discoveries trembling on the brink that involve the paradoxes and differences between terrestrial physics and galactic physics, to say nothing of the "nothing" in between the galaxies.

I have spent some time studying fluid dynamics and of course with several forms of healing. My studies in DNA have been extensive as well and there is more to do there. I have attended some symposiums on optics and the subtle natures of Light and I have had long conversations with several about family dynamics as well. I am free to pursue what interests me, as are all here. If all you wish to do with your Heaven is to catch up with all the television shows you have missed and speak with the deceased actors from your favorite movies, then that will certainly be your experience. Heaven is broad, vast, forgiving and highly interactive. And yet it is not the 4-D experience!

DL: Is Tesla working with Newton, Einstein, or others?

NT: Yes, certainly: I have seen and worked with many scientists known and unknown. Einstein has stepped back a bit for a little while: he is contemplating a life of simple pleasures and humor. Newton is still a man of great enthusiasm and energy, and has become quite good at presenting lectures. Yes, Time flows differently here: there is no time and yet your experiences unfold as though Time still existed when you wish. Newton himself has been recently fascinated with Time, so he and I intend to do some more work with it.

DL: Does Tesla argue and fight with other scientists as we do on Earth, or just discuss ideas?

NT: The discussions might become animated and energetic but there are only fights when all parties concerned wish fights to happen. As I said earlier: if you were a boxer or a martial arts expert in your incarnated life and you want to learn how to become better, then of course you will do fights. If you were someone who was always picked on, made the butt of bad jokes or even beaten up, you may learn techniques for self-defense, using humor to diffuse someone's rage, or a martial art or what have you. It is very hard to argue the nature of God's characteristics when you are within the presence of that Living Being in every timeless moment. But no, I do not fight with anyone: the final Arbiter is always there to settle any arguments.

DL: Does Tesla share his ideas with others?

NT: Of course! I have no need to be cagey here; furthermore, I do not have only one person in the world communicating with me though channeling, dreams, inspiration or other methods.

DL: Is there any human ego where he is?

NT: In the sense that I know myself as a self separate from the One Self, yes: I remember who I have been and contemplate whom I might become. But in the sense of having an animal-based brain that needs to defend its self against others, no. As I have said elsewhere: the human ego is only noxious when it is unrefined. I will add that an unripe ego is as different from a ripened one as an unripe persimmon is from a ripe one.

DL: Is it in the divine plan for Tesla to come back to Earth, and if so when and where?

NT: Forgive me, but I will not speak to this: any child that has even a part of my soul-self, a part of my worldview, might become trammeled by notoriety.

DL: Does Tesla remain in his human personality when he works on his projects in Heaven, or does he become part of the divine Being? Is this a multitasking function?

NT: I am human when I need and choose to be, though the Divine Being works through me when I am in resonance with it. "Multitasking" is one way to see it, but a real clue is in the truly timeless nature of this afterlife state.

DL: Does Tesla meditate and get easy solutions for his projects from God?

NT: Only when I wish! I still love puzzles and still love finding my own way, so that opportunity for enjoying mental challenges is certainly provided for me.

DL: Are you working to create things for human beings, or for other planets, galaxies or universes?

NT: Yes, for all of those and for myself as well. As it is with alternate realities, where any idea in one reality may transform its self in quite unexpected ways because of the different needs and circumstances of that reality compared to the source reality, there have been times when something that might seem simple and automatic for a human being may become the kernel of an astonishing revelation on another world; similarly, what might seem a simple, inconsequential fact in one universe may become the seed of a new science in another. I have spoken with what you may consider alien beings: some of them are profoundly different and some are amazingly human, whatever their forms.

But yes: I remain a being of service, for that is what God's Intention has refined me to be.

Glossary

Anentropy: an actual reversal of entropic processes, such as in spontaneous or miraculous healing, most usually through the M-D structures of Grace

Consciousness: focused awareness and the ability to interact within an environment intentionally

Dimension of Identity: A delimiter and a descriptive function of an enfolded dimension, functioning also as one of the Torsion Fields, this enfolded dimension *acts upon* the other dimensions in order to create the 4-D and M-D geometries and topographies upon which reality is built

Elementals: the spirits and intelligences that keep the coherent pattern beneath and within each of the five elements of Earth, Air, Fire, Water and Ether

Elves: conscious and intentional entities, taking any of various human-like or animal-like forms, whose overall rate of vibration makes them invisible to most human beings

Epigenome: The dynamic, living record of the changes an organism has undergone that can be passed to its offspring, regulating the genome's expressions in that offspring by suppressing certain transposable elements

Ether: a rarified substance similar to plasma that interpenetrates all matter, a step down from the infinitesimal bundles of energy that are the Units of Consciousness

Faith: courage and self-confidence; trust in the good intention that underlies all

Grace: a non-random, spiritual state of resonance between human beings and the Divine, and a structure created by the conscious areas or points of engagement and interaction between the Zero dimension and all other dimensions, that intersects with those dimensions as a result of the enfolded geometries

Light: composed of mass-less particles with wave-like properties. When "physical" is defined as the set of all fields that interact with each other primarily within the specific 4-dimensional matrix, light is simultaneously physical and not physical

M-D: Multi-dimensional, particularly as regards the enfolded dimensions that are tangential to physical reality in terms of form, which provide physical reality with its structure

Magic: an inner intention made manifest though specific ritualized actions that access or attempt to access higher-order realities and M-D geometries, that creates effects greater than the sum of energy in both intention and ritually patterned actions combined, manifesting a positive yield of energy

Mind: awareness; perception as in discernment; analysis; synthesis; internal patterns such as habits, or the automatic re-enforcing of a sequence; pattern recognition

Self: contains all aspects of mind, the emotions and non-physical data within the boundary of identity

Solition: a standing wave created when the wave's natural tendency to disperse is exactly balanced with its impulse to peak

Spirituality: being aware of, and interacting with, Divine Consciousness

Thought: the intentional and yet automatic expression of concepts within the framework of language, however rudimentary, usually given impulse by your mind or emotions.

Units of Consciousness: one of the most miraculous and essential Ideas of the One Source. So infinitesimal they are not only the "substance" of Ether's Torsion-field effects, these Units act as the "stem cells" of physical matter to give form to Time and Space, taking the forms of tetrahedrons to create all shapes and forces

Zero dimension: an enfolded dimension that is both a mathematical factor and an expression of reality; the dimension most like God, it is everywhere and nowhere, within every function and apart from every function, and the core of self

Biographies

Nikola Tesla was a visionary inventor of electrical devices. Born in Austria, just a few years before the origin of the Austro-Hungarian Dual Monarchy, July 10, 1856 in Smiljan, he studied in the University of Prague. First interested in physics, he became fascinated with electricity. Employed as a telegraph engineer for the Austrian government, he pursued his interests in electricity in Paris and Budapest. Going to the United States in 1884, he worked with Edison and Westinghouse; later he established the Tesla Laboratory in New York, devoting himself to electrical research. Disagreeing with Edison, who preferred direct current, Tesla created a genuinely workable method of using alternating current for electrical power; he also patented the induction and thermo magnetic motors, electric circuit controllers, the arc lamp, and many, many other truly innovative inventions. His impressive list of scientific discoveries include the principles of rotary magnetic fields and extensive work with high voltage, as well as various transformers, induction coils, dynamos, and condensers. Some of his ideas were considered too revolutionary, such as his deriving electrical power directly from the Earth's magnetic field. He died Jan. 7, 1943, in New York City, receiving a formal State Funeral attended by over 2,000 including as many Noble Prize winners as were able to arrive during the 1943 wartime travel difficulties.

Carl Gustav Jung, An eminent psychologist who worked with Freud for a time, Jung was born in Kesswill, Switzerland July 26th, 1875 as the son of a Protestant minister and died on Lake Lucern in Kuessnacht in 1961. Growing up, Carl Jung preferred solitude and was fascinated with both various scientific disciplines and religious history; this unusual synthesis made choosing a career difficult. He studied medicine at the University of Basel and graduated from the University of Zurich in 1902 with his medical degree, moving on to study psychology in Paris. A year later, he met and married Emma Rauschenbach, who lovingly and loyally worked with him in his scientific studies until her death in 1955. Living on the shores of Lake Zurich in Kuessnacht, they had five children. Exchanging papers with Sigmund Freud, Jung started working with Freud in 1907. Eventually the two parted because of irreconcilable differences in their approaches to working with the human mind: Freud with his structured understanding based on physical responses and Jung with his multi-faceted approach that led to his conception of the Collective Unconscious, and later ideas about the inner nature of man's psyche such as the concept of introversion and extroversion and human archetypes. He had to give up his psychological practice following a severe heart attack in 1944, though he founded the C.G. Jung Institute in Zurich in 1948, and in following years received many honorary degrees.

Note: The information in the articles with Carl Jung was created from discussions with Dr. Jung in the afterlife. Still interested in helping humanity, Tesla wished to share some of the many things he has learned from this eminent psychologist and is quite pleased that Dr. Jung was willing to discuss some of his ideas so that Tesla could communicate the information in those articles through me.

William H. Terbo is the Founding Director, Chairman and Executive Secretary of the Nikola Tesla Memorial Society Inc. He is Tesla's grandnephew through Tesla's oldest sister, Angelina, the mother of Tesla's nephew, Nikola J. Trbojevich (Nicholas J. Terbo), who was a mathematician, engineer and inventor of the Hypoid gear, the reversible worm steering gear and other inventions that are still in wide use today, and who held more than 150 U.S and foreign patents. As a graduate of Purdue University working with solid-state electronics and cryogenics as well as in the space industry, William Terbo followed both his father Nikola J. Trbojevich's, and Nikola Tesla's love for physics and inventions. Giving many interviews, presenting internationally at 100 symposiums and in 20 video documentaries, Mr. Terbo has worked diligently for over forty years to reestablish Nikola Tesla's importance in our modern world, and helps promote respect for his works, in accordance with the Society's ethical standards.

CPSIA information can be obtained
at www.ICGtesting.com
Printed in the USA
FSOW01n2344050717
35781FS

9 781513 620800